Unconditional-
Uncensored

Unconditional ~ Uncensored

By

Marybeth Sheridan

ISBN 978-0-557-69602-4

Dedication

This book is dedicated to my Mom
Thank you for inspiring me to be who I am

Contents

ACKNOWLEDGEMENTS

This book took me more than five years to write. It started out being a journal of the stories in which I learned from - in order to live by. My amazing mother encouraged me to write to help release my pain from knowing a disease that rocked my very core. She knew that writing was my, and still is my passion. She knew me better than anyone else in the world and she knew that if a battle were to be had that I was the person to be holding the sword. She called me her "Angel" but she was really mine. Thank you Mom.

There have been many people over the years that, in some way or another, contributed something to this book. First and foremost I want to Thank God because without him none of this would have ever evolved and because of him "All things are possible."

I want to thank my husband Jim and my children for the sacrifice you had to give in order for me to get here. I would like to thank the first readers who encouraged me to go onward and upward, Mary Bottini, Siobhan Fennely, Denise Ippolito, Matt Sekunna, Anita Piniella, you were my "Green Light"

To my sister Cathy: for always lending your ear and absorbing my pain whenever possible, for saving me at the expense of hindering your own self, and for being my friend and for your unconditional love and support no matter how many times I tried to "Burn The Bridge." I love you!

To my sister Rita: Who I have huge respect and admiration. You give the word "class" true meaning, you are the best mommy to your four beautiful children and I love you, I admire your bravery and strength. Your unconditional love for my children and me is a true gift from God. I am lucky to call you friend, privileged to have you as family.

To my brothers for loving me and being my brothers.

To Anita for letting me be my crazy unstable wacky self and loving me no matter what. For holding my hand and not letting it go even when I tried, and most of all for being the one who would always, always remind me to trust in God, I love you more.

To Carrie and Lisa for your friendship as you were the two people I first met when I moved to Florida 34 years ago and to this day remain my very best friends; for the road trips, for letting me grow with you, escape with you, change with you, and for being true friends.

To Denise: I used to say that I hate EB, but I have learned to be thankful for the people I have been privileged to meet because of EB. You are my soul sister, my warrior friend, and my partner in crime for the fight to eradicate EB. I love that I never have to explain my tears to you and I am so thankful that God choose you to be one of the first friends I made 12 years ago because of EB. Without you stem cell harvesting for EB would have never happened and I would not have been able to survive EB Boot Camp. Without you *Uncensored* would not be alive. Thank you – I love you!

To Fr. Tom Madden for helping me to breath through the absolute biggest challenge in my life, losing my mom. Your sense of compassion and your insight to life was a very special gift to me. God handpicked you to spend those last few weeks in our home before my mom passed away. I am so thankful it was you. You are confirmation there are no coincidences in life.

To: Fr. Bob Morris: for being the one who taught me to always do things with "love". You were also the one who first told me that my walk was a testimony of my faith, that the strange twist of events was not really all that strange but instead witness to the incredible awesomeness of God. I know, you do not know this - but it was because of our talks that made me realize that this story had to be told, shared because really this is God's story.

To Mon. Fr. McCahn with one promise to you – you opened the door to a remarkable understanding for me of not being or doing anything selfish. Thank you for that.

Travis Roth - for being my brother, little brother, friend, and ear to listen whenever I needed a friend.

Siobhan Fennelly for just willing to be whatever I needed and loving the story, the idea, and all that went into it. You get it, and you helped me to keep going, thank you.

Mary Bottini for standing next to me at church, and letting me crash into your world, and for being honest. For the long late night spiritual talks and the discovery of life through both of our eyes, you have helped me to find my way and stay grounded while getting here, thank you my friend I love you.

Matt Sekunna – thank you for being my friend, for guiding me when I got lost, for holding me accountable for making excuses, for letting me have tantrums and making sure that I knew that something good is always waiting for me around the corner, invaluable advice - brother, thank you.

Tom Langdon – I would not have been able to finish this book without you. You are in my new best friend circle and I feel so lucky to know you. You fit into the crazy chaotic life that I call "mine" and you worked relentlessly to help me make this a reality, thank you.

To My Dad: for being Popi, for being there from day one to carry Samantha on your back and walk her through her pain, to offer her your love at every turn, and for keeping Mom-moms in the present, I love you

To Dr. Patrick Yee – for becoming a Pediatrician. This world needs more doctors like you. I told you when I first met you that you are in fact a rare find and that you are the example to be set by other doctors who know nothing about human compassion. You jumped in and pulled us from the water many times. You are the same amazing person you were when we met you during your internship. God handpicked you to be Sam's doctor you do know that right? You have been one of our biggest supports from the day we met you and always, always, whatever you did you did it for the best interest of Sam – not yourself. You are my favorite doctor ever, thank you!

To our Honey Doctor, Dr. Dumois: For absorbing my abrasive attitude the day we first met on the floor of Tampa General Hospital, and staying calm through the storm. You never gave up on her, instead you looked forward and you took chances with Sam but nothing you wouldn't have done for your own child. There are no words for saving her life; for thinking outside the box because you took the time to think – because you care. Thank you!

To Dr. Susan Barker – I have so many things to thank you for Dr. Save Me, we could be here all day. You know what you did, the birthday party in your office when you found out that some members of our family did not care about Sam. You held my hand and you showed me the way through the most difficult time in my life. You taught me how to fight, when to fight and more importantly how to never give up. You showed me the roads to choose from and you opened many doors to give Sam a better way of life. I am forever grateful for you. God handpicked you Susan Barker to be in our life. We love you!

To Eileen Crawford: Thank you for being there always. You are an angel and without you this book would not have been a reality. You are the best friend anyone could ever ask for. I love you.

Inez – I know I make you crazy always waiting for the last minute on everything. Thank you for loving us, for the prayers and the friendship. We are so thankful for you.

Cynthia Petitjean – EBAN would just not be - without you. Thank you for believing in us and for your undying "Labor of Love." We are forever grateful!

To Jeff Angel: You are the Greatest OBGYN ever. Thank you for being a doctor. Thank you for the nights that you came to our home to help Sam, and for the years of support for EB – You are an Angel Jeff.

Tom & Kathy Shannon – Thank you for walking your faith. You jumped into our battlefield out of your love for human life. EB will never be able to thank you as thousand's of families today are still reaping the rewards of your kindness & generosity. We are so privileged to call you "friends"- we love you, thank you so much.

To F.A.D. – You are my Warrior Friend and my sister in Christ. Thank you for not giving up on the one thing I tried to forget –Hope! EB families will never know just how much you sacrifice to keep their Hope alive –I love you, I am on your side partner.

To Silvia- You are my Warrior Partner, My best Friend, My Italian sister and the best EB mom I know. You have given your heart and soul to help others and sometimes at a price. Thank you for staying in and never giving up. Thank you for doing all that you do to help EB. The Internet would never have been what it is today for EB without you my friend. I love you.

To E: You are forever in my heart, friend.

To All of the Wound Care Companies that I have ever had the pleasure to work with: You are the foundation of our EB world today and I will be forever grateful for your love and support. Thank you!

To Tim Wiebe: My wish is to one day be like you. Your generosity is something to mirror. You are an honorable man! God Bless you! We love you.

MHR Faculty & Families – Thank you from the bottom of my heart. Your school and all of the families who interacted in Sam's 9 years there have been a true gift from God. We could not have been luckier or more blessed than to have walked through your doors. Your acceptance and unconditional love for our daughter will never be forgotten. We love you! We are so thankful for you!

Claudia – for being my sister in Christ. Thank you! You helped to make the calm and clean in my life. You came even when I know the choice was trust, and I will forever be grateful to you. You always said yes to anything I asked for and because of you I am here. I love you and want you to know I would do the same for you my friend!

Mary Heston- Thank you for being my friend. You were the safety net that caught me just as I was about to jump. You're living your faith! I am so happy we are friends and blessed that our awesome God chose our paths to cross.

INTRODUCTION

A personal story about a disease called Epidermolysis Bullosa (or EB for short) - that came without conditions.

The journey that began with conditions.

The story is uncensored, but true and told in its most raw form.

The love is unconditional.

The pain is raw – I am telling my personal story about a disease that no one has ever heard of but affects hundreds and thousands of children. I have spent the past fifteen years trying to bring awareness to this disease hoping that the end result would be a cure for my daughter and all who suffer from EB, or at the very least a better life. In my attempts to raise awareness I have always been told what to say, what not to say, who to say it to, and how to say it – always having to leave out the most significant details.

I was inspired by thousands of people to share our story. In doing that not only did it help me and encourage our journey, but it also seemed to help many others.

The story is about the coincidental (and I don't believe anything in this life is by coincidence) meeting of different people and stories along the way that gave me courage and strength and a faith that grows into an unconditional love and trust in God, and a life of unconditional love for the child I always dreamt of having.

Chapter 1.

In The Trenches

Spiritual journeys usually begin with some kind of event that occurs in your life. At some point something will happen that will get your attention and take your breath away. It will stop you in your tracks and create a moment where you stop and question everything. Whether it is good or bad, at some point in our lives we go on a journey looking for answers to questions about our life that you never thought of before: Who you are and why we are here. My journey began after the birth of my first child, Samantha.

You know how it is when you're a little girl your head gets filled with all kinds of dreams: Romantic dreams, fairytale dreams, meeting prince charming, getting married, and having children. When I was a little girl these were the things that seemed to be talked about in my house and around me. You grow, you get married, most women instinctively want children, and then some women just think it is the right next thing to do. Some women don't have any children at all; either by choice or because for one reason or another they just can't. I was one of those girls who wanted to have a lot of children. My mom made it look so easy. Being the youngest of five was fun for me when I was little. I always liked the idea of "family." I remember being pregnant like it was yesterday. Eating absolutely everything I ever wanted. Gained too much weight, but I loved every second of it. I went to every pregnancy check up on time gleaming with joy and happiness. I kept notes on everything. I loved being pregnant.

As a child I went to church, but mostly for holidays and special occasions. My family is Catholic; however, while I was growing up, my mother let me explore other religions from time to time. That was mostly in part due to who my mother was. My mom was the smartest woman on the earth. She even studied theology for a period of time in her life. Sometimes my friends would invite me to come to their church service and I would go with them. I learned a lot about other people and their religions by having those experiences. My mom would also try to explain the differences to me. As I got older I just came to the understanding that there is a God, there are a certain set of rules we as humans are to live by no matter what your faith is, and prayer really works. I stayed with Catholicism mainly because it is what I felt most comfortable with. It is what I know. My grandparents from my mother's side were devout Catholics. They were very faithful about attending Mass every Saturday night without fail. They went to confession religiously and prayed before every meal. My grandmother would tell us to pray constantly. No matter what the problem was, or wasn't, prayer was the answer to everything.

When I was in my teen-age years, and even up into my early twenties, I really did not have a full understanding of the magnitude of God or prayer.

As a child our family only attended Mass on Holidays. My mom was very consistent about making sure we knew who God was and what role He played in all of our lives. We didn't go to church every Sunday, but she made sure we practiced what she preached. One of her favorite sayings to us always was, "With God all things are possible." Whenever any of us had problems, or felt like life was getting to heavy for us, my mom would always tell us to pray to God and ask him specifically to "please take these problems from me Lord. You take these problems from me Lord because I know only you have the power and strength to solve these problems. You are almighty and the most High Jesus Christ, thank you Lord." Whenever any of us, including my mom, would lose something (like the keys to the car, our favorite toy, book, or whatever it was), my mom would always say this: "Dear, St. Anthony please come around – something is lost and can not be found." These phrases of wisdom that my mother would frequently speak are the most powerful tools I would come to cherish and use to live my life by to this day.

I really started to attend Mass after I became pregnant. Shortly after I found out I was pregnant it was almost like I was drawn to church. Prior to my pregnancy and even as a child I never felt drawn to God's house in this way before. Praying for a healthy child became something instinctive I wanted to do. I am pretty sure almost all pregnant women feel this way at some point in their pregnancy. I don't know that I ever really thought that I would have an unhealthy child, but just prayed that the baby I was carrying inside me was going to be ok.

During my pregnancy it felt like everything about my surroundings became more real and intense. I wasn't responsible for just 'me' anymore, now there was going to be two of us to care for soon. I was paying attention to my surroundings more then I usually did. I had heard about new moms 'nesting,' which means you start getting really organized and prepared for your new child to come home. You clean the house - and I mean *really* clean. Then you get the room ready for the baby to arrive. Organizing every room and every closet to the point where you are asking yourself, "What am I doing?" I had not heard about your visual senses becoming so vibrant and on alert during pregnancy though. I started noticing things that I had never noticed before. All kinds of things: like people and places and colors and all sorts of things. Or maybe it was just that I picked this time in my life to slow things down a notch enough to stop and smell the roses for the first time. I am not sure. I just know that my house became a home, and everything in it was not only clean but organized too. This is also about the time that I can tell you "my journey" began.

Chapter 2.

"He Has What?"

When I was between eight and ten weeks along in my pregnancy, my husband Jim came down with what I thought was a cold, or maybe the flu. The only thing strange was that he was running really high fevers. I had never seen anybody that sick before. I was giving him Tylenol every four hours and making sure he was drinking plenty of fluids. After about the 2nd day of these really high fevers - I mean 104, 105 temps - I decided to take him the hospital. We went right to the emergency room. After waiting in the ER for about three hours, we were finally taken back into a room for a doctor to come in and examine Jim. Once the doctor came in and did his evaluation, he concluded that my husband had the flu. He thought that I should just take him back home and continue the Tylenol every four hours. The doctor also prescribed an antibiotic to give to him just in case it was bacterial. He had all of the usual symptoms of a cold: fever, stuffy nose, soar throat. I mentioned to the doctor that Jim's fevers seem to be unusually high and so consistent and asked him if that was something to worry about. He just said that sometimes a cold or flu can be that bad and to just make sure he takes his medicine and gets plenty of rest and fluids.

The next day my husband started running 106 temps again every four hours. Nothing seemed to improve. He was still taking the Tylenol every four hours, but his temperature would rise to 106 about every four hours consistently anyway. All of his symptoms were getting worse. He wasn't eating or drinking anything. I knew instinctively that something was wrong. Then oddly he started hallucinating. Nothing he said to me was making sense. When he told me that he felt like he was going to die I really got worried. Jim wasn't like that. He would never even joke about death - especially his own. He really thought he was going to die though and he repeated that to me a few times. So his brother (who happened to be living with us at that time) and I decided we would take him to a different hospital this time and see what they thought might be wrong. I felt that the previous hospital was in too much of a hurry to get us out of there, so maybe they missed something. Where we live in Tampa, Florida, there are three or four hospitals within 30 minutes of us in different directions. I was convinced that a different hospital would give us a different diagnosis. We had to lift him from bed and then we had to dress him - he was barely able to hold himself up. He had absolutely no strength at all. Then we had to carry him to the car. He could not walk. I was scared. Something inside of me knew that he was dangerously ill.

As we pulled up to the emergency room entrance at the hospital my husband started to vomit. We opened up the side door to the van and he fell slumped over in his seat. The emergency room nurse came running outside to help us with a wheelchair. He felt very hot - like his fever had just shot up high, however I had just given him Tylenol maybe one hour before. Clearly things were going from bad to worse in a short amount of time. As we were walking very quickly into the hospital the emergency room nurse starting asking me questions like: "How long has this been going on for? What are all of his symptoms? Is he taking any medication?" The ER nurse looked at Jim, who by now was almost unconscious, and asked, "Sir, can you touch your chin to your chest?" Jim could barley speak as mumbled, "No, I can't move my neck - or my head. My head hurts so bad I feel like it is going to explode." The emergency room nurse had a look of panic and fear on his face instantly. He looked at me and said, 'Stay back ma'am, I want you to go to the family waiting area I think he has spinal meningitis."

I said, "But I have been taking care of him, I have already been exposed!" The nurse looked at me with a very stern face this time and said, "I don't care, just stay back – this is very serious and extremely contagious! Please just go to the waiting room. We can take it from here, he is in good hands and a doctor will be out to talk to you shortly." Then they rushed him back between two doors that led to the emergency room patient area. Wow! - That was the fastest I have ever seen anyone go to the back part of an ER area.

I went to the family waiting area. I was so emotional. I just felt like crying, like, "Oh man, what is happening here?" Suddenly all my thoughts drifted to "very serious – highly contagious…." Oh, my God, was this really happening?

I waited for hours in the waiting room area, not sure if he was going to live or die. I kept going up to the information desk to ask how he was, but they would only tell me to just have a seat and the doctor would be calling for me shortly. I felt mad as I pondered the thought of how the hospital from the day before had just casually released us on our way - without even doing any test on him. I was very clear about his symptoms and the fevers. Why is it that no one at that hospital suspected anything this serious? Now here we are in a situation that could be life threatening. How does a hospital, a doctor in the emergency room no less - miss spinal meningitis?

I paced and walked, and tried to eat, but it was hard. Trying to remember that I was with child and needed to make sure that I got the food and rest I needed so that no harm could come to the baby. All the while trying to remain calm. I really wanted a cigarette but I quit when I found out I was pregnant and I knew smoking cigarettes while pregnant could only be bad for the baby so that wasn't an option. I was one of those "first time" pregnant moms who was a fanatic about doing everything right; especially what I put in my body. I would not drink a drop of wine or any kind of alcohol. I was extremely conscious about what I put in my body. I didn't eat raw fish or anything that the doctors said might cause some issue - nothing. If my OB doctor said there was even a slight chance of harm to the baby I stayed away from it during my pregnancy. I had heard about Down Syndrome, and babies being born with Cerebral Palsy, and some other birth defects and disabilities during the pregnancy course Jim and I had attended a few weeks back, so I wanted to make sure that I did everything by the book. I didn't want to take any chances.

The only thing I had ever heard about Spinal Meningitis was all bad stuff. The end result of that was someone always died. I never heard about anyone having Spinal Meningitis and living to tell his or her story. So I was a little bit scared that I might be having our baby alone. I was a lot more scared of losing my husband and that's not fair since we had only been married for three years and here we are about to have our first child together.

The door finally opened to the area where I knew they had taken my husband. A doctor peered out and called my name. "Mrs. Sheridan?" Oh boy, I knew this was going to be bad. I stood up and acknowledged him, then walked over to him. He walked me back into the emergency room patient area. We walked over to the middle of the room. There was sort of a circular area in the middle of the ER where it looked like all of the doctors and nurses gathered to look at their computers, make calls and write their notes. I think it was the nurses/ doctor's station. He sat down on a bar stool type of chair and offered me a chair. He was a tall man, slender in build, and his demeanor was very calm. He moved his computer so that I could see the screen he was looking at. He introduced himself to me and asked, "Have you ever heard of Spinal Meningitis?" I answered him, "Well, yes, but only on TV and in the news."I really don't know too much about it. I know I have heard that people can die from having it." He explained that there were a couple of different kinds of meningitis: A bacterial kind, and in that family there were a couple of different types. He said that bacterial kind was the worst and can be fatal and therefore was most difficult to cure. Then he said there was a viral type as well. He told me that the viral type was less severe but could also be fatal. Both kinds were difficult to treat. He said that he was not sure at this point which type my husband had, but he was pretty sure he did not have the most severe form of the bacterial one, however he might have one of the bacterial kinds. Mostly because he did not present any kind of rash on his body anywhere. I understood from the doctor that if someone had a rash with meningitis it is deadly and highly contagious. Then he pointed to his computer and showed me Jim's lab results on the screen and how he came to the diagnosis of it being meningitis in the first place. He asked me how long this had gone on for. I explained how we went to another local hospital just the day before and how they sent us home with an antibiotic and said to just continue the Tylenol every four hours. I told him that it was my intuition that told me to just go to a different hospital because I felt something else was wrong. As the doctor listened to me he did not show emotion one way or another regarding that situation, but he did say that he could not believe my husband was still alive. He said that maybe the antibiotic that the previous ER doctor put him on might have saved his life. He went on to say that we were not out of the woods yet, and that my husband may not survive. Jim was now in a deep sleep due to the high doses of Demerol they gave to him because of the pain and swelling causing pressure in his head from the meningitis. The doctor explained how with meningitis the brain swells and is very painful. There was only one IV antibiotic medication that was available to work for this meningitis. He explained how deadly this disease was. He was very curious as to where we had been and how my husband could have contracted such a deadly illness. He asked me where we had been in the past week. Did we eat out anywhere different? Did we travel to any place at all in or out of the country? I answered 'no' to all of those questions, but there was one thing that happened that was different from our normal day-to-day routine. My husband had been helping his best friend at that time, Sonny, do some renovations on his house. I remembered Jim telling me how they were digging in this one area and they hit a rat's nest. He said some kind of particles like dust were flying around everywhere in the air, and Jim joked that it was rat poop. He and Sonny were having a few beers that day. So the doctor thought it was quite possible that rat poop particles had somehow gotten into his beer and this is how he got this deadly illness. This ER doctor told me it is not very easy to come into contact with something like this. Usually that involves traveling to some other country, but rats do carry it. You have to have been bitten by a rat, or somehow ingest the rat fecal matter, in order to get meningitis. If you came into contact with a person who has it, then that affected person's bodily fluids would have to enter your body somehow in order for you to get it that way. At least this is how I interpreted this explanation.

He said he wouldn't know if Jim is going to survive for at least 24 hours. It all depended on how well he responded to this one antibiotic. I thought I would just stop breathing, right then and right there, in that emergency room. The doctor told me that they were going to move my husband to a different area and quarantine him. He did not think it was a good idea for me or anyone else to be around him, but I argued with him about that since I was the first person to care for him. He was my husband and we lived, ate and slept together. He finally agreed to let me see him, but I would have to put protective gloves, a gown and mask on to help prevent me from contracting it. At that point I did not show any signs that I had meningitis.

The ER doctor told me that a different doctor would be following Jim from here on out. This would be a doctor who specializes in these types of illnesses: An Infectious Disease Doctor. The title alone sounded so official and so serious. I knew it was serious but now we have a doctor with a specific title and that was scary. Finally he asked me how far along in my pregnancy I was. I think I was 10 weeks. I was so excited to be pregnant that I started to wear maternity clothes right away. Usually women don't start wearing maternity clothes until they are 20 weeks or more. For me wearing maternity clothing made being pregnant feel more real. I knew people were not sure if I was pregnant or not. I really wasn't showing at 10 weeks. I didn't care what anybody else thought though it's what I liked that mattered to me. I did feel as though all of the nurses and the doctors were wondering if I was pregnant. They were probably worried because what my husband had was so contagious.

After many hours - maybe even into the next day in the emergency waiting room - many horrible thoughts were roaming around in my head. The doctor finally called for me again. This time it was to tell me that the medication looked as though it was working, and Jim was responding well to it. In just a short while the new doctor in charge would be calling my name to meet me and update me on the progress. The new doctor was very nice. He told me that he was going to arrange a time in the next few days to meet in my husband's room. He asked me if it was all right to conference call my OB doctor at the same time so that we could discuss this disease and my pregnancy. "Hmm," I thought to myself, "why does he want to talk to my OB and what about my pregnancy?"

He then informed me that anyone who had come into contact with my husband from the time he first showed signs of the illness up to - two weeks prior should take this prescription antibiotic as a preventative measure to avoid getting the illness since this illness was life threatening and highly contagious. I thought of every person that Jim may have come into contact with in the past few weeks and gave the doctor their names. He then wrote out prescriptions for each person. He told me I could take the pills too, but he was not sure what it would do to my pregnancy. He said he thought that if I took the pills there might be a chance that it would cause me to abort the pregnancy. Immediately I said, "No ...no I don't want to do that. We really want this baby." I called everyone I knew to update them on Jim's status, and also to alert everyone that they should take this prescription that the doctor had given me to give to them because this is very serious and if they were to get this meningitis they could die.

Chapter 3.

"The Big Green Book"

A few days later we (the ID doctor and I) met in my husband's room. The doctor was sitting in a chair next to Jim's bed. He had an unusually large green medical book in his lap. The book was at least 8 inches wide by 12 inches long. The book looked like it was heavy, as well as very old, too. I had never seen a doctor's medical book that big or that old looking before. I walked into the room and sat down. The ID doctor had my OB on the phone and he explained that we were all meeting on this day along with my husband to discuss continuing my pregnancy or terminating it at that point since there was a possibility that the baby had been exposed to this deadly illness. I was a little shocked to hear him say that. Sitting in that room with that doctor felt like something out of an old movie of sorts. The doctor was a bit old himself, and he dressed the part. His suit was green and worn. He did not wear the typical white coat doctors normally wear. His face was round and jolly with a sense of warmth. His salt and pepper grey hair looked a bit messy as if his curls had been blown by the wind.

I'm a pretty stubborn person and I told him right out, "There is no way I would even consider aborting this pregnancy! You will have to prove to me there is no other way" He would have to know for sure without a doubt that I would be causing harm to my baby. I was not sick. I did not have symptoms, so I felt like we were ok: the baby and me. He sounded like he was scared for me to have the baby though, but yet he wasn't really telling me why. The phone was on the table next Jim's hospital bed. He explained the disease from the description in his book, which looked like it was a hundred years old. He said something about "there might be a chance of our baby being born missing a limb or finger or something like that," but that really according to his information there was not enough data to support that the baby would be born with a birth defect at all. The book only suggested it "could" or "might happen." Finally, my OB doctor interjected with, "You know Marybeth, I think everything is going to be just fine. After all, there are tests we can do and sonograms we can take to monitor the progress of the baby. There are no guarantees for any new parent to have a healthy child, but if you really want to continue the pregnancy, then I think we will be ok. It is yours and your husband's decision after all though." I answered with, "Well then that's that! We are having a baby." I didn't even give Jim a chance to say a word or have a choice. My mind was made up. The ID doctor closed his book and thanked our OB doctor for taking the time to have that meeting with us. He said he was only doing his job and he wanted to make sure that he explained all, if any, risks that may be possible.

I was really feeling more drawn to God now as I really did have a reason to pray. I prayed that my husband would get better and I was praying for a healthy baby. Praying for a healthy child became a daily ritual.

Jim ended up spending a couple of weeks in the hospital. Each day he got better and stronger. He ended up getting released and coming home. He still had an IV in for antibiotics for another week or so while at home.

At my next OB check up appointment we actually got to see my favorite doctor (Dr. Caps), which was my doctor to begin with anyway. These days, when you have a baby, your doctor is part of a group of OB doctors (usually 6), and you have to see all 6 of the doctors rotating each time you go. They do that so that you get a chance to meet all of the doctors in the event that you happen to deliver on a day when your doctor may be off. That wasn't my favorite part since I was so fond of my doctor. I think most of us can say that. Anyway, we walked in and Dr. Caps nearly fell over when he saw my husband. He told us that not too many people survive the kind of Spinal Meningitis he had, which was the 'strep de caca form', so he was happy to see him alive, and that walking around was even more impressive.

Chapter 4.

"Should I Ask or Should I Not?"

One other experience I remember quite well was a trip to the grocery store. My husband and I went for a few things. It was late in my pregnancy but not sure how far along. Since I knew I had never been exposed to chickenpox, any sign of them scared me to death knowing what it could do to my baby. When you are pregnant and it is your first pregnancy the OBGYN doctors cover a lot of information with you in your first few visits. They make sure to explain all of the foods you should be eating and all of the foods that you should not be eating. They tell you about how much weight you should gain and when too much weight can be dangerous. They ask you every question related to your health and your family's health that you could ever possibly imagine. You have to answer questions about your parent's health, and your sibling's health as well. All of this information is helpful to the doctors to determine what your percentages are of having a healthy baby is going to be. They want to know if there were ever any cancers, or birth defects, or what medical condition, if any, that any member on either side of our families may have ever had. Most health conditions that can be passed down to a child are genetic. Genetic defect, in a nutshell, means that either the mother or the father, or both in some cases, pass down a defective gene that then causes some kind of condition to the newborn baby.

In answering all of these questions it had been determined that I had never had the common chicken pox virus before - ever - even as a child. Most of my friends, including my husband, did have the chicken pox at some point in their early childhood life. I also had been warned that contracting the chicken pox virus during pregnancy could cause severe trauma to the fetus, or maybe even death to one or both of us.

We were going through the cashier line at a local grocery store and I noticed the cashier had what looked like the chicken pox all over her face and neck. She had tiny little red pinhead bumps and some of them had tiny, white heads. My OB doctors warned me about the dangers, so

I think I freaked out. Not to mention that my husband and I were not mentally recovered from the whole meningitis scare. How ironic that I had just been to a pre-pregnancy visit a few days before and been warned of these dangers, and then I find myself standing in front of some one who could potentially have the "chicken pox." I really didn't know what to do. I was afraid to ask her, but I was more afraid not to ask her so I asked, "I'm sorry to ask you this, but I am pregnant and it could be bad for me. Do you have the chicken pox?" She just stopped in motion what she was doing and took a deep breath. She did not say a word to me - for about two minutes. Everyone around us was just staring at me as if they all knew something I didn't - but should have known. Then she looked at me and said, "I have acne." My face turned every shade red there was. I was mortified, and I felt so bad that I embarrassed that sweet girl in front of everyone. Jim was trying to hurry me out of the store. He could not believe that I had just done that. I really wasn't trying to hurt her feelings and I would have never wanted to make someone feel bad, but I had to know. That day would soon come to haunt me forever. I would soon learn how I made her feel at that very moment for years to come. I will, for the rest of my life, not ever forget that young cashier or the way I made her feel when I asked if she had the chicken pox. Some lessons in life are so hard to learn. I would think back to this moment in time and, the meeting with the infectious disease doctor in Jim's hospital room on and off for years to come.

Chapter 5.

"The Delivery"

Being a first-time pregnant mom I did not realize at the OBGYN office how you can actually get herded in and out pretty quickly for check ups. There sure was a lot of pregnant woman in that office all of the time. You go in, you get weighed, and the doctor comes in, looks over your chart chats with you for a few minutes, then you leave. That is unless, of course, you are going to see a high risk OBGYN - which I wasn't. Or unless something was wrong with your blood work, or urine, or sonogram. I do remember in my 6th month that this time when the doctor came in he spent more then the usual five minutes with me. He wasn't my normal doctor but one of the six in the group. He told me I had too much water in my sack of amniotic fluid. He just thought the baby had a cold. He told me that usually when there is too much water in the sack this is usually a sign that the baby is not swallowing the fluid properly and could just be a sign that the baby has a cold. No one seemed to be concerned so, naturally, neither was I.

The holidays came and went. It was as cold as Florida gets in the month of February. The weather was refreshingly cool for my huge, pregnant body as I was feeling every bit of being past my due date. My stomach was so stretched out that the steering wheel in my car pressed against it. I was seriously ready to have this baby. By this time, I was the one badgering my OB doctors daily for a plan. We had a few false alarms but nothing was really happening.

I was four weeks past my due date. It was Feb. 13th and I was scheduled to be induced since the little baby inside of me, for some reason, did not want to come out. When we got checked into a labor room I had actually started to have some contractions before they were going to induce labor. The nurse had put this very big, wide belt around my HUGE belly (I gained almost 90 pounds - I don't recommend that by the way), that would monitor the contractions, and then she hooked me up to some other stuff that would monitor the baby's heart rate. I laid there in the hospital bed for a while waiting for the doctor to come so we could start to induce the labor. Suddenly my baby started to have some kind of fetal stress. Her heart rate was not stable. The doctor came in and told me that we were going to have to have a C-section for the safety of the baby. The baby's stress was worrisome and I was too far past my due date. At that point all I wanted was the baby out anyway. So I said, "Ok- let's do it."

I had the most wonderful team of nurses and medical personnel around me. The current "laid-back-everything's-moving-slow-and-we-are-just-here-waiting" feeling suddenly evolved into a whirlwind high speed of events that went spiraling out of control. We were running down the hall - it seemed as though right after the epidural (which by the way took forever since I was so big I couldn't curl that well for the anesthesia doctor to put the needle in my back for the epidural). They were racing to get me into the surgery OR area. Instantly I was terrified. Trembling and praying at the same time. I recall one nurse, who was steering the hospital bed I was on, whose name was Brenda. She was back by my head at the end of the bed, pushing the bed as someone else pulled the bed from my feet area. She rubbed my hair and assured me that everything was going to be ok. She talked to me in my ear the whole time she was with me. "Don't worry honey you are going to be just fine," she reassured me. "Things will move fast, and as fast as they move you will have your little precious baby in your arms before you know it. Don't worry you are in good hands and everything is going to be ok." I loved her. I wish I could tell her how awesome she was. I was grateful for her kindness. Like an angel on my shoulder she held my hand, talked to me, and calmed my fears. Just like that she was gone and I never saw her again. Her care, concern, and compassion for me were unconditional. I thought that at that point I was just going to pass out from pure fear. If you have never had a C-section before, then what I can tell you is that the first one is easier then the second or the third - keeping in mind that the first one is really frightening.

Everything was moving very quickly, and everyone around me was moving at the same pace - fast. They wheeled me into the surgical room. The very first thing I noticed were these two, enormous, bright lights above me on the ceiling. You couldn't look up or the brightness would blind you. They were so bright. The room was cold and grey and it was very strange in an unfamiliar kind of way. My angel nurse had to leave me, but I didn't want her too. There were other nurses in the room but they just didn't seem as loving or as caring as Brenda. The other people in that room just seemed to be moving about and doing their job like programmed robots unaffected by my presence. I was lucky to have Brenda there to comfort me on the way to the surgery room for those few minutes. People that work in the hospitals that really like their jobs make all the difference in the world when you are the patient there. It's like they, too, have been in the same situation as you so they know how you feel and can say words to provide comfort. They are not afraid to hold your hand and tell you everything is going to be ok.

The very thought of someone cutting into the very place where your baby is moving around and kicking you was plain terrifying. The doctor came in. He had his gown on and gloves and facemask, and hair mask. Then they brought my husband in to be with me. They let Jim sit on a stool behind me to the side of my head. As soon as he sat down I turned my head on my pillow so that I could see his face. I don't think there was ever another time that I saw Jim so nervous. He looked as terrified as I felt. I just turned my head back so that I was facing the ceiling and those horribly bright lights. I couldn't worry too much about Jim right now. First of all - it was a serious reality that in a few minutes my baby was actually going to be in my arms, and that was an excitement that I had been waiting for such a long time. The day was finally here and it was all about to happen. Second was the fear of knowing that this doctor was going to be cutting my stomach open and pulling her out. Panic crept into my body. I tried to take slow, deep breaths to calm myself. I had never felt so nervous and scared in my entire life.

The doctor, who was going to be delivering my baby on this day, was not a doctor that I knew very well. I think I had only met him once - maybe twice - during my OB check up appointments. I was wishing Dr. Capps would be there with me, but it was his day off. This doctor seemed to be nice enough, though. I felt a little uncomfortable with not really knowing him that well. At that point it wasn't like I had a choice either. He started to tell me the procedure and what was going to happen. He walked me through every step. He said, "Okay, I am cutting now," then he paused for a few minutes. He asked me if I could feel anything. I replied back, "No". Then he continued, "Okay, now you will feel some pressure, and then some pulling, are you okay, Marybeth?"

"Yes," I said.

I could actually feel the cut on my tummy, but not the pain just the pressure from it, which was totally a weird feeling. I could feel the doctor moving my body below my waist… then the pressure. I could feel the pulling and pushing, and I could feel the powerful force the doctor was using to pull my baby out. Like he was moving my entire lower body - from my waist down - and you have absolutely no control over anything he was doing because you are numb. Your mind can tell your hips to move but nothing was moving. All I could think of was, "I wanted it to be over fast."

It felt like it is taking forever. In reality, it's not. I know when we got into the surgery room it was noon, and when he pulled my baby out it was 12:20. How strange it is that time feels so different when all of those different emotions came in to play. Then something to do with the drugs they give you in the epidural that numb your lower body for the C-section delivery, you get the shakes. I mean uncontrollable shakes. I was shaking so hard that my jaw was shaking and I couldn't talk. The doctor was asking me questions and I couldn't answer him. I tried to talk, but my words were not making sense because of the shaking. I really thought that was just me freaking out. Maybe I was hyperventilating, but the anesthesiologist who was behind me monitoring the drugs in my IV said it was happening because of the drugs that they were giving me to numb my lower body. He told me to just be patient that he was going to put something in my IV to help calm me down as soon as our baby was out. I am not sure if all women get the shakes during a C-section, but I sure did. I felt like I was hyperventilating. I just started praying. I prayed The *Our Father*, or some may know it as *The Lord's Prayer*, over and over again. I was whispering it to myself. I wasn't sure if anyone could hear me and I really didn't care. All I knew at that moment was I wanted God to hear me. The next thing I heard was the doctor saying how big our baby was, "Wow this is the biggest baby we have delivered yet this year!" He was laughing and joking about how my doctor (Dr. Caps - the one I loved) was too old to have pulled a baby this large out of me, and that he is lucky it was his day off. We found out she was a girl when I was about five months pregnant, so we already knew we were having a girl. As it turned out she was 10 pounds 3 1/5-ounces and 22 1/5-inches long.

Ya' think four weeks past my due date was a little long?

She was a big baby. That wasn't surprising since I was so far past my due date. Most newborn babies weigh between six to nine pounds. Ten pounds was huge. My friends asked me why I went so far past my due date and I just told them that I didn't know why. I assumed it was normal to go past your due date. I had always heard that you could either deliver a baby two weeks early or two weeks late. I knew I was four weeks late, but never gave it a second thought. I just thought it was ok.

Then I heard my baby crying. Oh, the sound of my baby crying was a good sound! It was a great feeling. I felt relieved because I could hear her; she was alive and she sounded good and strong. The doctor became very quiet. Silence crept into the room like a fog for a couple of seconds, but what felt like ten minutes. My baby became quiet too. I couldn't see my baby, and I couldn't tell what the doctor was doing or looking at. I could only move my head from left to right and see the room I was in to the right or left from about my chest up and back of me, but I couldn't see anything in front of me. I could see the nurse walk over towards the doctor to look at my baby. All I could see was their hats on their heads. Then I heard the nurse say to the doctor, "Well maybe she was sucking on it in her womb." Then it sounded like they started to whisper to each other. Then I said, "What? What are you talking about? What is wrong? Is there something wrong with my baby? I can hear you whispering, what is going on?" Confused, the doctor responded back to me," We are not quite sure Marybeth, just hold on a few minutes and let the nurse examine the baby."

"Oh my God! All I could think of was - is my baby okay?"

I wasn't really paying attention to anything else that was going on with me, but more concerned for my baby at that moment. What were they whispering about? What could be wrong? Why not tell me? Then I asked, "Does she have all of her fingers and toes? Is something wrong with her?" I was wondering if maybe something was wrong like that. Like maybe she had some kind of birth defect. After all, my husband did come down with that Spinal Meningitis around my 8th week of pregnancy. Maybe something happened as a result of that. The doctor with the very large, green, very old book said that there was a possibility of some kind of birth defect. He said something about a missing arm, or leg… Oh my God, was this really happening? I was starting to feel panic. Could this be because we were warned and did not want to abort this pregnancy? All I could think was panic: "Please God, do not let this be happening. Oh please, God, make everything okay with our baby girl." My mind was scrambling for answers to the questions racing through my mind.

Chapter 6.

From Happy to Horrified in Ten Seconds

The nurse told me that something was wrong with my baby's left hand. She said that sometimes babies suck their hands in the wound, and so maybe that is why there seems to be some skin missing from her left hand. I had heard that babies could suck their thumbs - but their whole hand? Is this nurse crazy? She said it was not common for the skin to come off due to the baby sucking - but it could be possible. So she was cleaning the baby off to get a better look. The nurse stopped communicating with me. She was solely and intently attending to my baby in the back corner of the room. Since I was lying on my back, and the nurse was directly behind me, but towards the right corner of the room, I looked up over my right shoulder directly behind my head and could see the nurse cleaning my baby. My neck hurt stretching it that way but strangely my pain was not important. I noticed the white, milky, thick substance covering my baby's body and the nurse very gently rubbing it off with water and some sort of cloth. The nurse looked like she was going very slowly - as if she were watching something that she had never seen before. The nurse seemed to be moving in slow motion. Panic and fear were starting to control me. I thought the nurse was too quiet. I also thought the nurse was looking at my baby very intently like there was something else going on. Something was wrong - horribly wrong. My doctor did not say a word; he just kept his head down and looked like he was working on me. I got the feeling that he didn't want me to talk to him. My chest felt like it was palpitating so hard that my body was beating with it. I never experienced any emotions like this before. Not even the time Jim was fighting for his life with meningitis. Everything in that surgery room that day felt like it was magnified about hundred times. Every emotion I was having was one of terror and fear. Like it was the very first time I ever felt that way. My mind was spinning so fast I could not keep up with any one thought. They had not shown her to me yet, and I kept asking to see her. "Please can I see my baby?" The nurse replied, "Hold on a minute, honey, I am trying to get her cleaned up."

I thought in my mind, 'bull shit!' In the movies and on TV you always see the babies being put butt naked right on the mom's chest. So why then was this different? Don't they just pull the baby out and then give her to the new mom? It was not supposed to be this way. Or was it? I didn't know for sure because this was my first baby. My husband sat quietly behind me, not saying a word. Maybe he said a few words but I couldn't hear him. I was fixated on my baby girl. The minute I knew she was ok, I was going to be ok. No one was telling me that she WAS ok. That was the problem.

I saw the nurse wrap her in a blanket, and then she walked over to me. She said she was going to show me my new baby. The nurse seemed nervous. I could feel it. I could hardly wait to see my baby and look into her eyes. I dreamt about this moment for months. I used to tell my baby when she was in my womb how much I loved her and how I couldn't wait for her to be here in my arms. I told her how exciting it would be for us to meet face to face and just speak to each other with our eyes. My mom used to tell me that our eyes are the windows to our souls, and I believed that to be true. I always could get a lot from someone just by looking into their eyes.

The doctor was still doing whatever it was he was doing to me. I knew he had to stitch me up. From the time the surgery began he had a blue sheet of some sort draped across my lower tummy area and up so I couldn't see anything down below my waist - except for the top of his head and the blue sheet of course. The nurse walked up to the spot where the doctor was stitching me. As she lifted the baby over the blue sheet, I had this really weird feeling that something was going to happen. Like she was moving in slow motion. I wanted her to move faster to just get my baby on my chest so I could hold her. But I had this weird feeling that the nurse would change her mind at the last minute and take my baby back and make me wait more. Then she sort of lowered my baby over the blue sheet for me to see her face. She had one hand supporting my baby's head and one hand supporting her body. She tilted my baby so that I could see her face. She was lowering my baby so that she could place her on my chest. My babies face was the only thing I could see. She was - in a word -beautiful. Everything else was wrapped very snug in a baby blanket. The moment my eyes caught my baby's eyes she knew it was me: 'Mommy." We named her Samantha. I knew Samantha knew it was me, and I spoke to her with my eyes. We did have an intense eye contact moment. Then - just like that and all of the sudden - very abruptly blood came spilling out of my baby's mouth onto the blanket on my chest. I just started saying, "Oh my God, oh my God!! There is blood coming out of her mouth! What is wrong? Is that normal? What is wrong? Please someone tell me why blood is coming out of her mouth?" The nurse looked horrified.

No one said anything. I went right into sheer panic mode. The nurse very quickly pulled the baby back up, and then, from slow motion, we went into high-speed motion. I heard someone page the neo natal doctor to our surgical room. "Neo Natal to surgery room 3 stat!" I knew what 'stat' meant, and I knew I was in room 3. I could hear them talking about transporting my baby to NICU. NICU was short for Neo Natal Intensive Care Unit. I also knew what that meant. Jim and I did go to the pre-pregnancy child birthing classes together and they did go over some of these things there. Only babies that had some kind of serious problem at birth got rushed stat to NICU. What I didn't know was what was wrong with my baby. I was trying to piece it together in my mind: "Okay, so she was missing some skin on her left hand, and when the nurse was cleaning her up, the silence from the nurse told me that maybe something else was wrong. Then when the nurse went to give me Samantha- blood starting pouring out of her mouth and I knew that was not normal, but what could it be? What were they thinking? How serious was this? Did they think she was going to die? Why didn't she have skin on the back side of her left hand?"

I was trying to move to look and see what was happening but my body was numb. I kept turning my head all over the room to see where my baby was and what they were doing. My vision was getting blurry from the tears forming in my eyes. I started to feel really emotional and confused. Finally, I looked up over my left shoulder and there was my husband, tears welled up in his eyes. I knew he was sitting there the whole time, but I was so focused on Samantha and what was happening to her, that nothing else mattered. He could barely speak to me, as he asked me, "What should I do? Stay with you? Or go with the baby?" Tears were rushing down his face. Tears were rushing down my face too. Adamantly I told him to go with our baby. I said," You stay with her Jim... no matter what - you stay with her. You find out what is going on, I will be ok."

I really wasn't sure if I was going to be ok either. I just said that because I didn't trust anybody at this point. No one was telling us anything, and I knew in my heart Samantha needed him to be with her more then I did. I was scared to death. The last thing that I wanted was to be alone and I knew I didn't want to be alone with this doctor either. He clearly did not want to talk to me. Every second he did not talk to me just made me not like him all the more.

The Neo Natal doctor came into the room and went right to the baby. He was very quiet. I couldn't hear anything he said. In my mind I was thinking, "This is bullshit that they are whispering. This is my baby and I am her mother and Jim is her father and we have a right to know what they are saying. We have a right to know what they are thinking." I stopped talking just so I could hear. I couldn't make out one word they were saying. My emotions were rotating between fear and anger. At that point they rushed my baby out of the room in one of those little baby carts they put newborns in that have the clear acrylic sides all around the bed. Off she went to the NICU. Jim followed. I did take some comfort from knowing that her daddy would be watching over her.

Chapter 7.

OK, I'm Leaving now

I actually tried to get off of the table before the doctor was done sewing me up. I knew I made him mad at me. He yelled at me. He yelled at me like I was a child. He behaved like this might have been his first time having something really messed up go on during a delivery. I really felt like he was a very experienced doctor due to the way he walked me through the whole C-Section process. I was wrong. And he was an idiot. At that moment, anger just took over and the fighter in me came out. God, I wished Dr. Caps could have been the one to have been there that day. He would have known what to say to me. He would have treated me like I was one of his children, and he would have comforted me instead of reprimanding me. He would understand. This doctor here was a jerk. Not only did I not know him very well, but now I didn't like him either. I was totally losing it. I did not know what emotion to have next: fear, anxiety, worry, panic – you name it, I was having all of them at the same moment. I remember feeling embarrassed and really mad at the same time. I was going to get off that table whether he liked it or not. He kept telling me to stop trying to move. I completely ignored him. Then he gave me a shot of some sort – something I am sure to mellow me out. I don't remember a lot of what I said at that moment. The only memory I have was the doctor yelling at me for freaking out and me not really giving a damn what he thought. I had one thing on my mind and only one thing: To see my baby. To get to her, hold her, and find out what was wrong.

To this day, the one thing that I know that would have made all the difference for me in that delivery room at that moment would have been for that doctor to just talk to me. All he had to do was to tell me everything was going to be ok, and I would have been ok. I panicked because he panicked. No one was prepared for a problem. I'm sure he was probably afraid and, not knowing what was wrong with my baby, he didn't want to make any assumptions. He probably had never seen anything like that before and I think he was panicked as well. Maybe medical school doesn't teach doctors the human side of unexpected complications of a newborn. Maybe they don't learn how to have care and compassion for another human who has just been hit blind-sided with trauma and devastation. It could just be that he did his job. I mean, after all, there I was lying on the table cut wide open after the C-section and all he really knew was that he had to get me put back together while maintaining *my* health. I don't know the answers to all that. All I did know was that on that day, February 13, 1995, my life would change dramatically forever.

I knew something was wrong. I knew something really terrible was wrong. I could feel it in the pit of my stomach. Everything felt like it was taking such a long time. I wanted to see my baby, but the doctor told me I had to go to recovery for a short time before I could do that so that the nurses could monitor me. My health was his concern. I just had a major operation and they needed to make sure that I did not have any complications. "Well how long will I be in there?" I asked, and he answered, "Maybe for an hour or so, it all depends on how your body responds to this surgery." Recovery felt like forever, even though it was actually only one, maybe two, hours. I could not wait to get to my baby.

I kept asking any nurse that walked by, "Please, please can I go see my baby now?" They would just tell me, "Please be patient, just a little while longer. You have to be in recovery long enough for us to know that you are ok." Then I would ask, "Please can someone tell me if my baby is ok? Is she still alive? Something happened to her, she has something wrong with her and I just want to know if she is ok? No one will tell me anything: please!" I asked these questions over and over again, and to anyone who would listen. I was sort of parked in a corner spot in that room so nurses were walking by me to get to other patients. I was talking to anyone who walked by. They all seemed to be so busy. I felt like I was talking to myself as if they could not hear me. Some of them just kept walking by me… ignoring me. If I weren't numb from the waste down, I would have gotten up off that bed and ran to where my baby was. All kinds of thoughts were going through my head, and none of them were good. Fear can really do a number on your mental physic. I started thinking, "Is she ok? Is she still alive? If she is, is she going to be ok? Why would she have blood spilling out of her mouth like that? What was wrong with her hand? Why? Why? Why?!"

Chapter 8.

From Recovery to Discovery

Finally this nurse came to get me. She told me we were going to a room on the maternity floor. Then the nurse started to roll me down the hall out of recovery and down another hall into NICU so that I could see my baby. The nurse said, "Ok, honey, we are going to roll you right down to NICU where your baby is so that you can see her okay? But we can't stop there, we have to get you settled in your room first and update your nurse on your status before you can go into NICU and see your baby." Oh, this was such torture for me. I was not known for having any patience and that was because I didn't have any: Plain-and-simple! We started down the hall towards NICU. As we got closer it felt as if we were moving in slow motion. We were moving past all these babies hooked up to all kinds of machines. I knew this was NICU and not the regular baby area from all of the machines and monitors. There were tubes and wires coming from different parts of their tiny little bodies and then from their bodies they were plugged into those machines. In-between the babies and myself was a huge glass window. I guess families could go there and stand by the window to look in and see their babies. Finally, mid-way through the unit, I could see her ... there she was. My eyes were immediately drawn to her. She was so big compared to all the other babies in there. Mostly all the babies in NICU were tiny, preemie babies, maybe 4 pounds, 5 pounds, it looked like maybe a few were really tiny - maybe 3 pounds - they were in incubators with bright lights on them. Then... there amongst all these tiny, tiny babies... was my 10-½ pound baby girl. She looked so much older then all of those other babies. She also had these tubes hooked up to her. The tubes were on her chest and then attached to some kinds of machines and monitors. My mind was going a hundred miles an hour and in a hundred different directions. No one said anything about her heart, so why then were there tubes connected to her chest and then to a machine as if they are monitoring her heart? Does she have something wrong with her heart? Could that be why blood came flowing out of her mouth? My mind was racing, but then I focused back in on her again and I could see that she was screaming her head off. In my mind I was like, "Oh my God, please let me just touch her; let me get to her now. I need to hold her!" She needed me. My heart was wrenching in pain. This was terrible. This was torture for me. All I wanted to do was to go to her, hold her and comfort her. I knew I could comfort her. No matter what was wrong with her, I knew I was the only one who could make her feel better. I just wanted to hold her. I just wanted to feel her skin against my skin. I wanted to kiss her and talk to her. I felt like I was letting her down. I promised to take care of her and that I would be the best mommy ever. Now, for the first time in her life out of my womb, she could not find me. She could not hear my voice. She must have been terrified without me.

The nurse who was rolling my bed slowed down slightly but she wouldn't stop. She told me that we were not going to stop. I guess she was in a hurry to get where she needed to be. She didn't care that I had not yet been able to hold my baby, or really see her at all. Not being in control right then was making me crazy. As we rolled past Samantha, I could see her naked body in the little acrylic like baby bed they had her in. Right away I noticed some sores on her stomach and chest area. Then my eyes caught her left hand, "Oh my God - her hand, what is wrong with her hand? It was bloody and raw! It looked like there was no skin on the backside of her hand! What was wrong with her? Please tell me?" The nurse who was rolling my bed assured me that everything was going to be ok, "Lets just get you to your room and get you settled and then you can go there and be with your baby." But what that dumb nurse didn't understand was that I really didn't give a shit about getting *me* settled into a room right then. I wanted to know what the hell was wrong with my baby, and I wanted someone to tell me right then, damn it! It didn't look like Samantha was sucking on her hand to me! What the heck was that nurse in the delivery room talking about? Did she think I was stupid or something? Telling me my baby probably sucked her hand and the skin came off? I mean, what kind of wacky crap is that? Her left hand looked like a patch of skin was completely missing on the back. It was red, raw, and bloody, like some kind of wound. It was as clear as that. There was no question: She was missing skin there and something horrible was wrong... but what?

Just like that we were rolling again down the hall and around a few corners to some more hallways, then to my room in the maternity ward. I had never been good with direction, or having a sense of direction, ever in my life. Right then, however, I was trying very hard to pay attention to where we were and where we were going so I could get myself back to the NICU. The only thing on my mind was getting to Samantha. Her screams and cries were playing over and over again in my head like a bad song. I was really trying to stay calm. That nurse who was rolling my bed warned me that they would not let me go into NICU if I didn't stay calm. Next thing I knew I was in my room. The maternity room felt unfamiliar - so cold and empty. It was quiet. The only sounds you could hear were the sounds of laughter and joy coming from both sides of my room on the other side of the walls. You could hear new families bonding with their babies. I could hear people talking and laughing. I felt like I just found out that my best friend had died. I mean it really felt like someone close to me had died.

My baby was not in my room, and I knew that the other new moms in the rooms right next to mine on either side had their babies in their rooms with them. You could hear the sounds of joy from new parents talking and laughing and crying with such happiness of their brand new babies. I could hear their family members congratulating them. I could hear the sounds of the infant babies crying and then the sounds of comfort coming from their parents. All right, then, just kill me. What in the world could possibly be any worse then having to sit in my cold, quiet room baby-less, not knowing when I was going to see her or, really, what was going on. To top that off, I was surrounded by other mothers who were happy. My mind was racing again, and my emotions were out of control. Samantha's cries were different than what I was hearing from the rooms on either side of mine. It was one that struck a cord so deep inside of me that it just shook me... rattled me.

My faith had definitely been shaken.

My husband was in the room waiting for me when I first got there. He was sitting in a chair in the corner of the room. I looked at him for a long minute - but I couldn't speak to him. I was choked up with tears and pain. His arms were folded together like he was waiting for something or someone, but he wasn't waiting on me. He was just waiting. It was such an awkward feeling. A bad feeling. We both felt some kind of loss, or pain, or sadness. I am not sure that I can explain it but, whatever it was, it was painful. We couldn't talk to each other. We just stared at the walls waiting for anyone to walk through that door and tell us what was going on with our baby.

I asked him, "Did you go to be with her like I told you to?"

He replied, "Yes."

I asked, "What is going on?"

He answered, "She is beautiful Marybeth, so beautiful, but something **is** wrong with her. She has little sores on her body all over. No one knows what it is yet, or maybe they just aren't telling me, I don't know. They told me to let them examine her and that I should wait for you in your room"

I just couldn't understand that. I didn't comprehend any of it. Nothing made any sense to me at all. We sat in there: waiting, numb, lifeless....

Chapter 9.

Happy Devastation

Flowers started to arrive in our room. I felt like there was nothing to celebrate. I was angry and confused. I didn't want to see flowers and I didn't want to read the cards. This was not a happy time. This was tragic… devastating. Then finally after what seemed like another very long wait in our cold, lonely room, in walked the neo natal doctor. He was the same doctor who came to the surgery room when I delivered her and took Samantha to NICU. We will call him "Dr. Grim." Because Grim was how he made the situation feel. He was tall and thin with dark hair, and he had some sort of hospital cap on his head. His bedside manner was awful. He was very matter of fact. He spoke without emotion or feeling. He was like a robot. He really pissed me off when he handed me a picture - yes, would you believe? - A *picture* of my baby! I wanted *my* baby, not a meaningless picture. All I could think of was - either this man had lost his mind, or he is a complete idiot with no sense of compassion whatsoever! He must have taken the picture with a Polaroid camera. You know the really old Polaroid cameras where you have that one-inch white strip on the bottom of the picture? You shoot the picture with the camera and then the picture comes out of the bottom of the camera instantly. The white strip read on the bottom, "Sheridan baby 2/13/95." We did name her! Her name was Samantha. Didn't he know she had a name?

She was the biggest baby born that day, or that year, from what we were told. She was also the largest baby that had been placed in the Neo Natal Intensive Care unit that day as well. I was speechless as he handed me the picture. He told us that it was likely that our baby was born with some kind of genetic birth defect. He said that it was caused from a gene that must have been passed down by one of us (Jim or I), or both of us. He said that this is how genetic conditions occur: By the parents passing down a defective gene at the time of conception that then causes certain illnesses and birth defects to occur. I could not believe what I was hearing. This was a nightmare. This was not happening. But it was.

Ok, well, you might as well have just killed me right then and there. Somehow, guilt crept into my emotions and my thoughts. What did I do during my pregnancy to hurt my baby? Or is it something I did before I was pregnant? Maybe it was because my husband got sick? I know Jim was thinking the same thing I was. I knew he was feeling like it was his fault too, and at the same time I was thinking it was my fault. The mood in the room felt that way. My mind starting going back to my high school days. My mind was everywhere. Was it possible that I did something that caused this to happen? Maybe because I used to smoke cigarettes. Or maybe it was because I smoked pot a few times when I was younger. What was it? What did I do to make this happen? Somehow I passed down a bad "something" to my baby girl and she has to suffer from something I did? Oh my God, why didn't someone tell me this could happen if I had a baby? Then again, maybe it was Jim's illness that caused this to happen. That made the most logical sense. That doctor did warn us, but damn it… I didn't listen. I was so stubborn. My desire to have a child outweighed everything else, so now this was my punishment. I didn't even give the ID doctor a chance to see his side of things. I just shut him down and told him I was having the baby no matter what. But now the unthinkable was happening. So now what? How was I going to forgive myself? How was Jim going to forgive me? How would we forgive each other? Where was God right now?

Well, what if it was Jim, and he was thinking what I was thinking? How was he going to forgive himself? Our relationship had always been a little stormy before this, so maybe he will leave me. I knew he loved me as I did him… but was our love strong enough to with stand something like this? Maybe he wouldn't want a baby that has some kind of problem. God wasn't really a part of our lives at that time in our life - so would God help us now? Where was God anyway? Why did He let this happen to us? To our baby? My mind was racing with all of these thoughts. I couldn't focus on anything.

This was supposed to be the happiest day of our married lives together. We were supposed to be laughing and cooing and loving our brand new baby as first time parents do. We were supposed to be smelling those flowers and figuring out where to put them in our room. We were supposed to be answering the phone in our room and sharing our good news. Jim was supposed to be calling all of our family and friends to tell them about Samantha. He had a list of people to call. We talked about him calling them. We had a plan. Now what do we do?

What would we tell everyone? Would we tell them that, yes, we had a baby, but she was missing skin on her left hand, and for some unknown reason she is getting little sores all over her body and nobody knows why? Would we tell them that she was scooped up by the Neo Natal doctor and rushed to NICU - and we are not sure if she is going to live or die? We didn't even know what was going on ourselves, so how would we be able to tell anyone anything? I know everyone was waiting to hear from us. This was not supposed to be happening. This was not what we had planned for. We had not prepared for tragedy. No one told us this was ever remotely close to how it was going to be... or did they? We were in new, unfamiliar territory and we were terrified.

Dr. Grim told us that our baby was placed in the NICU unit for observation. Further testing needed to be done to determine what exactly was wrong with her. He said he thought there might be a chance that she has the "flesh-eating virus," and explained what that was to us for a few minutes. We were speechless. We had no questions. We were clearly in shock. Then he walked out of our room. I just wanted to throw something at him. I wanted to scream at him. He was delivering very bad news so he was the easiest target for our anger. He just dropped the bomb, and I didn't like him. I didn't like God either at that moment.

All I knew was that I wanted to go to sleep and try to wake up and pretend I was in a bad dream. Maybe if I went to sleep I would wake up and realize that I had been dreaming the whole time. Or maybe they could just move me to a different room. The joyful sounds coming from the two rooms on either side of us was more then I could bear. I felt like someone was rubbing salt into my wound. I had physical pain, I had emotional pain, and my heart was broken. I picked up the phone and called down to the front desk check-in area and asked them to send away any more flowers that were to come to my room. I didn't want any more flowers. I didn't want anyone to visit me. I had no idea what to say to anyone, so I told the operator, "Please do not put any calls through to this room for any reason."

The operator responded with, "Are you sure? People are already calling the switch board and asking us about you and your status."

I told the operator, " I am sure. Please. I just can't talk to anyone right now."

"Okay, then you just let me know when it is okay to put calls through again."

Then I added, "And please, no more flowers - just send them away"

"Oh but I can't do that!" she replied.

I rudely interrupted her, "I don't care do whatever you want with them…JUST DON'T SEND THEM TO THIS ROOM, please!"

I thanked her and hung up.

Not knowing what to say to our family and our friends was stressful. I mean, we didn't even know ourselves what was happening. So much drama had just transpired in such a short amount of time we couldn't even process the whole thing. I felt as though I just couldn't talk to anyone at all anyway. Even if I would have had the answers the whole experience was just too traumatic to repeat. I was so tired and drained and overwhelmed. I felt as though I was sinking into a very deep depression and I had only just had my baby four hours prior. I was angry with God. Very angry! I went to church and I prayed for a healthy baby - what happened? How could He have let this happen? Why?

My husband and I had very little to say to each other. We couldn't look at each other. We were blaming ourselves for this disaster privately - I just knew it. And at times in the room it felt like we were blaming each other, too. It was a very doom and gloom mood in our room. I was thinking in my mind, "Oh my God, how will our marriage ever survive this?" We'd had so many ups and down in our marriage before this that now we were having our first child together and she has something serious wrong with her. This was really going to be tough to survive. We couldn't talk about what just happened. One of us did this to her. One of us had passed down this horrible "thing" to our brand new baby girl - or at least that is how we processed what was told to us. We were sick in our hearts and in our souls. We were in pain. I was certain my husband was going to just walk out the door.

I tried to tell myself that I couldn't worry too much about that right now because, more importantly, I needed to get to my baby. I prayed to God that if He was actually there… if there was a God… that I hoped He was holding our marriage and our life in his hands.

Chapter 10.

Who Said I Can't Go to the NICU?

I started asking the nurses, "When can I go and see my baby?" I felt like everyone was trying to keep me from going to see my baby, as if there was something really bad happening and everyone was trying to keep it a secret from me. I knew it was a conspiracy. I was so paranoid. Looking back it was probably the drugs from the surgery and the pain medicine that enhanced those feelings of paranoia. I had just had a C-section so there were all sorts of rules I had to follow, and the more they tried to tell me what I had to do – before I got to go down there to NICU to see Samantha – just made me all that much more mad and angry. I mean, for goodness sakes already, just let me get down there to be with her. All I wanted to do was to see her and to hold her. I hadn't even been given the chance to see her body naked. I wanted to check her out. I wanted to see who she looked like more: Jim or me. Whose nose did she have? I wondered what a combination of Jim and I looked like anyway. All that stuff you do when you first get to meet your brand new baby for the first time. I did get a brief glimpse of her at delivery, but with the drama, it just wasn't the same. I wanted a long look at her.

I really didn't know what was wrong with Samantha. I felt like nobody really cared if I got down to see my baby or not. And why not? I was the only new mom on that entire floor who was not getting to have my baby in my room with me, or at least that is how it felt to me. That separation anxiety I had was ripping me apart and making me crazy. Like nothing I have ever experienced before. There were other babies in NICU, but it seemed as though every room anywhere near my room had really happy sounds coming in through the walls. I felt like crawling into a hole and dying. Everyone else near me was overwhelmed with joy of their brand new babies. Don't get me wrong, I was happy for them. But the extreme opposite emotions that Jim and I were having – compared to what we could hear – were just torture. I don't even like to go into maternity wards to this day just because the memory of that time was such a deep wound that still hurts. I am not sure how, or even if, hospitals are doing it today, but there should be a special place for moms who deliver a baby that is not healthy, or appears to have some kind of complication, to be separated from the new, happy moms who are celebrating their new 'healthy' babies. To be so close to such happiness in the wake of what was feeling like the most tragic thing to happen in my life was unbearable. Unthinkable in terms of life and reality.

I have always been a fighter, and my personality was strong, so I had those two things on my side from the beginning. My husband grew up similar to the way I did, so I knew he was tough too. I wasn't sure exactly how tough or strong he really was, but I prayed for God to make him strong. I did have thoughts running through my head that my husband Jim might just get up and run out the door. I was worried. When I would worry, I would cancel the thought and ask God to help us get through this nightmare together. I prayed to God and I screamed at him at the same time. I guess it was a good thing I was even still talking to him at all. I could have stopped. You could say my relationship with God at that time was one of doubt mixed with certainty, so although I questioned whether or not He was there or listening, I prayed anyway just in case He was real… and He was listening.

I am not sure exactly how I got to the NICU floor to begin with, but I do know I walked there and I wasn't supposed to. The nurse from the maternity floor I was on came running after me with a wheel chair. By the time she reached me I was already in NICU. My physical pain was not as strong as my emotional pain or my desire to be with my baby. Nothing was going to keep me away from my baby right then: nothing good or bad. No matter what anyone had to say to me, no matter how bad it was going to be – I was going to handle it because I knew Samantha needed me. She needed my milk and she needed my love. I could feel her screaming. I could feel her pain. I needed to get to her fast.

I immediately went to her and reached down in her bed to pick her up when a nurse rushed towards me. The nurse said, "Please you need to sit in the wheelchair." So I did. The nurse explained to me how I could hemorrhage and that I needed to be careful with my incision. I nodded to let her know I understood and would follow her instructions. I felt vulnerable and I wanted to comply with their rules so I could be with my baby. Then I stood up to hold my baby and yet another nurse came running over and said to me, "You can't hold that baby!" I was ready to fight. I thought to myself, "Who the hell does that nurse think she is?

Telling me that I can't hold my baby. She must be out of her mind!" I answered her, "This is MY baby and I am going to hold her." Ok – enough was enough – I wanted to do what they said, but give me a break for goodness sakes. I just gently held Samantha. I didn't put her down or have a reaction. I just sat there holding her. The nurse stood over me – watching me – I didn't care. I just ignored her. What a wonderful feeling of joy… to hold my baby. Then the nurse said that her skin was really fragile and getting badly damaged and no one knew exactly what was wrong, so they wanted to keep her handling at a minimum. I looked at the nurse in her eyes and said, "Well then I guess you will have to let me do all the handling because this is my baby and I am going to hold her!" I think from that moment on that particular nurse and I did have an understanding with each other. What I was not prepared for was the other nurses changing shifts and new nurses coming in and switching places.

Samantha was wrapped up very tightly in this baby blanket and I wanted to see her body. I was so curious. I was already very annoyed that anyone would try to tell me what I could or couldn't do with my baby. The anger that had already found a home in my mood was about to unleash itself on the next person who tried to stop me from holding her or from just being with her. I did open her blanket and very carefully I looked her over. I could see what looked like little patches of raw, open skin around these little, blue circles of tape on her chest where they had taped probes to her. They were – for some reason – monitoring her heart. It didn't look like a rash at all, but instead little, round areas that were either a blister or an open wound. Like the skin in that spot ripped off. She also seemed to have little, red bumps on different parts of her body, or maybe they were blisters, too, I couldn't really tell. At this point I knew something was seriously wrong, but unsure of what we were dealing with; I just tried to stay in that moment. I wanted to keep Samantha calm and happy.

It was clear that I needed to make friends with the nurses on this floor if I wanted to find out anything, or get any information. Years of being in sales and being trained by the best had taught me that you get more with honey then you do with vinegar. I think the nurse on this day was starting to actually feel sympathy for Samantha and me. She started to warm up to me. Knowing in my mind that I was on drugs from just having a C-section, not even five or six hours ago, I was trying to be very careful how I handled myself so they would let me stay in NICU with my baby. I wanted to know everything and I wanted to ask as many questions as I could so that I could get a better understanding of what was going on. Samantha was born at noon, and I think I finally really got to see her around 3 or 4 o'clock. It was probably around 5 or 6 o'clock now and my nurse was informing me that her shift was almost over and that a new nurse would be coming in to replace her. She told me that the nurse who will replace her will be with Samantha until the morning and then there will be another shift change of nurses around 7am. It made sense. But I thought, "Oh, God, I have to have all these different personalities to deal with and while I was in the worst place in my mind I could be."

The nurses, overall, were pretty nice, but what made them not so nice was that they had 5 or 6 newborns to monitor instead of just mine. They were always rushing and made me feel that, although warranted, my questions were not convenient. After I understood that, it was easier for me to understand their personalities. Prior to my baby being born, the only other hospital experience I'd had really was when my husband was in ICU quarantine for spinal meningitis.

That was a much different situation than this one.

Chapter 11.

Baby Blanket Battle

Although they didn't want me to hold me baby, I did it anyway. I think the first nurse realized how good it was for both of us when I held her. The whole mother-baby bonding issue was completely necessary. When I held her, she calmed down and stopped crying. It intrigued me how Samantha always knew I was there and sometimes at the sound of my voice she would calm down. I tried to breast feed her, but her lips seemed to be so fragile, they would tear and break as she sucked on my nipple, so I pumped every couple of hours and I learned how to feed her with a syringe. Eventually, we figured out how to lubricate the nipple of a bottle so that when she sucked it, it would be okay on her lips. Well, the new nurse arrived and clearly she had her own way of doing things. I learned everything that the first nurse had done and taught me. I made sure I knew every detail so that I could tell the new nurse incase someone were to have forgotten. They were so busy that I wanted to be helpful in writing down every detail because I knew it would only be better for Samantha. Sometimes little things would get lost in the translation between shift changes, so I wanted to make sure for Samantha's sake that nothing got missed.

The second nurse and I didn't seem to get along at all. She absolutely had no personality. I don't think I ever saw her smile. Everything about her was so serious and uninviting. I felt like maybe she didn't really like her job here in NICU. She made me feel like I was in the way. She also made me feel like she had absolutely no interest in hearing anything I had to say about Samantha prior to her shift starting. Like maybe I wasn't qualified or experienced enough to translate to her since she was a nurse. Who knew what her problem was? But she had one with me.

I only sat with Samantha in a rocking chair or near her bed. I never wondered around the unit or got up and went anywhere except to the restroom. Whenever the nurse would come to take Samantha's vitals I felt awkward and uneasy around her. She wasn't friendly, but instead cold and stuck-up: like she knew everything and I was just some poor, pitiful mom hovering over her sick baby. A couple of times when she would go to do something to Samantha, I would very gently try to tell her that the nurse before her thought that maybe doing it (whatever it was) this way was better for Samantha. Man, I think that just made her more mad and mean. This nurse was mean - period. I had to watch everything she was doing to Samantha. I had to protect Samantha. It was uncomfortable for me to be there when I clearly knew that this nurse just didn't like me being there. She didn't want me to be there in NICU at all. She would walk by me and tell me, "Oh, maybe you should go back to your room now and get some rest." Then I would say to her, "Well… can I take Samantha with me?" To which she would respond, "Uh… no, she has to stay here in NICU. Don't worry I know what to do. The nurse before me left notes for me, so I know everything that is going on with her care." "Okay," I replied, "But the nurse before you had forgotten to put down there in your notes how she and I figured out a better way to wrap Samantha up with the baby blanket so that it is less traumatic on her skin, and I have to show you that."

The nurse looked like her face was red with anger. She glared at me and said nothing. I was scared to leave Samantha in her care. Sure I was exhausted and my body physically was in agony and pain. I had no choice but to stay. This one nurse could really maybe hurt her or cause more wounds. Oh, heck no! I was staying, so I said to her, "You know what? That's ok - I am fine. I am going to stay right here, thank you."

I am not sure about the time, but a little while later, during one of the routine vital checks this nurse was doing on Samantha, she had to unwrap her to get a temperature under her armpit. I was standing there next to Samantha, watching to make sure that this nurse was gentle. This nurse was in such a hurry that she would just rip the baby blanket right off of Samantha and I would just cringe as if I could feel Samantha's pain. Samantha started to cry like it hurt, and I looked at the nurse and said, "Hey - she obviously has something wrong with her skin. Could you please be a little more, gentle with her?" So, boy, was I surprised when the nurse took Samantha's baby blanket and threw it at me… in my face. As she did that, she said to me in an angry voice, "Well, then, you do it!"

Oh, boy, that was it! I was steamed. I was done taking crap from her. I quickly wrapped Samantha up, but very gently as to make sure not to cause any more boo-boos, and I walked over to the nurse's station there in NICU, raised my voice loudly and said, "Did anyone see that? Is this how parents get treated here in NICU? I demand to speak to your supervisor!"

A few minutes later this wacky nurse just told me, "Go to your room!"

"No," I demanded, "I want to speak to your supervisor right now!"

A few minutes passed and this young girl came out from the back room and walked up to me to talk to me. I knew she was a nurse, but she didn't look like she was old enough to be a supervisor. Anyway, no one else was in NICU when the mean nurse threw Samantha's baby blanket at me except for the mean nurse and me. What was I thinking? That someone was actually going to believe me or listen to me? Well, this new nurse asked me to go to my room.

"Ma'am," she said, "I am sorry you are having such a difficult time. I am sure this is a very hard for you. The nurses have told me that you have been here in NICU the entire time since you were released to the maternity ward from recovery. You must be exhausted. I am sure if you get some rest this will all seem better tomorrow."

All I could see was red. I was so mad. This was so unbelievable that I couldn't believe it. Well, I knew that I needed to go because clearly this mean nurse and I hated each other and nothing good was going to come from me staying. For Samantha's sake I better go and just pray to God that someone was watching the mean nurse.

It freaked me right out at how rough I thought she handled my baby. We actually had a knockdown, and we yelled at each other. That was the first time I felt the need to fight for my baby. I felt like a lion protecting her cub. I think at that point I was in and out of NICU periodically throughout the night, not really sleeping because I wanted Samantha to know I was there and that *I* was watching over her. I did go back to my room, but then I would walk back down every hour or so just to check on Samantha until the morning. I had noticed by this time that the slightest touch would cause an open sore or a blister on her skin, and these blisters were starting to appear randomly all over her body. It seemed to me that you had to be very gentle with her. This new nurse was so cold to me. She behaved as though she really didn't like her job. She didn't like me asking her any questions, and she made me feel like I was an imposition. Every question I asked her she tried to ignore me, or she would just rudely walk away from me. I demanded to speak to the head of the hospital after my battle with the mean nurse, but to no avail. I think they all just thought I was a crazy mom in NICU - loosing my mind which, looking back on it now… maybe I was, or… maybe I saved Samantha from undo trauma because of a nurse who really didn't like her job.

I never did get to speak to anyone of any authority in that hospital. It never occurred to me that another woman could be so mean to a new mom. Especially someone like me who just had her whole world turned upside down. I don't know what kind of people she was used to dealing with, but under the current circumstances I thought I was being very calm. I was walking on eggshells around that nurse. Nevertheless, I had waited all day to speak to, or to see face-to-face, or hear from by phone - our pediatrician. By the way, we got our pediatrician from an interview I had with him prior to Samantha being born. So, before this day, I had only met him one other time. He was the only pediatrician I interviewed. That whole process of interviewing a pediatrician before your delivery to find the right one never really worked for me. I mean, how do you know if you have the right one until you try them, right? So I wasn't going to interview five pediatricians. I just didn't see the sense in it.

I was anxious to see Samantha's doctor, hoping that he would tell us something… anything. Almost an entire day had passed and not one person had anything at all to tell us. They were not necessarily telling us anything bad, either; they just were not saying anything. I kept asking the nurses, "When is the pediatrician going to be here?" They kept telling me around 5am or 6am when he does his rounds, so I waited. Come to think of it, I do not remember sleeping at all that night. I just kept going back and forth from the maternity unit to the NICU unit. The nurses on the maternity unit were great, so every chance I got I would ask them when our pediatrician would be there.

Chapter 12.

UH-OH - Who Is This Man?

To my surprise, the pediatrician walked into my room around 8am or so, and the first thing I got from him was a lecture about my behavior in the NICU. He told me that the NICU nurse complained to him that I was rude to her. He told me that he was not going to allow me to behave rudely to his nurses. He didn't even ask me how my night was, or what happened, he just walked in - slamming me with accusations. I thought, "Ok, this relationship is going to last about a day and then I am going to fire him." It actually lasted a bit longer than that but, seriously, who comes into a hospital room to greet a brand-new first-time mom who had her world tossed up side down with a lecture about her behavior with a nurse in NICU? I know the answer to that but will, respectfully, hold my tongue.

All because the mom was franticly worried how the nurse was handling her baby. Knowing that handling her baby - even the slightest bit roughly - could result in blisters and open wounds? Who wouldn't freak out? I was neurotic - definitely neurotic - but who wouldn't be? Only the doctor I chose would turn out to be such a jerk, right? I didn't care much about the way he was treating me. All I really wanted to know was what the heck was going on with my baby? How can we fix my baby and make her better and get the heck out of there? Surely there is a pill or something they can give her, right? Well, guess what? He had nothing to offer us either - except that they do believe it is some sort of a genetic condition and that they were leaning away from it being the flesh eating virus. I knew it wasn't the flesh-eating virus. He told us that he was going to find a local dermatologist to come in and exam our baby. That turned out to be the best thing that doctor ever did for us.

I spent every second in NICU rocking Samantha and trying to do all that I could so that the nurses would not have to do anything. I would feed her, change her diapers, and hold her. Once I started holding her I never put her down. If they weren't touching her, I was happy. She would get new blisters and wounds all over her body every day regardless. Every other second of the day I was praying for God to help us. Praying that He would just let her stay with me for a while. "Please, God, don't take her from me God. Please." I would repeat that over and over again in my mind. I would say that constantly to myself whether I was awake or about to go to sleep. Watching Samantha get all these wounds and sores on her body made me nervous she was going to die. I didn't want her to die.

My mom was there beside me reassuring me everything was going to be ok. "Oh Samantha looks beautiful Marybeth," my mom would say. And I would think, "Does she not see what I see? Sure she is beautiful, but something serious is wrong with her." Now that I look back on it, my mom saw what I saw and more. She was so wise, and a pillar of strength for me. My mom was so smart to always keep me focused on the good and the positive ... and God.

Chapter 13.

"Dr. Save Me"

It was now a few days into what felt like a complete nightmare. It was later in the afternoon, and into the NICU walks this woman dressed in beige, kaki pants and a button down top. She didn't look like a doctor. She didn't have one of those long white coats on. She had short blonde hair and a smile on her face that told me right away that she was going to be kind to me. I really needed someone to be kind to me at that point. She had a calm, casual demeanor, but the nurses were very respectful of her. Everything I knew up until this point about my life would be changed forever. The only thing that was certain right then was that I just gave birth to my first child; the one I dreamt about for 10 months, the one I felt move inside me that gave me so much joy and pleasure while pregnant, was just born a few days ago and I was not sure if she was going to live or die. Every tiny touch to her skin anywhere on her fragile body would look painful and cause sores that were raw and open. I had a constant stream of tears rolling down my cheeks at all times. Tears seemed to flow so easily then. My eyes were just constantly swollen and red from crying so much.

I want to call her "Dr. Save Me," because she really did save me. She was like a beam of sunshine that just radiated the whole NICU. She walked over to me and started talking to me right away as if someone may have described what I looked like to her and told her that I was the half crazed mom in NICU all of the time holding her baby. Dr. Save Me told me that she thought our precious beautiful baby girl might have something called, Epidermolysis Bullosa. Ok... so that was a foreign language I had never heard of before. I had a blank stare on my face as I looked at her. "Huh," I said, "What did you say? And how do you pronounce that?" She repeated it again, "Epidermolysis Bullosa. It is an inherited genetic condition and it is very rare." That is a word I would soon hear a lot -"rare." "Oh," I said, "what does that mean?" "Well," she said, "it means that she may have a problem with her skin that has been passed down to her by both you and your husband or by just one of you." She asked me if anyone on either side of our families had ever had this or any skin conditions that we knew of before, and I said no, not that Jim or I had any knowledge of. Usually when a disease like this one gets past down by one or both parents it could mean that there is a family history of it somewhere down the line. Usually you would have heard of some family story or some one in the family who had something like this. Jim and I had not ever even heard of anyone even having any skin issues ever, not even acne or rashes, or anything.

It also means that there are not too many children affected by this disease in the world today, which is what makes it - rare. This disease does not discriminate, it will occur in any race - in any family – in any culture - and in any income bracket. She went on to explain that this was going to be challenging to figure out. No surprise to me considering my entire first mommy experiences were challenging to figure out.

So I told her how the other Neo Natal doctor had told us that one of us had caused this to happen to our baby, and how neither one of us, Jim nor I, had been able to speak to the other about it all. I think that my husband and I both felt as though what had happened to our daughter was caused by one of us, and it was a kind of pain that is almost unbearable to think about, unimaginable to think that we may have caused this to happen to our baby.

Wow - news flash bulletin for Neo Natal Doctors around the world: Please don't do this to brand new parents ever. Is there not another way to tell brand new parents about genetics? Instead of making the parents feel as though they committed some kind of crime. Thank God we were both fairly strong people, because I am not sure anyone else could handle having just delivered a brand new first baby with some kind of severe problem and might not live… and then to find out on top of all that, that one of the first time parents might have caused this to happen to their baby. WOW - that is all I can say is - wow.

So this Doctor (sent right from heaven above) proceeded to tell me that there was further testing that needed to be done to confirm what she might have suspected to be the problem with Samantha. Dr. Save Me needed my permission to do a three-whole-punch biopsy to be sent away to this EB specialist doctor in North Carolina. The Doctor in North Carolina apparently was the only person in the entire country who could read this test. The test was called an Electron Microscopy, and the doctor in North Carolina was the EB expert. I guess the test was unusual in that it was extremely difficult to tell where the blistering originated. The EB expert was going to have to take the tissue sample from the biopsy, put it in the "Electron Microscopy" machine and try to make that determination. That determination would tell him what subtype our daughter has. We agreed and signed the papers for this test. She told us that after the test results came in it will confirm that she has Epidermolysis Bullosa, and that it will also help determine the subtype of this disease, which was very important. There was also some DNA testing that we would need to get done, but that could wait a little bit. The DNA testing and the three-hole-bunch biopsy, together with a clinical evaluation, will give an accurate diagnosis. Getting the proper subtype diagnosed will determine how we will care for our baby. She said that every subtype of this particular genetic condition was different and required different kinds of daily care. Some babies required bandaging and some did not, depending on the subtype and severity of the disease.

I know that I spent five days in the hospital when Samantha was born; partly because I was not taking care of myself properly while trying to make sure that my baby was not going to die, and partly because I knew my OB felt great pain when trying to tell me that I was going to have to leave the hospital and leave my baby behind in there in NICU. One thing for sure was that our insurance company at that time wanted me out of that hospital no matter what. The Gloomy Day of Departure was coming and I knew it.

At some point Dr. Save Me did confirm this diagnosis to be Epidermolysis Bullosa but she gave us hope that there were over 60 different subtypes and that Samantha could in fact have one of the less severe subtypes. Maybe if we were real lucky she might even escape the life threatening subtypes. Meanwhile, my husband and other family members began to hit the Internet and library to find out as much information about this disease EB as they could. No one could even pronounce "Epidermolysis Bullosa" - let alone comprehend it even existed. Knowledge was power and we needed all the information we could get our hands on if we were going to help Samantha. I don't think any of us were fully prepared to learn about EB. The information they uncovered was unthinkable. The dark side of this disease, EB, was hovering over us like a black cloud. At first everyone seemed so eager to get information and give it to us and find out everything about EB. Then, strangely and almost suddenly, everyone just became quiet. They almost seemed to avoid the subject entirely. When I would ask what or if anyone had found out anything, everyone just ignored me purposely. Later, I would understand why. No one wanted me to read the words printed about EB. No one wanted me to know the truth about EB. I guess they thought that somehow they could just keep it from me… I guess.

The first document I read was horrible, and devastating. All I could see or hear was death. Death before the age of one if the subtype was Junctional. And death before the age of 20 if the subtype was Recessive Dystrophic. Either way it was death with a life of endless pain and suffering. No method of treatments, apparently no cure, and no medicines were available to make it all better, and most definitely there was no magic pill.

Oh boy! Never in my life had I ever heard, or read, or ever witnessed such horrific details surrounding a disease. The information was beyond any thing my mind could wrap itself around. The slightest touch would bring painful blisters, and open wounds. The slightest touch? The skin is our largest organ, how is that possible?

Well depending on the subtype it looks like children with EB are either born with not enough collagen number 7, or they were missing the collagen number 7 gene all together.

The eyes were affected, the mouth, throat, esophagus, hands, feet, bowls, every single part of their bodies… except their minds. The mind was not affected, and in most cases reports indicated that most children with this disease were far more intelligent then children in their age groups. Far more intelligent then the average child for sure. All I could think of was that this was the most tragic horrible disease I had even heard of and now… it was in my life. More tragic then anything else I ever knew about. If they (EB children) had their minds, then they knew they were doomed for a life of hell. If they had their minds, then they knew how much pain they were in. Finally, if they had their minds, then at some point in their lives they would learn that their time here on earth was terminal before the age of 20 with no hope for a cure. How could being smart or intelligent be anything to be happy about if your life was going to be true torture all of the time? There was nothing positive or promising about any detail of the disease that I read. The more I read and saw as we explored the internet and different articles and books, the more like hell it seemed to me. It was no wonder everyone tried to hide the details from me. Oh my God this was insane. There was no way I was actually awake and living this. I know…. I am asleep… I am dreaming - I just need someone to wake me up.

I prayed all the time. Non-stop. I was constantly talking to God, sometimes even yelling at Him, but never-the-less, talking. While we were in the hospital no one really knew to pop the blisters that just kept appearing all over her body. The blisters would just appear and then burst on their own - I guess from friction or from someone handling her. There were blisters all over her body scattered in various places. Every day new blisters would appear... no... every hour. There wasn't even one area that did not get a blister. The blisters were inside her mouth, on her tongue, and inside her ears. My baby's body had an odor of puss that you could smell when you were holding her. It was really gross and weird at the same time. Weird for me to say it was gross - considering I was talking about *my baby*. We had to cover her hands with mittens because she wanted to touch her self with her hands (like new born babies do) all of the time, but her nails were scratching her and causing wounds and more blisters. She was hurting herself so we had to discover new ways of keeping her from doing that. We had to bandage her heels and feet because she would kick and thrash around and then her feet would get blisters that would burst and turn into painful bloody wounds. We had to bandage her left hand that did not have skin on it to get it to heal. Her hand was bloody red and raw and it was like... I could see and feel her pain. She definitely had pain. Some people thought that because she was born with boo-boos that maybe she was used to the pain, or somehow didn't feel the pain. No... I don't think as humans we ever really get used to pain. Plain and simple: pain is pain. I had heard of a rare disease in which a child is born not able to feel pain, but not with this disease EB - everybody was in pain... including the parents. You could tell Samantha was in pain. It was heart wrenching to be witness to her suffering.

The doctors put her on Benadryl right away to help her from itching the wounds that were trying to heal. That was the next big issue. Healing skin itches, so she was always itching herself because some spots on her body were always healing and others were becoming new wounds and new sores. Some days felt like we would take three steps forward, finally getting some areas healed up, and then ten steps backwards with new wounds appearing. For the most part Samantha seemed to be a pretty happy baby. Watching her little body so battered and sore all the time was heartbreaking for everyone... especially me. I was never the one who could handle blood or bodily fluids either. If you knew me, then you didn't throw up around me. And if you cut yourself and blood was flowing, then a doctor's office or a hospital was your safest bet. I had no intentions of being a nurse. The thought had never entered my mind.

Every day we had blood or puss oozing from somewhere on her body and at multiple places at a time. It was disturbing and nerve wrecking. It was getting really hard for me to function. I was literally afraid to do her bandages. I was freaked out at the sight of her wounds. My reality was disturbed and twisted. Nothing was making any sense to me at all. This was a whole new ball game and the territory my husband and I were in now was totally unfamiliar.

Chapter 14.

Leaving Her Behind

So the day came that I had to leave the hospital without my baby. Oh, my goodness, you might as well have just cut my head off. The torture was unforgiving and relentless. Every time I turned around a new heartbreak was waiting for me around the corner. The fear of leaving her there in the hospital and not being able to just be there every second was really a frightening feeling. I felt so powerless and not in control. What if something happened to her while I was not there? I guess I should have considered myself lucky since I knew that some moms had to go home without a baby at all. Some moms gave birth to babies that were stillborn, and/or had some complication and the baby just didn't make it out of the hospital at all. Their pain must be far beyond what I had experienced, so I was thankful that she was still alive but fearful she would die at any minute. Maybe that was why leaving the hospital without her was so hard. I don't know. All I do know is that was the worst feeling.

I prolonged my departure for as long as I could that day. I thought of every reason why I should have to stay until late that night. Every time my OB doctor would see me and try to talk to me about leaving I would have a new reason why I should stay. Although - unless I personally wanted to pay the hospital bills - I had to go. The Insurance Company said I had to go. So finally the day came that I had to leave. That ride home from the hospital that night was such a long ride home and so emotional at the same time. Jim had left our Van at the hospital the day before and rode home with my sister, Rita. I am not sure why - maybe it was just out of plain confusion. My sister had given him a ride to the hospital that next day so that he could get and take me home. Somehow they left the keys to our van at home or with my sister Rita - I am not sure which one. Jim did not realize that he did not have the keys until he got into the hospital and up to my room. My sister had already left the hospital. Then something had happened where my sister went out to eat with some friends. She thought she would be doing us a favor by giving us some time alone. When we tried to reach her by phone we could not get in touch with her. So my husband had to call one of our employees at 10pm at night to ask for a ride home. It was like my husband couldn't function either. Neither one of us was functioning.

We couldn't think or solve simple problems that we were previously so good at doing. Here I was one week post C-section delivery - a major surgery on top of coping with a baby whose prognosis was not too good and I could barely walk due to the pain from my surgery. Well our employee, Jeff, had a two-door, two-seater little sports coupe car. I took one look at that car and I thought, "Oh no this is not going to be fun." Just sitting in there all squashed up in the same seat as my husband was painful. When he hit a bump in the road I thought I would die from the pain. I had weaned myself off the pain pills so that I could be coherent and intelligent when anyone was speaking to me about my baby. Although the pain pills did help the pain, they were not so good for the mind to digest medical terminology and information that could possibly save my baby's life. Someone should have told me that night to take a pain pill just for that ride home. But then no one would have ever had any reason to think I'd be sharing the front seat of a tiny sports car after major abdominal surgery either. Ok - that night was bad. I was really angry with God - cried myself to sleep. I was even mad at my husband for the ride home too. I was just mad at everyone. Total insult to injury. All I could think was, "Man - just when I thought things could not possibly get any worse, they were sinking deeper and deeper into a pit of bad getting more bad and the light was fading."

Hope was fading.

Chapter 15.

God, Can You Hear Me?

The agony of being at home without Samantha was more than I could stand. The next day, just before getting in the shower, I called both Dr. Save Me, our dermatologist, and our pediatrician and begged both of them to please consider letting Samantha come home with me. I really felt like no matter what I said they were not listening. It was very frustrating. I gave the pediatrician a really hard time. I was not taking "no" for an answer and he was not budging. He just kept telling me that she needed to stay in NICU until "they" felt she was stable. Later that morning as I was in the shower all I could hear was Samantha screaming in my head. When I closed my eyes and let the water flow down my face I could hear her scream. It sounded so real to me. It was so alarming. I had to keep telling myself it was only in my mind and that I wasn't really hearing the sound of her crying. I just started to pray, and ask God, "Please, please let her come home with me. Please God, just let her come home with me. I can take care of her, I know I can." I think I was in the shower for 20 minutes crying and praying then finally screaming at God, "Please God I need her here with me. I can't take any more pain, I need her with me." I went on and on for at least fifteen minutes ranting and screaming at God. My mom always reassured me He was always listening. She always told me to pray and never give up that God would take care of me. I am not sure that she ever told me it was ok to scream at God... but darn it, He wasn't listening to me.

That warm water running down my face in the shower was so comforting to me then. Just as I got out of the shower and wrapped the towel around myself, the phone rang. No one was home but me. Everyone left the house to give me some time to myself. I will never figure out why anyone would think that time alone was even close to something I needed at that point. I am still not sure why they did that, because I felt like I was losing my mind being home without my baby. Time alone was not good for me then. The past eight days were so exhausting for me. I think I might have only slept a few hours total those whole eight days. This was the first morning at home without my Samantha and I was not doing well at all. I was beginning to loose my breast milk, and I was so fatigued I could barley function.

I answered the phone. "Hello", the voice on the other end said, "Hi Marybeth this is 'Dr. Pediatrician,' I am calling to tell you that you can come to the hospital and pick up your baby today. We have decided that Samantha will get better care at home with you then in the hospital where there is one nurse for every four or five babies." I was stunned… shocked… speechless really. There was a moment of silence on the phone.

"Are you there, Mrs. Sheridan?" said the doctor.

"Oh yes, I am here, I am just in shock. You told me just this morning that this was not going to happen."

"Well the other doctors and I gave it some thought and we realized that you were right. Your baby does belong home with you. So what time shall I tell them you will be there Mrs. Sheridan?"

"Right now," I replied. "I will be there right now, and thank you."

So my sister Rita drove my mom and I to the hospital. I was still not allowed to drive a car from my surgery. My mom tried to keep things upbeat and light in the car. Happy and always with a smile on her face, she told me how wonderful this was going to be that she was with me to help me care for my brand new baby. My mom said she couldn't wait to show me all of the tricks she learned being a mommy to her five children and how exciting this was to be here with me now as this was my first child. I was the youngest of five children and I was her baby. I could tell my mom was scared too, but she never showed that to me. Fear was not part of my mother's game plan and my mom always had a game plan. My mom always wore her brave face in times of trouble. My mom prayed a lot as well. She would be the one to always direct me back to God and the power of prayer. She always believed that miracles were possible. She always told me, "With God all things are possible." Right about now I was even wondering if there was a God. I mean how could God let something like this happen? I felt like I was losing my faith. I think my mom was worried about that to.

All I did was cry. I still felt like at any moment Samantha was going to leave me, and that very thought alone haunted me constantly. My mom kept up the cheery mood. "Oh honey, did you see how Samantha smiled at me in the hospital? She is such a beautiful baby Marybeth, and strong as a horse. Did you see how well she holds her head up? Oh,

Marybeth, she is still so young to be holding her head up. She is going to beat this thing she has, you must have faith child."

My mother would repeat this to me over and over again. Samantha was developing perfectly. She was doing all of the things that babies do like smiling and cooing, beginning to hold her head up. Developmentally she was right on track.

Every minute I was away from my Samantha felt like a lifetime that had passed. It is hard to explain really unless you have walked there before. All I really knew at this point was that I wanted to have a baby at this time in my life more then anything else I had ever wanted. I enjoyed every second of my pregnancy and every pound I gained. I got such pleasure from feeling this living being inside my womb and I talked to her every day all of the time. I waited for 10 maybe 11 months and then here we were at the hospital to finally take her home, and all I could think of was, "Will she live to see her first birthday? How will we survive this as a married couple? How will I survive losing her?"

Chapter 16.

Nurse Karen

We walked into the hospital ready to pick her up. The exit nurse was waiting for us. She was so kind as she had everything ready for us. As we gathered all of our belongings, a new nurse that I had not seen before this day came up to me. "Hi my name is Karen. Is Samantha your baby?"

Curious, I replied, "Yes."

"Well," the nurse continued, "I have a nephew who was born with this very same disease."

"Oh really?" I said.

She started to show me pictures of her nephew. She told me that her nephew had Epidermolysis Bullosa. I think up until this point I was thinking that either my Samantha was going to die, or there was going to be some sort of medicine that was going to make her all better, or better yet, maybe my child would be one of the lucky ones to have the least severe form of EB. The one that completely goes away with age and leaves no sign of the disease behind at all. No scars, no more boo-boos. So as she showed me these pictures, questions started rolling out of my mouth that I didn't know were there before that day. I asked her, "Well, does this disease go away in time?"

She said, "No, I am afraid not."

"Oh," I said. "Well what are those brown spots on his arms and skin?"

"Oh those are scabs," she replied. "Yes, he gets wounds, then they heal and scab up and then new ones appear and the process repeats itself."

"Well, can he have children?" I asked.

"Well... yes," she responded, "But that depends, and more than likely he will hand it down to his children."

Ok - that was enough for me. Oh my God, scars, scabs, and he looked different, not normal - just different. My poor baby girl. What kind of a life was this? No children of her own? No hope for her future? Oh no....

No one - not even Dr. Save Me - could tell me the answers to these questions, so why then is some nurse who I have never even met before in my life coming up to me on the day I am taking my baby home and telling me all of the things? I didn't want to hear any of this. Did someone put her up to this? Because they could not tell me themselves? All kinds of thoughts were traveling around in my mind. I was so upset, and so confused. I really think that Nurse Karen thought she was helping me by sharing her story. She seemed so confident and sure of herself. But little did she know she just shoved an arrow through any hope of a normal life I had for my daughter. My sister wanted to strangle that woman. I know we had some words for her and I don't think it was "thank you."

The rest of that day was a blur. Later we confirmed that the mysterious nurse Karen really did tell us the truth about this disease Epidermolysis Bullosa (otherwise known as EB). What Karen didn't know is how bad we would truly find out it was for us. I know now that Karen's nephew was a very mild case of EB. I do know that Karen tried to help us, but it was too coincidental for me. I don't usually believe in coincidences anyway so I was really having a hard time with this one. I was trying to piece things together again. It just felt like every couple of days everything just sort of fell apart again.

Sometimes I think back on that day often and wish I could go back and find that nurse, Karen, to tell her "thank you," and to tell her that I am sorry if I got her into any trouble at all for sharing with me about her nephew. I knew my entire family was upset that a strange person approached me with photos in hand to tell me of this horrific disease that doctors had not yet confirmed to be true with me... but yet she was confirming. I also know that when I got to a phone I immediately called all of our doctors to ask them why this person Karen made it a point to share her story with us. It never occurred to me that she thought she might be helping me. I felt like I was under attack... all the time.

Chapter 17.

Finally Home: "Don't Lose Your Faith"

So we get home and we really have no idea what we are doing. We were afraid that we were going to do something wrong. The wounds and the blisters were intimidating, and honestly I was the more scared one between Jim and I. Jim had to do the bandage changes the first day we got her home. That whole thing just made me queasy. Still we had no idea what the heck to do. We didn't know where to get the bandage supplies and, even if we did, neither one of us had any knowledge of how to use them. Thank God someone thought to send a nurse out to our home. A nurse came out for about the first week everyday. She would show us simple wound care techniques. Boy, did we have some learning to do. Even some of the other nurses who came out had some learning to do. It was crazy. Not only were we first-time parents, but also we were first-time to any kind of nursing care or wound care. This particular nurse is the one who showed us how to bandage these wounds, and open sores on Samantha's tiny body. She was amazing. She was calm and patient. We would sit on the floor and she would slowly give us instructions on how to wrap the wounds and what bandages to use. I wanted her to come everyday, but our insurance company would not allow her to come everyday. Then one day we had a nurse come who insisted on giving Samantha a bath. We tried to tell her we knew how to do the bath, but we felt that the bath was painful for her so we wanted to wait until our appointment with our Dermatologist next week. Anyway, for the most part we were giving Samantha little sponge baths so it wasn't like she was dirty or anything.

This nurse was so insistent on the bath, so we said, "Ok - we would let her if she really felt like she needed to." After all, we didn't want to argue with the very people who were coming to our home to help us. Well, the nurse -without asking - started to rub Samantha with this sponge that she must of pulled out of her bag (because I never saw that sponge before), and just as we caught her rubbing her... she made an open wound. Samantha started crying and we were yelling. Our home became pure pandemonium within a matter of minutes. The nurse was shocked and horrified at what she had done, and we were calling her supervisors making sure that particular nurse was never to come back. She moved so quickly and seemed to be in such a hurry… and she had no interest in listening to a word we said until it was too late. The nurse got to experience EB first hand and I guarantee you she will never forget that day at our house. She did phone us later that night and apologize for her abruptness and for her mistake.

We learned that we had to be super careful with everyone who came into contact with Samantha. Even if that person was a doctor or a nurse at that point we realized that medical people were not exempt from being ignorant about EB.

Our appointment with Dr. Save Me to get a full overview of how to care for our little baby was not for a few more days so we have to make the best of it till then. At that point, Samantha was about two weeks old, and my mom was pushing me to have her baptized. I was from a big, Catholic, Italian family. Having your newborn baptized in the first few months of life was one of the most important religious sacraments we followed in our Catholic faith. Most families would wait a few more weeks, or maybe even a couple of months. Our family was in fear that this child was not going to live a few more weeks, so my mom kept pushing me to get things done. She phoned our church and told the priest of our situation and asked if a priest could come to our house and baptize Samantha. I was not up for arranging anything, so I just asked my mom to do it. She was happy to get the ball rolling there.

That morning, Jim and I were changing her bandages and covering new wounds. My parents, brothers and sisters, as well as Jim's parents and some of his siblings, were all at our house to celebrate Samantha getting baptized. Jim and I really had no idea at all what we were doing in terms of Samantha's wound care. We were just going through the motions and pretending to be calm for everyone else's sake. Since we didn't really know what we were doing, we were not aware that bandages could get stuck to a wound. The day of her baptism was also the first time a bandage had gotten stuck in a wound. There was this one bandage that was stuck and we both started to panic thinking, "Oh my God this bandage is stuck and we need to un-stick it so it doesn't heal into her fragile skin." I tried to pull it, but it was wedged so deeply into the wound that blood started dripping from the edge of the bandage out. We started fighting about it. Jim wanted me to back away so he could handle it since

I was so weepy about all of the wound care stuff. He was getting mad at me because I was panicking and crying and tying to tug at it slowly. He thought I was making everything worse by going slowly and he wanted to just rip it off. I started yelling at him, he was yelling at me - so much stress. All I know is that I begged my husband to just leave it alone and he was determined to get it off. Next thing I knew was that there was blood everywhere. He was just standing there holding this bloody bandage in his hand and I was screaming at him. Samantha was screaming and he was yelling at me. Wow - our first bandage feud was happening and we were only just beginning. "Panicked and Furious" managed to consume my emotions. So much stress. So much tension. So much pain. After we got it bandaged back up and the blood cleaned up I was so tired. I felt so drained. Totally drained emotionally. I felt like the world, my world, was getting ready to end. I was definitely not in the mood for a Baptism or celebration of any kind.

My husbands' best friend called a little later that day and I remember answering the phone and telling him (as I was crying), "Oh good! I am glad you called because he needs a friend right now. We have a really horrible situation on our hands," and just passed the phone over to my husband. I was still furious about the stuck bandage. Jim didn't really want to talk on the phone either, and I knew that, but a part of me knew that it would be good for him, and since we were not talking to each other, I knew it would be good for him to talk to someone.

The second phone call we got that day I will remember until the day I die. My dear friend Kelly called. Kelly was a friend that I had known for years. We worked together at a large Wholesale Distribution Company for some time together. She was one of those friends I managed to stay in touch with throughout the years. Staying in touch with people can be challenging - especially when you move to different cities and change your line of work. Somehow Kelly had heard that we had a baby and that something terrible was wrong with her. I never asked her from whom, or how, she found out. I just took a certain comfort that she was calling at all. Even though I didn't want to talk to anyone, there was a part of me that needed to talk about what I had just been through. I was tempted not to answer the phone at all anymore, and then another part of me said 'just answer the phone.' As I answered the phone, "Hello," on the other end I could hear the tears flowing as Kelly said, "Hi Marybeth, its Kelly." I could tell Kelly was struggling to talk and I started to cry with her before even speaking. For a few minutes there were just tears, then I found that no words would come out of my mouth.

My friend simply said these few words to me, "Marybeth don't lose your faith."

"What…? What did you just say?"

She repeated it again, "Please promise me… do not loose your faith"

I thought, "Well, that's strange." I guess I was very angry and faith was the last thing on my mind actually. But I told her I wouldn't, that I would be ok. That is all we really said to each other that day. It was as if Kelly was meant to tell me that. In all the years I had known her we never really talked about God. I didn't go to church with her. So how did she know that my faith is exactly what I would be losing right then? How did she know that those words she spoke to me would be words of strength for years to come?

That is how I believed God works for us sometimes. Kelly wasn't someone that I talked to every day. So for her to call that was just strange, and after that call from her I don't think I heard from her for months, maybe years. Sometimes it is just the words people tell us that are the signs we need to hear. Those words may not have any meaning to anyone else, not even the person speaking them but huge meaning for us. God uses people in this way to speak to us, or at least that is what I believe.

For days after her call I would reminisce about her phone call and really give deep thought to "Don't lose your faith Marybeth."

Well, the bloody bandage drama seemed to be okay after all, and all was calm again in our house as we prepared for the priest to come to baptize and anoint Samantha. Here we all were in our home with Samantha on her baby changing table and my mom, dad, sisters and brothers, and Jim's mom and family were there to witness the baptism of Samantha. She was only wrapped in her bandages, which covered her legs, hands, and bottom. Her tummy was usually left unwrapped. I think the priest may have even felt as though Samantha might not live very long. She was a big baby and strong and so sweet. She was so calm and at peace with the priest and everyone there. She just kept looking around as new babies do. Everyone knew why we were rushing the baptism, but yet no one said a word. Everyone just acted like it was a normal day. Nothing could have been further from the truth. It was far from the normal. EB was in our lives, and no one knew when it was going to take

Samantha's life. I guess a normal survival technique would be to act as if all was normal in the midst of disaster. Everyone took turns holding Samantha and rocking her. The priest that came to our home that day was not someone we knew. He officially baptized Samantha and went on his way.

We learned how to dress her in boys T-shirts with the necks cut out and the shirt turned inside out so that the seams did not rub against her skin to give her blisters. We dressed her in one of these T-shits for her Baptism. There was no fancy dress on her that day, as a fancy dress would have caused boo-boos. We learned how to pick her up in a way that would not hurt her. Other new parents (of children who do not have EB) would pick up their babies by lifting them from underneath their arm pits and holding the back of the baby's heads at the same time. We could not do that or we would rip the skin right off from under her armpits. We knew that because we actually did it once. The skin under her armpits seemed to be one of the more fragile places to blister easy. If you had ever caused a major sore or open wound on your new EB baby, then chances are you would not make that mistake twice. So we had to find a new way of picking her up. We would put our hands behind her back gently and support her head at the same time. Everything had to be done differently than my mom or the birthing classes had taught us. With EB in our life everything changed. Nothing was easy and everything we did to Samantha, even little things like diaper changes, had to be done differently. Every little thing had to be altered to adapt to Samantha's fragile skin. Feeding our new baby was different. We had to use a special shaped nipple and then we had to lubricate the nipple. If the nipple caused her lips to blister then we had to use a syringe. Diapering our new baby was always a challenge. In the beginning we would just lay her on an open diaper. If you attached the diaper on normally, like you would another baby, Samantha would get blisters everywhere the diaper rubbed or was close to the skin. The plastic material of the diaper would rub against her skin and cause a blister. Oh - and if you happen to get the tape stuck to her side as you were fastening the diaper, then don't pull the tape off. That would be traumatic for you if the tape you pulled off had her skin on it. We learned that if tape got stuck to her for any reason we would get a lubricant like Vaseline or Aquaphor and spend four or five minutes gently getting the ointment up under the tape so that it would slide off.

We learned about wound care products that would help us. I remember this one called an EXU-DRY sheet. It was about the size of

Samantha's body and she could lie on there and wiggle and squirm and not get a blister. That was a lifesaver because babies like to wiggle and squirm. When Dr. Save Me first showed it to me I touched the product and said, "No way! I am not putting this against her skin. It is so coarse and hard it feels like it will cut her skin." It was a very sheer almost silky but coarse and sharp material; it almost felt like sand paper. This product was made to absorb drainage from wounds and also to reduce friction to the skin. I always found it so fascinating how a product that is made to do one thing, looks and feels as it would do just the opposite. Anyway that product worked like a charm and we would sometimes just lay her on her back or side just on one of those Exu-Dry sheets naked and free from the confining bandages. I learned very quickly to trust Dr. Save Me. She was always researching for us and trying to find new ways for us to give Samantha more quality in her life. In the beginning, Dr. Save Me researched every medical supply we would come to know and use. She was a great teacher and a wonderful doctor.

It seemed as though everyday was a challenge to just care for her. I finally lost my breast milk in the first two weeks. I wasn't sleeping for fear that Samantha would die in the middle of the night. I wasn't eating or drinking properly so no wonder the breast milk vanished. I was in the middle of a war to keep her alive, and my own needs became secondary to Samantha's needs.

Chapter 18.

Brother Gerry to the Rescue

We had not gotten her properly diagnosed with a subtype, and there were some doctors who told us that she would die before she was a year old. It was clear to everyone involved that Samantha had EB, but what wasn't clear was: What kind of EB did she have? We had learned that there were 60-plus different types of EB. Of those 60, there were two lethal forms. One was fatal before the age of one and that was called Junctional, and one was fatal before age 20 and that was called Recessive Dystrophic. There was also a very happy subtype of EB that was in the Simplex family. A form of Simplex called Dowling Mira Simplex. As the child grows up most of the time the disease gets better and eventually goes away. This is the least common of the subtypes, but at least there was one subtype that actually had a chance to get better and possibly go away. Still there was hope for Samantha that maybe she could be one of the lucky ones to have this subtype. All the documentation I had read indicated that the two most common sub types of EB were the two fatal forms, Junctional and Recessive Dystrophic.

Every physician we had met believed that our daughter had one of those two subtypes based on her appearance and the way she was blistering. Usually with the Junctional subtype there is excessive throat involvement, which would include gagging and choking on liquids and foods. Samantha did have those symptoms, which is why the doctors from the very beginning could not make up their minds which subtype she had.

My brother Gerry and his wife Anna came to our home just shortly after we came home from the hospital. Bags and suitcases in hand, and baby in tow, (my sister-in-law had given birth to a baby girl, my niece, Casey, exactly one month to the day and within one hour of Samantha's birth). Casey had been born on January 13th at 11am, and Samantha was delivered on February 13th at 12:20am. Gerry and Anna stayed with us to just help us function. I would sleep during the day for a couple of hours here and there. At nighttime I had made a make shift bed in the living room set up that Samantha and I lay on. She slept and I watched her sleep. During the daytime, if Samantha was sleeping, everyone watched her sleep for me. Someone was with her at all times monitoring her. Her room had now become the living room, and her bed was our pull out coach sleeper-sofa in the living room.

One or more of the doctors we had met made the most unfortunate mistake of telling me that she would probably pass away in her sleep, so I decided that I would not sleep when she slept. I was so determined to keep my baby alive. They thought she would die in her sleep because they were assuming she had the Junctional subtype due to the extensive throat and esophagus involvement. Samantha would gag on her milk when she drank it and sometimes spit up blood. When we started her on rice she would choke swallowing the rice that was a creamy texture. So, based on the information the doctors had, I think they were just trying to prepare us for what could happen.

My sister-in-law, Anna, would lay her baby Casey down to sleep next to Samantha. It was sweet and they seemed to bond naturally. It was difficult for me to see and hold Casey. She was normal and healthy and I knew she wasn't going to die. I was happy for my brother and his wife, but at the same time I couldn't help to wonder why my baby had to be born with such a horrible illness. Watching those two babies side-by-side was a bittersweet emotion. It was painful and comforting at the same time.

Don't get me wrong - I wouldn't have traded one moment my brother gave me, ever. I think he is responsible for saving our sanity, and maybe our lives. Who knows? Because Jim and I were so vulnerable and so weak. Up until the moment my brother walked through my front door, we were not functioning at all. I wasn't eating, or showering, or thinking period. Jim and I were barely communicating. Jim would get up early in the morning and go to work and not get home until after dinner or late at night. I think his way of dealing with it was to just not be home. My way of dealing with it was not to talk about it. I was barely staying in the reality of the situation. My mom was watching over me and trying to be at my home as frequently as she could.

When Gerry came over he cooked for us and researched data on the disease to help us get more educated. He had been working in the medical field prior to this happening to us so he knew how to get the information. He also knew whom to go to where he could get the right information. He tried to explain it to us. It was like everyone was speaking some kind of a foreign language and we had to learn how to speak their language. It was very frustrating to me. He forced me to talk about it with him, and that was a good thing.

The first doctor's appointment Jim and I took Samantha to was to our dermatologist, Dr. Save Me. She was beyond wonderful and gave us so much of her time and love. I think sometimes doctors forget they are human too. But this doctor made us feel like she was walking this nightmare with us. She empathized with us and she went out of her way to help us cope with the realness of the disease. She found names of Specialists who were experts on EB. Of course none of the EB specialist were in Florida - they were all out of state. She even found the name of an EB organization that she told us were maybe trying to find a cure for EB, and maybe contacting them could lead us to a better way of life for Samantha. She told me when I felt strong enough, and when my head was focused, that I should explore the possibility of serving that organization in some way. That in maybe helping the organization, it could help me. At that time in my life I didn't know what an "organization" was. I had never even heard of one before. I had no idea about non-profits, either. I did know what a 'for-profit' company was because I owned one, but I never became familiar with the words 'not-for-profit' before. I certainly didn't understand how my participation in some organization that I had absolutely no clue about could help me with anything. But my trust in this doctor was growing quickly, and so I knew that in time these questions of mine would get answered and then, someday, I would understand what she was talking about.

On this particular day Dr. Save Me showed us how to properly lance (pop) the blisters that had fluid in them. She used a long sharp needle. She would poke this needle into the edge of the blister and then use a tissue to drain out the fluid until all the fluid was gone. It really looked painful. She continued on that the blisters required popping or correctly lancing them, because if you failed to lance the blister it would only get larger and larger due to the disease. I knew I wasn't going to be able to do that. I sort of backed away from the table and pushed Jim in front so that he could be the one to do it first. Then we had to learn how to bandage the blisters and the open wounds as well. Dr. Save Me told us that when we lanced these blisters that we should try to keep the top layer of skin in place. Sometimes on these blisters the top part of the blisters skin was very fragile and would slide off very easily. She explained that if we kept the skin intact it would make the blister heal faster than if the skin came off - thus creating an open wound. The very thought of popping a blister made me sick, let alone dealing with blood or oozing sores. The fluid that came from the blister, she told us, was protein, but to me it smelled like puss. Now I know this was my baby, but I never signed up for nursing... or so I thought. I mean, up until now I was a professional businesswoman. I never had the least bit of desire to be in the medical field - at all, whatsoever. Being forced into wound care and medical terminology was terrifying for me. I started praying for strength because all I really wanted to do was run away and hide. I started praying specifically for God to help me to be strong enough to deal with all we had to do to help Samantha.

Chapter 19.

Did You Say Its Fatal?

My husband was actually the one who stepped up to the plate and started to pop the blisters and do Samantha's wound care. I firmly looked at the doctor and said, "Oh no, not me! I can't do that. No way! I can't stick a needle in those blisters. I will hurt her and I can't do that." I'm not talking about just one or two blisters, there were a lot (like 20 or 30), and they would just pop up all over her body all day long. It was crazy, like nothing I had ever heard of before. This disease affected every part of her body; well of course we have skin all over our body. What I was beginning to understand here was that ANY friction to her skin would cause either blisters to form, or in some cases the skin to just tear and come off. All I could think of was, "Is this really happening to me right now? Can something so horrible really exist... and why my baby?"

Dr. Save Me also told us that from the preliminary lab work that was done that it did appear that Samantha could have the Junctional form of EB, which would be fatal before the age of one. Babies with Junctional EB usually die from an airway closure. Because of the involvement with the throat and esophagus, it is common for the airway to close unexpectedly and without warning. If the airway closes they will not be able to breath resulting in death. It was explained to us that if the doctors all agreed that Samantha did have Junctional, than a tracheotomy tube could be placed in her throat which could eliminate the air way closing and prevent death.

She believed she had this form due to the fact that from the very beginning Samantha had involvement with her throat area and a lot of complications with her esophagus. One of the indications for Junctional, along with blood work, is how a patient presents. Having trouble swallowing anything and GI issues are usually a good sign of Junctional EB, but not always as it was complicated and tricky to really know. However, Dr. Save Me also told us that there was another possibility that Samantha might have the recessive subtype. That subtype is fatal before the age of 20. Somehow in my mind that actually sounded better to me.

She explained that the only doctor who could confirm or deny this would be the EB expert in North Carolina, Dr. Fine. Apparently he would need to see Samantha and get clinical data on her, compile all of her medical data, and then make a judgment call. Dr. Save Me told us that this particular doctor did not favor patients and families coming to visit him. He would rather just communicate with the patient's doctor and make the diagnosis from the information the child's doctor provided. Looking back, I think Dr. Save Me wanted us to go see this expert for peace of mind, and because she knew he was the best in the EB world. That doctor had no desire at all to meet with us in person. He even told us that when we phoned him.

Dr. Fine did receive the three-hole-bunch biopsy that our Dr. Save Me sent to him the first few days after Samantha was born. Examining that tissue from the biopsy is extremely difficult for most doctors. Apparently there are only two, maybe three, doctors in the world who can read this test. One of which was Dr. Fine, who was a very well known and highly respected doctor in his field of dermatology who, at that time, was working at Chapel Hill University in North Carolina.

The Electron Microscopy, or EM, determines the layer of skin where the blistering occurs. When they look at the skin specimen they are looking through a special microscope to determine where the blistering originated from: meaning which layer of skin (out of the seven layers) did the blister first start out of the seven layers we have. I guess that was extremely difficult to determine. Only a very well-trained eye that has read many of these EM tests can actually make an educated decision. So sometimes it is a guess, and in most cases DNA blood samples, along with clinical presentation (which simply means a doctors observation of the child's skin and body symptoms at the doctors visit), are used together to determine this subtype. Getting the right subtype was extremely important. We were going to need as much information as we could get in order for these doctors to make a decision. We needed to collect blood from Samantha, my husband and myself, and that had to be flown overnight to a lab in Philadelphia so that the DNA experts there could determine if Samantha's subtype was recessive or dominate. This was also a very complicated test to read. Not many doctors were able to find the defective gene in the DNA. We were told that our test could take a few years before we would get the results. Actually, it took two years, but I will tell you more about that a little later.

Knowing that our trusted Dr. Save Me thought Samantha could have the terminal type before the age of one was terrifying. We were once again devastated. I was praying so hard for this not to be true. I prayed she had the other type: the recessive one that was fatal before the age of 20. That was better because it would give me more time to be with her. I could not lose her right now! No way! It would kill me. I felt like I was in prayer constantly, saying, "Please God, don't take her away from me, and please make me strong." I would just keep repeating this in my mind over and over again.

Every time she choked or gagged on her formula we would have this fear inside of us that was so profound it would stop us in our tracks from whatever it was we were doing at that moment - just long enough to remind us that this disease EB was in our life and could take our daughters life at any moment! We were always on the edge - as if something was jumping out in front of us, scaring us. We were always jumpy and nervous. We got rattled very easy and we had a tendency to rattle others just as easily. Friends and family had difficulty being around us. Loosing her was not an option for me at that time in my life. The fear of losing her haunted me every second of every day.

Chapter 20.

Second Opinions Are Not Always Better Than the First

Dr. Save Me suggested that we meet with a Gastroenterologist doctor (GI) to discuss possible ways to treat Samantha's throat problems. We knew she had difficulty swallowing. I think the doctors thought her airway was affected. Sometimes she would almost get a tint of blue to her skin. My brother Gerry was always worried she was not getting enough oxygen and that's why her skin looked a faint blue. No one ever found out why that happened. It didn't happen all the time - maybe every couple of days, and at different times of the day. Sometimes she would be lying on her back smiling and happy and then you would notice her skin all over her body just looked a sort-of shade of light blue. When this did happen, the doctors thought it might have something to do with her circulation and or ability to breath in air. At this stage in the game I don't think anyone thought Samantha was going to live for very long.

So when she would sleep at night, I would watch her to make sure she was breathing and I would listen for the sound of her breathing. I began to learn the rhythm of her breathing very quickly. My brother tried to show me how to do an emergency tracheotomy a few times, but I really didn't pay attention to him because I knew that if I couldn't pop a blister and deal with blood everywhere and oozing wounds, there was no way in hell that I could forcefully shove some straw or tube through her throat to keep her breathing. Oh no - by this time I had already told God that I would do my part in taking care of her the best that I was capable of doing, but that if He (God) decided to take her home, it was going to be all God's decision and out of my control. Then, and only then, I would have to cross that bridge when we got to it. So we left Dr. Save Me's office that day with even more new news that devastated us. Hope slowly began to be disappearing every second of every day.

The next day, I took over all of the bandaging and care for Samantha. I just thought if this is what I am supposed to do, well then,

I am going to do it. Something inside of me just snapped and I just decided to jump in with both feet. It was not about me anyway, or what I can or can't handle. More importantly this life, my life, was now about this beautiful little angel I just gave birth to. It was my responsibility to make her as comfortable as I could given her circumstances. So I became a nurse, a student, and a mom. Samantha was my teacher. Together, we began a remarkable journey together into the unknown.

Jim and I had decided that we would find another dermatologist in town to get a second opinion. Even though we really did like our Dr. Save Me, we just felt like maybe there was a chance that she was wrong about Samantha's subtype, and maybe there is still a chance that she might have one of those other subtypes, you know, like the one where the disease gets better as they get older and then goes away. So we looked to our local University. By this time Jim's mom had come to visit us and shared in our joyful bliss of our first baby. We really were trying to find the joy in all of the sadness. I mean watching a baby, your newborn baby, suffer and have all these sores and blisters all over her body was really, really hard. Close to impossible really. The fact that it is your child was even more difficult to process. It is like someone taking a knife to your heart and very slowly pushing it through. I am really not sure if there are words to describe this kind of pain. What I was sure of was that we were living it.

We went to the local University for a second opinion. It was one of the first times we were really out in public together with our little bandaged-up Samantha from head-to-toe. It was a very strange feeling being stared at. Not just by one person, or even three or four people, but anyone we came into contact with stared at us. We would walk past someone and their heads would turn in our direction and their bodies kept moving forward. Some of them you could see the look on their faces; their thoughts were expressed through their facial expressions. Some people would ask us if she was in a fire. Or did we beat her? And at the same time give us a dirty look or tell us "shame on you for hurting that baby." It was awful and embarrassing. We were so new to all of this ridicule from the public.

We arrived at the University Medical Center building. Before we got to the front door we told each other, Jim and I - that no matter what happens today we will agree that we will walk out of there happy. That no matter what the doctor tells us, good or bad, we are going to be ok. My mother-in-law, bless her heart, just slowly walked behind us not saying a word. The worse thing they could tell us anyway was that our child would not live past the age of one, and we had already been told that so we were ok ... or so we thought.

Well - we were at a teaching hospital. Do you know what that means? It means that alongside of the established, experienced doctors, you have young people still in school learning to be doctors. The older, established physicians asked if the young men and women interns can come into our room so that they can be witness to one of the rarest, fatal, genetic conditions known to man. This older doctor explained that it would be a great opportunity for these young intern doctors to see an actual newborn baby with this suspect, genetic disease, EB. We said 'ok.' We thought that was the right thing to do. So the doctor walks in. He asks us a few questions and we answered him. He reviews the lab reports and other medical records we brought and probably medical records he obtained on his own of Samantha. He examined our sweet little baby. We took her bandages off so he could see her blisters and her open wounds. Then he looked at us and he said, "Well, I have to concur that I think your daughter has the Junctional form of this disease EB too. She will not live past one year of age." He further explained that most likely she would die from her airway closing off and that, in his opinion, there was nothing anyone could do about that. After he explained his opinion, he then asked us, "This is a teaching University would you mind if our students could get a closer look at your baby so they can see what a baby with Junctional EB looks like?" As he was asking us if it was okay for the students to come in, everything around me felt like we were in slow motion again and I couldn't hear anything. No sound at all. I could see his lips moving and his face, but I could only feel a pain in my heart and a sickness in my stomach. I could feel my eyes getting blurry from the tears filling them. I had tears falling so fast from my eyes that I couldn't really see. I couldn't get words out. My mind was telling me to tell this doctor to "get the hell out of our room and leave us alone, oh and take your interns with you asshole." My mind wanted so badly to speak those words... but I just couldn't talk.

My husband couldn't speak either. I was numb again and struggling to gather our belongings. I was fumbling with the bandages as I tried to quickly bandage her up so we could go. I was careful not to hold my head up because I didn't want anyone to see my pain or my tears. We really felt like we were on display, and at the worst possible moment you can imagine. Some doctor just confirmed, as a second opinion, that our beautiful baby Samantha was going to die with no hope at all to live past the age of one. Oh shit, and in that split second, 10 to 15 young adults stood there silent staring at us. Staring at our beautiful daughter. No one said anything for a moment - just silence.

I tried to collect myself. I felt like my knees were going to buckle under me at any moment and I would fall to the ground crying. I am not even sure what came out of my mouth at that point, although I think I said something like, "Sure we would like to help in any way we can so that maybe other families will not have to go through this." Not one of those students asked us a single question. I was so thankful for that. They could tell we were in tremendous pain. They could tell that my tears were creating a puddle on the floor between my feet. I knew they felt horrible to be witness to that. Hopefully, that moment in time will be the memory of pain they felt for us so that in their future as doctors they will be sensitive to first time parents of a child with any kind of disability and not invite their own students into a room just after they have delivered such devastating news. Hopefully....

How we made it through that day is still a mystery to me. Looking back now I think, "Geez - can you give a family a break? Do you have to tell brand new parents of a three week-old baby that not only was their baby going to die? But, oh yeah, can my team of students come into the room to see what this kind of disease EB looks like?"

Wow - it was unreal. We walked out of that appointment dazed, in pain, numb, confused and thoughtless. Death seemed to be following us.

Chapter 21.

I Cannot Find Peace in the Shower

The next day, as I was taking a shower, I had another episode of hearing Samantha scream when she was not really screaming. For some reason when I would take a shower I could hear my Samantha screaming. I started to have anxiety about taking a shower because I was afraid I would hear her cry and scream and my mind could not tell between it being real or not. She wasn't really screaming, but for some reason while the water was running down my face in the shower, I could hear her screaming in my head. It was scary and it made me feel jittery. I would have to tell myself that it was ok, that I am just hearing things because Samantha is ok and my mom and my mother-in-law, Judy, were with her and watching her, so it was ok. Mom would always tell me, "Mind over matter child. Pray, pray, pray!" Having my mom there was such a comfort to me. I knew my mom felt like she was interfering all the time, but I always told her how much it meant to me to have her there. She was my rock and my biggest fan, and her strength and faith in God was unwavering all of the time.

I was in the shower and just trying to pray and ask God, "Oh please just keep her with me, Lord, I need my baby to stay with me. And Lord, please help this screaming in my head to stop. I need your strength Lord, please make me strong. I am so weak I cannot handle this. This is too much for me, I feel like I am going to die, please help me God." I liked to pray in the shower. It gave me a place that no one else but me was in. Water was always soothing to me so after the screams stopped in my head, I would always pray. I prayed at bedtime too but lately I found my self praying any second I could. Praying also gave me peace and comfort. I would calm myself down and feel brand new by the time my shower ended. Just as my shower was ending, the bathroom door flew open.

My mother-in-law Judy burst through my bathroom door yelling, "Oh my God the baby is spitting up blood!" My heart skipped a beat, but I stayed calm. Judy looked like she had just seen a ghost. Her face was pale white with horror. I told Judy, "Its ok, I will be out in a second just let me get my towel and dry off and I will be right there!" I threw on a towel and went to Samantha. My mother and Judy had a look of disbelief and panic on their faces. They didn't even need to speak to me. I could tell what they were thinking. I really didn't think she was going to die at that moment, but I knew spitting up blood wasn't good, either. She didn't look blue and her color was good, but she was spitting up blood and I didn't know why. She didn't have a fever and everything else about her seemed just fine. She wasn't even crying. I think all of us looking at her made her scared. I was very connected to every emotion she displayed. I called the pediatrician and, of course, he didn't know why either but told me to just stop feeding her for a while and sit her upright and see if it stops. I was going to the GI doctor tomorrow anyway so that was a comfort that maybe someone would be able to explain this new spiting up blood incident to us. My mother-in-law stayed with us for I think about two weeks. I think the whole situation was so alarming to her... alarming to all of us.

All I knew at that point was that I had a brand new baby that I had waited for to come out of me for so long. Since the day she came out of my womb she was constantly getting blisters on her body that would pop and become open oozing wounds, or her skin would just come off at the slightest touch or bump. Her little body seemed to be so fragile, and now her mouth and throat area and maybe even her stomach were having issues. Everyday something new would happen that would unveil a new fear or a new sense of freight to all of my senses. Even simple things like taking a shower became hard to do, and just for the mere fact that something might go wrong for those 15 minutes I was in the shower. I learned very quickly to sleep a couple of hours at a time and still function. I started to train myself to not have a reaction when something alarming happened. I continued to pray for peace in my mind and in my heart.

Chapter 22.

God - She Is Your Child First

The next day we were scheduled to go for our first Gastroenterology appointment. We had our own business at that time in our life, so on one hand we were lucky we could financially take care of our selves and take time off when we needed to. But on the other hand, three weeks into to our new baby and my husband had taken too much time off work - it was becoming a problem, so my brother said he would go with me to that appointment. Besides, I still could not drive due to my C-section, so someone had to drive me there. My brother wanted to go anyway because he was concerned that Samantha looked blue and he wanted to ask someone about that. I really couldn't see what he was talking about. I just figured that by now, with everyone saying that she was going to die, it was going to be an airway closing issue and that maybe she was starting to look blue to everyone but me. I know my brother was freaked out and scared for me and for Samantha, but he did a good job of hiding that.

We met the GI doctor. After evaluating Samantha and looking over her medical records (which by now I was starting to carry with me), he told us that he also thought it was safe to say that Samantha had Junctional EB based on her symptoms. He said that he has seen these kinds of kids (EB) before. He explained how the airway closes off due to blisters forming in that area from constant friction just from eating foods. He told us that he could take her into surgery that very next morning and he could prevent her from dying by placing a tracheotomy tube into her throat so that if her airway did close she would still be able to breath. He explained that children with this disease and with this subtype do this all of the time, and that it was perfectly common.

I was numb again. I told the doctor that this was not an easy decision for me to make, and that my husband, of course, has to also want to do this. I told him that we were just really freaking out and that we could not believe that we were even in this position. I mean, we wanted to have a baby. But we had no idea this could happen. My brother of course starts to ask all of the normal questions: how, when, all of that. I just sat there and thought, 'Wow.' This doctor appeared to be so confident in his findings and evaluation. He just spoke like he was so sure of what he was saying. He told me to my face, "You have to do this or she will die." So he scheduled the surgery for 8am the next morning and told me to be at the hospital at 6am. My brother reassured me that everything was going to be ok, and that we have to do this to save Samantha's life. It sounded bad to me, and I was still trying to process the information in my mind. I asked the doctor if he could give me a number that I could call if I had any last minute questions. He said sure, and gave me his number. I think it was his cell phone. We left there to drive home. It was an hour drive from my house. Something just didn't feel right. Something just didn't feel good. I called Jim to tell him what was going on and words mixed with tears of pain were all I could get out. "Oh my God, how can they do this to her? How will the tube that is placed in her throat be able to stay in place? The skin there is fragile too and it blisters as well. It seemed to me that the tube will just become a bigger issue." When I went to bed that night I prayed that God would help me make this decision. I told God that I did not feel like I could even think. "Help me, God! Help Me," is all I could say. I lay in bed awake pretty much all of that night. At 5am the next morning I sat straight up in the bed, woke my husband and told him, "You know what honey? We are not doing this surgery. I am going to call this doctor right now and tell him so."

"Why?" Jim asked.

I said, "Because, Jim, if God wants to take her so bad, then he can just take her. We are not going to make her life a living hell or worse than it is now, and it feels like this tube sticking out of her throat attached to skin that will break down into wounds at the slightest touch could just be a brand new nightmare."

He agreed, and so I called the number the doctor had given me. The doctor answered right away. I told him, "I am sorry doctor, but after giving this some thought, we have decided not to have this procedure done this morning"

"May I ask why?" the doctor asked.

"Well," I replied, "I am not sure what your spiritual beliefs are, but we feel like if God is going to take this baby home, then that will be up to Him, we do not want to make her life a living hell trying to stop him"

The doctor replied, "Well, then, I think you made a wise choice"

"Really?" I said. "Then why did you push me so hard to do this in the first place when I was in your office yesterday?"

He replied, "Because I am a doctor and that is my job. To try and save lives. But you are right - it would be a whole new set of challenges for you, and doctor visits, and hospital visits. Yeah - it would not be easy."

I felt such a sense of relief to hear him say that. He did tell us that the blood that kept coming up from her mouth was probably from her stomach. I was not aware, but when you swallow blood it will make you nauseous and you will vomit it up. Blood can't just sit in your stomach. So apparently what was happening was that she was blistering in her mouth, throat and esophageal area, and when the blisters burst they created open wounds in that area that bleed and went right into her stomach. So his remedy for that was to give her some medicine called Zantac at the very first symptom of vomiting blood and the Zantac would coat her stomach preventing her from vomiting. The Zantac worked like a charm.

Chapter 23.

North Carolina Bound

That evening following that appointment, Dr. Save Me, called and told us that she thought we should go to visit the EB expert doctor she had been communicating with. He wasn't local, he was in another state, but it was definitely worth our time to go and see this doctor. I think she was thinking that maybe if Samantha was seen by a physician who was well versed on this disease, EB, that maybe that physician might have a different outlook on things. So she gave us his telephone number and we called the next day. Much to our surprise, this particular doctor did not want to see us. He felt that sending the lab work to him, and getting doctors' clinical data report, was really all that he needed to make a good decision on what subtype she had. After all, that was really what we were after anyway, right? Some "expert doctor" to tell us that she was not going to die in a year, or that she did not have either of those two, horrible, terminal subtypes. We insisted on going there and this doctor insisted that we not come. We went the next day. We figured we didn't have anything to loose and nowhere else to go for those answers. So we hopped on a plane and we went to North Carolina to meet one of the experts in the field of dermatology and EB. "Dr. Bow Tie" - I am going to call him that because he always wore a bow tie. These days you don't see too many doctors wearing a bow tie. I knew we were in trouble when he walked in the room. Or maybe it was when we arrived at the medical office building and they start with their series of questions off with:

"Are you married?"

"Yes."

"Are you related?"

We both looked at each other stunned. Oh my goodness - are these people serious? I think we asked them, "Are you serious?"

The nice nurse who was filling out the paperwork, replied, "Oh yes, this is a standard question, and you would be surprised at how many people with genetic conditions will answer 'yes' to that question."

We were stunned and of course it took us both a few minutes to regroup after that. NO we were not related! It is my personal opinion that Dr. Bow Tie was maybe a little shy, and maybe not very good with the patients or their families. His bedside manner was strange and not one I was used to. I was starting to get the sense that a lot of doctors dove so deep down into their professions that they in fact had forgotten that they themselves were human too. You could tell that this doctor knew what he was talking about and that he had studied this disease for a very long time. He was thorough and organized. He was patient and thought before he spoke. When we asked him a question he would pause a few minutes before answering, so I knew he thought before speaking. I liked that about him. He didn't rush us and he didn't make us feel like he was too busy for us, either. I could tell by watching him and listening to him that he was one of the smartest people I might ever meet in my lifetime. He told us, in his opinion, that he thought Samantha did not have Junctional. He explained that he understood how the doctors back home could easily have made that diagnosis, but he really felt that Samantha had Recessive Dystrophic based on his observation. As I said earlier, one of the indications for Junctional EB is the throat, and airway issues. Since Samantha had always presented and even at birth with substantial throat issues it was easy for any one to make that mistake. I am glad he explained it this way to us. It made me feel less angry with everyone, but helped me to understand the human nature side of doctors. He told us that there was a chance it could be some less severe form of EB, maybe in the Simplex family, but only time would be able to tell that. He explained that the Recessive subtype is terminal - usually before the age of 20. He said that based on his findings, with regards to her lab work, that being the 3-hole-bunch biopsy or the electron microscopy we did when she was a week old, and the way she presented clinically, that he felt that it was possible she had the Recessive type. He really had a lot of information about EB. He was better then the computer and Internet. He explained that there are a lot of different subtypes with this disease and sometimes patients will end up with an even better one as they grow older, but that you really don't know that until you get DNA testing done, and until the child begins to grow and develop. He told us that sometimes when children present severe at birth they usually end up being milder as they grow older and, in some rare cases, the disease would go away with every year of age. He did explain that those cases were rare. The very last thing that happened was my husband asked the doctor, "What is involved in a cure for this disease?" The doctor replied, "It will involve gene therapy and, in my opinion, a cure for EB will not happen in my lifetime."

That was the first time I had heard those words before - gene therapy - and I wasn't too sure exactly what that meant anyway. But I did understand what 'not in my lifetime meant.' I was trying to figure out how old he was to see if he looked like he was going to live for at least 20 more years and, well he looked like he might be in his mid-to-late 40's, so I assumed that he meant not in Samantha's lifetime either. Considering her life expectancy was 20 years old that is.

I really didn't care what he was saying anymore, I was so relieved. All I knew was that my sweet baby girl was not going to die before the age of one. Oh what a relief... like a huge weight had been lifted from my shoulders. He did assure us of that. As we walked out that building that day it dawned on me that although she would not die before the age one (so now I could finally sleep through the night), 20 years old also felt a bit scary. How would she die? What did I need to look out for? Why are we going through this? Why?

Chapter 24.

Time To Say Goodbye To Dr.....
Who Is This Man?

It did feel like I was in some kind of trance or dream. Like life was not actually real. We would spend entire days caring for Samantha, feeding her, trying to find new and better ways to use diapers so that her entire upper legs were not total open wounds, cutting collars out of boys white T-shirts, popping blisters, fixing wounds, searching for bandages that would not stick, learning new ways to bandage new wounds in different spots, and research any and all information we could find on this little known disease, EB. The daily grind for us meant me caring full-time for this little baby who, everyday it seemed, new issues would arise and new challenges would stand in front of us. As for my husband, he was lucky to go to the office everyday and run our business. I was learning how to brace myself for every scare and every scene of drama that occurred daily. I knew I never really bonded with our pediatrician, so that was probably the first sign there were going to be problems with him. I admit... I did call his office frequently, but heck - who wouldn't have? I don't know too many people who can be handed such a challenge in their life totally unprepared and not ask the so-called experts for help and advice at every turn.

In the beginning of Samantha's life her nutrition and GI tract were of the most concern. Sometimes she would just start vomiting blood for no reason, and let me tell you something, I am not the person for this. I mean, who ever thought I'd be a nurse? It is not what I signed up for - or trained for. I was a self-made businesswoman. I started my own business when I was 25. I only handed my husband the keys to the doors when Samantha was born. I knew that she was going to need my full attention and running a business also requires your full attention, so I choose her. Besides, what I really did best was start the business and get it running, but the day-to-day managing I was horrible at, and I am not sure if there was ever an employee that really liked working for me. I am the kind of person who, at the very site at some vomiting, you can just go get two buckets - because I will be doing the same exact thing. If I see it, smell it, or have to clean it up, you will have to clean me up because I, too, will start vomiting… Yuk!

Samantha's teeth were starting to come in at just three months of age. I found a dentist through the recommendation of EB doctors who might be able to help us. We went and met him and he was very nice. I knew instantly he would be able to help us and stay with us. I was starting to learn this as I met doctors now.

On one of our visits to the dentist office I had just pulled into a parking spot and turned the car engine off. I went to the side of the van to open the door to get little Samantha out and take her in for her dentist visit. As I opened the door, she started to vomit blood. It startled me so abrubtly that I thought I was going to stop breathing. All I could think of was, "God why me?" I am like the worst person on the planet to have to deal with this and try to be calm at the same time. Well, I just called my husband and told him, "You need to get to us right now! Samantha is throwing up blood and I can't deal with it and I don't know what to do! Help me!" So he did. Like in 5 minutes he was there. He had to do that frequently with Samantha and me in those first couple of years. I had to learn the hard way to pack a bag just for the car. I also had to learn not to leave the house with out the Zantac. With every new issue that would unfold I would call the pediatrician to inform him of what was going on. Just after Samantha was three months old, I noticed that our pediatrician was charging us for calls he was making to other doctors to find out about this disease. The invoices would read: Calls to Dr. so-and-so for information on EB - $300.00. I paid a couple of them, but shortly after the invoices starting really trickling in I felt angry. I thought, "Oh great! Not only did my life just get turned completely upside down, but now the one doctor that I rely on for so much is going to make us pay for it - literally."

That was it. I fired him. I thought we don't want a doctor like that helping us. He is in it for all of the wrong reasons. I am all for someone making a living, but lets be fair here. We were brand new parents playing a whole new game of parenting that was far beyond the normal, and up until this point was costing us an awful lot of money: Airfare here and there, co-pays, medicines, special clothing, special nutritional supplements, and bandages. We hadn't gotten a bill for bandages, yet, but I was sure it was going to be huge. I hadn't even had time to really look into anything. Because we owned and operated our own business (which, by the way, I was still managing the financial aspect of the business and being a nurse at the same time), we could afford to pay for whatever we needed. So the investigation issues with regards to bandages, and how to buy better, was not so important. Those issues only become important when you don't have the money to pay for them. Still, I was not going to be a part of giving doctors money to learn about a disease to help me. It just felt all wrong. Anyway, he didn't have the decency to pick the phone up and call me to talk about why I was leaving his practice. I think he just really didn't care one way or another, and that was another reason we left his office. When you have a child with special needs you need special people, including special doctors to help you... support you.

Chapter 25.

The Best Blessings Come in the Strangest of Places

I also decided to get to know this not-for-profit organization that Dr. Save Me found on the Internet a little better. It was called DEBRA. Stands for: Dystrophic Epidermolysis Research Association of American. I called and asked how I could be a board member. I remember it wasn't easy. It was not like anybody really wanted a parent there, or at least that is the feeling I got.

I asked the girl who answered the phone, "Well, do you have EB?"
"No" she said.
"Well does anyone in your family have EB?"
"No," she answered, "Why do you ask that?"
I said, "Because I figured that only people who have EB or were related to a person with EB would be working for this organization."
"Oh, no," she replied, "I am an employee here."
I am not sure why, but I thought that was strange. I asked if anyone who worked in the DEBRA office had EB, and she said, 'No." For some reason I guess I just automatically assumed the office raising money to find a cure for EB would have people with EB working there.

After a few trips to New York to visit the organization, and a few persistent pushes to get on the board, I was voted on the Board. My initial attempts to be part of that organization were strictly to have access to any and all information that might give us a better way to live this life and at the same time, maybe in some way, I might be able to help someone else who was in the same boat as I am. Helping other people was always a therapeutic remedy for me as I am sure it is for most people.

Since I had fired our pediatrician and Samantha was now due for her four month-old shots and check up I was in a bit of a dilemma. No doctor. No Shots. No help – period! That was not a good place to be, and probably not the best decision I had made the day I fired him. Find a new pediatrician first then fire the old one. I never thought things through (I am always jumping-in-before-I-look sort of thing).

I spent the next month trying to find a new pediatrician. It was not fun and, much to my surprise, no one wanted us as patients. I think I met four or five, and every one made me feel like Samantha had AIDS or some kind of really bad disease that they felt would not work within their practices. So after I pretty much went to every doctor that was even close to us with in 30 minutes, I ended up at the University's Medical Center where they did indigent care children. I knew we were not in need financially, but we were in need of a doctor and at that point I didn't care about anything else except trying to get Samantha her four month-old shots. So here we were at a teaching hospital again. In walks the older, more distinguish physician, and right behind him were the intern doctors. Little did I know at the time but it was about to be the best day of mine and Samantha's life yet… to this day I will never forget that day. The older doctor who appeared to be in charge of everyone else was repeating what I was telling him to his students. He was bewildered that any physician would discriminate against us for having a child with this disease, and he was even more baffled that not just one but all of the doctors in town I had seen would not take us on as patients. By this time in the game, my tears were not so plentiful during the daytime, but mainly at nighttime after I had put Samantha to bed, and I lay down to pray. I would cry then. Somehow the constant pain and drama of our everyday struggles managed to suppress my tears.

Hearing the doctor repeat my story was sad and overwhelming for me. I knew I was living it, but to hear someone tell it was awkward and painful. That was the first time I heard someone else tell my story to other people in front of me. I kind of felt like I was going to pass out, but I didn't. I kept my composure, and just then I noticed that one student in particular really seemed to take an interest in us. I saw a look in his eyes and a sound in his voice that told me, "He cares about what he is doing, and he wants to be a doctor so that he can help children." His name was Patrick Yee. He immediately walked through the group and came into the room and he told me he could not believe what we had been through. He said, "I'd like to help you. I am not sure I know anymore about this disease then anyone else, but it sounds as though you really know more then anybody here. Between the two of us I bet we can take good care of Samantha." I said, "Yes, you are right, thank you. I have spent time learning as much as I can about this disease so that

I can take care of her the right way." I went on to tell him, " There is a National EB conference coming up soon in North Carolina and I am going. My whole family is going and I intend to learn even more information there. I could bring some information back for you if you are interested?" He said, "Yes, I am interested, and I will read anything you have to give me. I can be your pediatrician because I have a few more months here at this clinic as an intern and then I will be a doctor and move on to an official practice." A Prayer was answered in the form of help and once again we were being rescued.

I was so happy. You would think that I had just won the lottery. To actually have someone want to take care of us, and then to have someone who was even remotely interested in learning about this disease EB so that he can help us, (and he wasn't even going to charge us), was an incredible feeling. Like, "Thank you God!" That is all I could think to myself. "Thank you God!"

So Samantha got her shots and we got a new pediatrician that we could depend on and count on for help, and for the second time since Samantha was born we felt a sense of relief being sent to us in the form of a doctor. Like a prayer being answered. I was realizing more and more that God's grace would come to us as He saw that we needed, but how strange - because sometimes not as I was asking for it. We needed a good doctor, and one who really cared about us. We needed this doctor, Patrick Yee, in our life more then he knew, or more then we knew. It is… what God knew. This doctor was a blessing we would come to be forever grateful for. Our team was being built. Our new pediatrician communicated with our dermatologist as if they had been good friends for years. Sometimes when you think the worst things are happening the most beautiful gifts magically unfold.

Chapter 26.

The Reality Of It All

Now I felt more awake and in-tune to what was going on around me then ever before. For the first three months of Samantha's life I felt like I was in a dream. You know the one I am talking about where you are in a very deep sleep, but your mind is dreaming and in your dream there is realness… the dream is in color and you feel like you are there in the present. And then at the very pulse of your heartbeat, you are awakened for whatever reason and you realize that in fact you were dreaming and you are in your bed, in your room, not in your dream. While you were dreaming you were asking yourself, "Is this real? Or am I dreaming?" Then when you wake up you ask yourself the very same questions. Almost every person I have ever met has told me that they have had this kind of dream. I have had them as well so I am really in-tune to them. I am thinking that after about the fourth month with Samantha I realized I was awake and this was really happening.

Being a Board member for this organization, DEBRA, would require me to travel to New York every three to four months. On top of caring for Samantha, which was already an incredibly demanding job in and of itself, I was still managing the finances at our business. I hired a personal assistant to work with me at the house to help me with the books and various other business related issues, and then I decided I would hire a nanny as well. I wanted to have my hands in all of it and still keep Samantha with me as much as I could, so I knew I would have to have a second pair of hands and a second pair of eyes. Probably five to six months into this disease and this new life with EB that we were living, our insurance company canceled us. I could not believe that they could actually terminate our coverage, but they did and it was without warning or notice.

We got insurance with someone else right away, but it wasn't easy and, clearly because my daughter had EB, it was a challenge. We were charged more then the average business because of our special needs child, and therefore so were our employees. My husband and I had to pay

75% of the cost of the policy for all of our employees so that their portion would feel like half, because the rates were so inflated. Our insurance rates went up about 60%. On top of rates increasing, now our bandages were not being paid for at all. This is when we had to pay the full cost of the entire order of bandages for Samantha's wound care supplies.

Shortly after the first insurance company terminated our policy, I received a bill from the bandage supply company indicating that we owed them 15 thousand dollars. Because the insurance company canceled our policy on a particular date everything that was shipped after that date was our responsibility. We were not informed that the coverage had been canceled for maybe about two weeks after the actual date these products were shipped. Within that two week time period there were quite a bit of supplies that got shipped to our house for Samantha's care. I remembered how the letter said that we had better pay or they were going to hire an attorney and make us pay them for every dime they ever spent on our daughter's bandages since technically bandages are an "over-the-counter-item" and insurance companies do not pay for "over-the-counter-items." Isn't that crazy?

I think that was about the time I started to wonder and worry about how other families were doing this. It felt like the exorbitant expenses to keep our child alive, along with unusual products needed to help make her life easier, was hardly believable. I think for me this was the start of my engine in my mind working and wondering how families could afford such exorbitant expenses just to give their child quality in his or her life due to EB. The whole insurance problem seemed so over whelming and daunting. But I knew I had to go through it because really we had no other choice. I had my own business at this point and I knew that getting and keeping health insurance was going to be tricky and it was.

I think we had to go through this insurance drama because it was the fuel that flamed my desire to help EB families figure out a better way of life - realizing that money really was the main issue for most families. When you walk through a certain obstacle in life it makes you more aware of the issues that need to be resolved. That goes hand in hand when saying that unless a particular situation affects you personally you really don't ever 'get it' or understand or have the desire to fix it. When I would form a judgment about a person or a company who I thought could help EB, but wasn't helping EB, I quickly retracted my thought or feeling because I realized it wasn't their fault - and maybe instead of placing blame or getting angry, a better plan should be to let it go and find someone or some other company that had a reason to jump into our cause. In my mind it was God's way of saying you have to walk there to empathize in order to help. At the end of the day we are all here to help each other anyway aren't we? I think it is safe to say that this 'termination of insurance' opened up my eyes to the financial hell EB families were already living.

With each passing year with Samantha, her disease revealed new challenges almost constantly. It seemed as though that with every year some new issue would occur and we were constantly trying to find solutions to new problems. At first it was with her clothes, then shoes, then foods. When she was younger, she would throw up blood a lot. She would choke on her foods almost daily, and some days she would even choke on liquids. Almost everything we learned was by trial and error. At some point her hands started to web together making the ability to use her hands more difficult for her. She lost all of her fingernails. I remember being so sad, thinking that one day Sam would wonder why she didn't have any fingernails and I would have to tell her about this horrible disease she has... I was dreading that day. It felt like as things progressed and her disease became more and more involved, I kept pushing away the day I would ever have to tell her anything about her disease at all. I would often ponder the notion that one day she might ask me how long she has to live. Oh, dear God, how will I tell her this answer?

Chapter 27.

The ER Drama

There were countless situations with medical personnel that were just unbelievable. I had to find out the hard way that not very many people, *including* the medical community, had very little to - no - knowledge of EB. We were in the car driving somewhere. It was in the early afternoon and in the middle of summer. That meant it was about ninety-five degrees outside with a feels-like temperature of 110, and the sun was shining without a cloud in site. I had my nanny, Carol, with us, and she was sitting in the back seat with Samantha. Suddenly Samantha started to complain of stomach pain, and the pain seemed to worsen as the minutes passed. This was not her regular tears of pain, this was alarmingly different. So I quickly phoned my pediatrician and he told me to take her to the nearest Emergency Room. He wanted me to do that because he was too new to EB, and since Samantha had been having so many unexpected issues with her throat, esophagus and GI he just wanted to make sure we were not dealing with a more serious situation.

I knew that Dr. Yee was worried about how we were going to be treated blindly walking into the ER. He had already experienced some other instances where medical staff had behaved badly just because they didn't know about EB. He told me that he would stay on the phone with me while we walked into the hospital so if a situation did occur he could help me handle it. Well, we walked in the ER and clearly you could see that Sam (probably about one year of age then) was wrapped in bandages from her neck all the way down to her feet. Seeing a child wrapped in bandages from her neck down can be cause for instant curiosity or alarm for anyone... even a well-trained nurse.

Calmly, I walked up to the triage nurse station to sign us in and explain why we were there. Samantha was screaming and crying from the pain, and she was saying, "Mommy it hurts so bad. My tummy hurts so bad, mommy, please make it stop," over and over again. Clearly she was in some kind of pain. The male triage nurse took our immediate information and then took us right back into a room. He said he wanted to get her vitals and a weight so he could at least give her some medicine to help relieve the pain. It was clear that she was having some kind of abdominal pain. He took her temperature and her blood pressure as she was thrashing her body around, making it difficult to just get those things done. The pain was making her hysterical. Then he said he needed to get a weight. I knew that he was going to want to get her weight by placing her in this standard weight bucket sort of thing they put babies in. I saw the bucket weigh scale there behind him to the left corner of the room. I was trying to explain to the nurse that she was too upset to sit in the bucket, which could result in unnecessary trauma or injury to her skin so isn't there another way to get a weight? He seemed annoyed that I would even suggest something different. I didn't care, though, because we had used this weight bucket before on calm days and it had caused some unneeded boo-boos. So I already knew that in this "emergency type of situation" we had better have a different plan.

He acted like he just wanted to do his job and he really wasn't interested in any ideas I had. I knew I had to press for a different plan or Samantha was going to get hurt. Through trial and injury living with EB, I had learned how to always have a plan A and a plan B in place. I said to him, "Why not just get her weight with me holding her and then I can hand her to my nanny and then you can just get my weight and then subtract my weight and then you will have her weight." We have had to do that before, which is how I knew to do it in the first place. There were times she couldn't lie in those baby buckets before due to something on the bucket that could have caused her a tear in her skin, or she either had some kind of wound that would have caused her pain from the position they would have had to lay her in - in the bucket. I explained that to him, but as I was talking to him he just sort of ignored me, as if I had no idea what *I* was talking about. I asked him if he heard me, but he didn't respond. So I started to repeat myself calmly giving him the benefit of the doubt that maybe he just wasn't paying attention to me for whatever reason. I told my pediatrician on the phone that things were getting too complicated, and that I was comfortable handling things, so I would call him back the first chance I could.

As I was repeating my thoughts once again to the ER Triage nurse, he interrupted me and said, "Ma'am, we need to get her weight and the only way to do that is in this bucket, which is how we get weights on children this age."

I replied, "Well, no! You can't do that. Not only is the bucket not safe for her, but she's thrashing around and she could damage her fragile skin being in that bucket because clearly she is in some kind of pain, and she is not going to sit still, did you hear that...?" He interjected with, "Ma'am, I am putting her in this bucket. I have to do my job."

"Sir you are not listening to me, please..."

Just at that moment, he grabbed her lower legs (which had bandages on them) with his big hands to hold her down in the bucket. He just grabbed her and pulled her into the bucket with her legs as I was holding her. I think from disbelief I was in complete shock. Samantha let out a loud scream. I knew she was hurt. I knew he hurt her without even looking at her lower legs. I could see his hand grab her legs. His hands were the size of her whole lower calves. I saw his hand wrap around her legs with force and I knew. I knew she was hurt. We were sort of standing next to the bucket weigh scale and, in that split second, he tore the skin from her calves. The bandages slid down from the skin on her legs as it tore and slid down. Just like that - in a matter of a split second - he ripped the skin on her lower legs off into an open wound. With most EB children, or at least I can say with mine, if a wound is caused by blunt force it is either a blister that fills with blood, or the skin just comes off and the area just starts bleeding. My jaw hit the floor. I went from calm to irrational and angry in five seconds. I think my nanny, Carol, was crying. Samantha was screaming. His face revealed the horror that was felt by his hands. He was speechless. In a fury I ran out of the door towards the entrance to the parking lot. I was yelling at him as I left. I was yelling loudly, "You're an idiot! I tried to tell you, but you wouldn't listen to me, and now you have hurt my baby. I am going to make sure someone knows what you did and you can count on that buddy!" I quickly called our pediatrician back and he started telling me, "Get out of there." I told him, "I know Dr. Yee - we are already leaving - don't worry, we are leaving. Can you believe what just happened?" Dr. Yee replied, "No I can't. I mean I heard a little bit of what you were going through, but I just can't believe that you just went through that. I will handle that don't worry just get her here so we can evaluate her now."

We ended up going to the pediatrician's office to get vitals and get checked out, but after a while her pain seemed to vanish, and what appeared to be a moment of "Go to the ER" turned out to be an ordinary day in the life of a child with EB. Her legs seem to be what were hurting the most after all that anyway. In the midst of the furry, the abdominal pain subsided and just went away. We never did find out why or what caused the pain.

Consequently, the ER drama that day infuriated her doctors so much so that a formal complaint was made. Upon reviewing the complaint, the hospital administrator organized a formal meeting in which they invited me to go there and speak about EB to the ER staff. They said they realized that their staff did not act appropriately and they asked me if I would be willing to do an EB information session just for the ER staff. I knew that the only reason we went through that nightmare was due to the fact that no one was familiar with EB. I knew then that even the medical community was capable of making mistakes because of their lack of knowledge about this disease EB, and if I didn't do my part then I, too, was just as much to blame. I didn't really want to go and do the lecture about EB, but I also realized how much good could come from doing that and ultimately it would make Samantha's life better. The more people we could educate about EB, the more chance she will have at having a normal life. All the children that suffered from this disease had something to gain from this opportunity.

I did as they asked. They set up a specific time and place for me to go inside one of the hospital facility's conference rooms. I gathered as much information as I could with the help of the DEBRA organization. I even called some EB doctors and nurses and gathered information from them that I knew would be helpful in this environment. I put together a wonderful lecture with a slide show to accompany. I wanted to take that negative experience and turn it around into a positive experience. I guess I was the only one who felt that way, though…I was the only one who showed up for the EB information lecture for the ER staff at that hospital. The director of the hospital and some of their administrative staff came to the lecture and they urged me to start anyway. I told them I was insulted. No one from the ER bothered to show up. I guess their egos were in charge of their schedules. They all apologized and asked me to do the lecture anyway. I declined, expressing my gratitude for their presence, but really there was no point to their understanding of EB as they were not the ones who caused the incident, and further more they would not be the ones to deal with an EB child, or their families, in the event one should ever have to come to that particular ER again anyway. My time was too valuable and if they didn't care to come then I was completely okay with that, as I no longer had use for their hospital anyway. There were three or four hospitals around town, and one even about one hour away that specialized in children, so I just thanked them packed up my bags and went home. I have not had to return to that hospital for any reason every again. Thank you, God!

We did have a few situations similar to that one but nothing as dramatic or as hurtful to Samantha. Having EB in our lives changed everything. Absolutely everything we did became a challenge. Who would have ever thought that going to the ER would cause trauma and drama? Every single day of our life was a day we would learn new things because of EB. Going to the grocery store was almost comical. I had no choice, right? I mean I had to shop for groceries. We would get stared at all the time. People would follow us through the isles and ask us questions like, "Did your husband do that to your baby? Does he beat you too? Did you burn her? Was she in a fire? Did you start the fire? Did you beat her?" All kinds of strange and unusual questions. At first I never knew how to respond. First of all, when I looked at Samantha she was just my sweet, adorable, precious baby. I didn't see the bandages, even though I was the one putting them on her. So it was kind of weird to always have so much attention drawn to us and almost always I was caught off guard. Responding to strangers about EB was always challenging.

It wasn't like I could say, "Oh yeah - she has a skin condition," because it was so much more than that. Most of the time I didn't want to respond at all. There were even times when strangers would follow me around the store, and I knew they were following me but it was so uncomfortable I just didn't know how to handle that. Mostly though, I think people were just plain curious.

I would pray about it at nighttime. Every time I was praying for God's help to make me strong enough to get out of bed the next day and face my EB life. I would also ask for God to help us get through the public discrimination of EB as well.

Samantha was becoming so shy from everyone always approaching us and staring at her all the time. This wasn't just the small, "oh-what's-that?" kind of stare. This was the long gazing stare. I started to notice that she would just clam right up and not say a word. I knew I had to do something. I had to find a way to bring awareness of EB, not only to our community, but also to the world. I knew I needed to do this to help Samantha. I also knew that in helping Samantha it would help all the other EB children out there who must have been experiencing the same types of situations we were.

Samantha was always so fun, loving, and cheerful. I didn't want people in our society to change her spirits. I didn't want Samantha to ever feel ashamed of who she was just because she had EB. I really didn't want Samantha to go through what I was going through. I knew there must be some way. I knew I had to do something. My mind started spinning with ideas and ways to get awareness all the while knowing it would not be easy. Thank God we at least had a choice. We could choose to be quiet and say nothing when people stared, or we could tell them off. We could be mean to them and tell them to mind their own damn business - or we could consider this a chance to educate and inform these people about EB. This issue was reeling around in my mind as a way of taking strangers stares and questions and informing them about a disease that no one had ever heard of. Sounded good, huh? But the reality of it all, for me, was talking about something so personal and so painful was not easy.

Through meeting other families with this same disease, and spending some time navigating around DEBRA, the not-for-profit organization (I was now a Board of Trustee for), I was learning new ways of educating people and answering the questions that were so often asked. I was slowly learning how to answer questions without tears rolling down my cheeks. Tucking your pain away and putting your happy face on is a learned behavior. One I was about to get a lot of training on. More training than I would ever have imagined in my life.

Some EB families would hand out little small index cards with a brief description of what EB was and how people can help to find a cure for EB. I really liked that idea, but it always seemed that I never had the cards on me at the right time, so even though I didn't really want to talk to anyone I put my happy face on and did it anyway. The happy face was for Samantha's future. That is what I would have to remind myself of everyday because I was in so much pain and no one had a clue.

My heart was getting ripped apart from watching my baby girl suffer in ways that no one could ever imagine, and yet every single day that I had to go to the bank, or go to the grocery store, or any store for that matter, no matter what it was I had to purchase I would have to put my happy face on and, in a positive manner, deal with the public. I will admit that some days the happy face just couldn't be found, and sometimes I would be as rude as the person was that approached us... but for the most part I really tried to be a role model for Samantha. In my heart, I always wanted her to know that no matter how people treated us, we could still be gracious and kind back to them. The problem was that my heart and my mind were not always on the same page when someone would approach us.

My mind became entrenched in solutions to this public awareness mission I knew we so desperately needed. I looked at everything and tried to see it as an opportunity to educate and bring awareness to EB to the world. I remember at one Board meeting asking the Board to replace their bandaged stick figure logo with a picture of a real child with EB. I offered Samantha as a solution. I thought if they had a real, live version of what EB looks like, it would be so much better then a stick figure image that no one could really identify with. Everyone else apparently thought so too, and thus Sam became the logo child for EB with the DEBRA organization back in 1997. People were staring at us everywhere we went anyway, so why not just use her picture to show what EB looks like and help the cause?

Chapter 28.

The United States Department
of Defense and EB?

In 1997, the acting Executive Director of the DEBRA organization had gotten a call from someone at the Department of Defense asking if an EB family could go to the Capital Building of the United Sates and testify before congress about EB. I am assuming because at that time I was on the Board and becoming more of an advocate about EB. The director of DEBRA phoned and asked me if our family would consider this invitation to the Capital. She explained that a representative of the American Academy of Dermatology would accompany us. She went on to tell me that DEBRA, the organization, could possibly get five million dollars for research from the DOD because of an agent used in war called Sulfur Mustard Gas. What I know about Sulfur Mustard Gas (SMG), or what I think I understood about that, is: Sulfur Mustard Gas is an agent used in war today, and when a soldier is exposed to the agent the soldier will automatically get EB (or something very similar to EB) and then die. It was my understanding that our government wanted to find a cure for EB so that we could also help our soldiers in combat who may get exposed to SMG.

The DOD had requested to speak to a family member of a child afflicted by EB to explain what it was like to live with this disease. Of course I agreed. Wow - this seemed like such an amazing opportunity to get some awareness right?

The challenging part for me was that the DOD asked me to explain our life with EB in "five minutes." I couldn't even answer the most commonly asked questions from strangers about EB in five minutes. I had no clue how I was going to tell our Legislative friends about EB in five minutes. Apparently this was a well-disciplined rule when you testify before congress. I mean, it takes me 30 minutes just to answer the most basic question, which is: "What does she have?" or, "What is wrong with her?" Oh - she has EB. "Oh… what is that?" I mean, that answer alone is a ten-minute discussion, so can you imagine how challenging it was for me to tell Congress about how EB affects our life... in five minutes?

I knew I had to do it. I knew it was important for all EB families, not just us. I even had to fax a copy of what I was going to talk about prior to our visit to the office of the congressman with whom I would be speaking. At that time, back in 1997, The Honorable Congressman Bill Young was the Chair for the Appropriations Committee for the DOD. He was also the Congressman who just happened to be in my district of the town I lived in. Sometimes I think "things" just happen for a reason. The whole five minutes we were given to talk about EB before Congressman Young actually took a good month to prepare for, believe it or not.

The DOD made calls requesting all sorts of information. We had to show proof of residency and identification. We even had to give a little history on ourselves.

As it turned out, Congressman Young and I had a few things in common. The Executive Director of the DEBRA organization was spearheading this event and doing most of the organizing and planning. I know we would have never been able to pull it off if it had not been for her. Her name was Miriam. I remember calling Miriam and saying, "Geez - why are we only given five minutes to talk when there is clearly more information than five minutes will allow?" She responded, "Well you are going to the United States Department of Defense and that is what they requested." They wanted to know everything about us: what schools we went to, and in what year did we graduate, and what grade did we get to? I didn't actually graduate from high school, which wasn't something I was proud of either. Nonetheless, we had to divulge any information they wanted... truthfully. When the representative called to ask me all these questions I came right out and told the Congressman's Aid that I wasn't happy about answering so many personal and private questions. He told me that these were standard questions and a common practice for "anyone" coming to the Department of Defense for any reason.

He asked me why I was so uncomfortable and I answered him by saying, "Well, I really am not proud of the fact that I did not graduate from high school. As a matter of fact it is one of my biggest mistakes in life that I wish I could go back and change."

Then he said the most amazing thing to me, "Well, Marybeth, you and Congressman Young have something personal and private in common then."

"Oh?" I asked, "What is that?"

"Neither one of you graduated from high school," he replied.

Wow - that was pretty inspirational then. A Congressman, as amazing as he was, and he didn't graduate from high school. Stunning.

So, we finally got to Washington and went before The Honorable Congressman Young I did the best job I could explaining this horrible tragic disease EB to him in five minutes. After we were done, Congressman Young invited us to eat lunch in the famous Senate Quarters. No one - especially people just visiting - were ever allowed to eat in the Famous Senate Quarters. What a treat! We were tickled that he would have invited us into his private sector of fellow Congressmen and Senators. Samantha was the star and she stole every person's heart with her tender, sweet smile and her beautiful, brown locks of long, shiny hair. No one in the Senate Quarters stared at us, and no one in there asked us weird questions either. Some of the staff told us how lucky we were to be in there, but mostly we were just thankful. The food in the Famous Senators eating-place was impeccable. I will tell you it was some of the best food I have ever tasted in my life.

After the tragedy of the World Trade Center attacks on September 11th, the funding for our EB research was cut.

Shortly after that visit, I ended up going to our local County Commissioners Council and asking for an EB Awareness Day. Again, I had to go before the entire Council and speak about EB and why we needed awareness. That was fine since I was becoming a professional about EB anyway. My Awareness Day was granted - but when I found out that I would have to re-appear before the County Commissioners every year to approve this Awareness Day, I decided to just relish in this present year. I knew there was not going to be any way for me to be appearing before them yearly. My goodness, I barely had time for anything. We were doing bandages everyday, and what little time I did have I spent strategizing plans and ideas and ways to implement new strategies on how to bring EB out into the public's eye. I was calling newspapers to try and get someone interested in doing a story. I called TV stations and, literally, I would talk to just about anyone and collect ideas on how to bring awareness of EB out to our community.

We were hoping to get some local media attention about EB from having this Awareness Day granted from our local, home town County Commissioners Council, so we called the news papers and TV stations to see if they would come out and do the story. Much to our surprise they did come out and interview us and, as a result of our efforts, Samantha and I ended up on the front page of our local newspaper, "The Tampa Tribune." We were told that we were going to be in the Metro section of the newspaper. Boy, were we surprised when we saw our full size photo on the front page of the whole newspaper. I was told that apparently the News Paper Editor at that time was taken with Samantha's photo, and he thought she was adorable so he wanted to put her on the front page of the whole newspaper – not just the Metro section.

Chapter 29.

"Wake Up"

One hospital stay that stands out very clearly and present in my mind was, and still is, a constant reminder that God was, and still is, in our life watching over us. We took Samantha in because she was vomiting blood and her doctors wanted to monitor the amount of blood she was throwing up. It was our first time spending the night in the hospital with both Samantha, Jim, and I. Knowing that no one had any knowledge of this disease, both my husband and I were extremely weary of all of the nurses and we wanted to make sure we kept our eyes on everything, and anyone, who came in contact with her at any time. After our ER drama we were now super-careful with everything. So I think she was about three years old at that time. The hospital bed was about three feet high, and we decided, or I guess I should say that I decided, that I would sleep in the bed with Sam so I could stay awake and watch over her. I was on the bed and my legs were v-shaped spread open with Sam lying in-between my legs just perfect with her little head resting on my stomach. I told myself that I was going to stay awake so that I could make sure no one did anything to hurt her during her stay in the hospital. Jim was sitting in the chair. He fell asleep pretty quickly that night. The stress this disease brought into our lives devoured our energy. Jim and I both always felt so tired and wiped out. You can imagine this being our first time in the hospital with her and us not knowing exactly what was going to happen, or what new problem was going to reveal itself - it just drained us. I prayed that night (as I did every night) for God to keep us safe and protect us.

At this point in my life with my husband, I wasn't really sure what his spiritual beliefs were. I wasn't even sure if he really believed God existed at all. I think EB can definitely rattle your faith, and if your faith is not solid to start off with, it can downright make you wonder if there really is a God. Jim and I didn't bring God up in our conversations that much. The only real memories I have about talking to Jim about God were the ones where Jim would ask me, "How can God let something like this happen to our beautiful little girl?" I didn't have the answers to those kinds of questions, nor did I want to pretend I did. I would just tell him, "Hey Jim we just have to pray and have faith… we have to do it because it is all we have to hold on to."

I remember going to church by myself a few times and asking God to show His face to my husband, and just asking for His help to make Jim a believer. Well, I think that night in the hospital pretty much did it for my husband. I can't say that just that one night made him a believer, but I can tell you that it definitely gave my husband plenty of reasons to question his faith. Sometimes those things - those unexplainable weird things that happen to us in our lives - are just enough to kick-start our faith in God.

Sam had an IV in her tiny little hand. She was getting IV hydration because of all of the vomiting. The doctors wanted to make sure she stayed hydrated. At some time after about one or two am in the morning, I must have fallen asleep with Sam as she was lying in the middle of my legs on this hospital bed. Next thing I know Jim was very gently touching my leg and whispering, "Shhh… honey, you need to wake up. Stay calm. Samantha fell out of the bed…. Marybeth wake up. She is on the floor. Shhh… stay calm. I need you to not freak out. Marybeth … wake up." I remember waking up. As I think about it now, it was as if the whole thing had happened yesterday. I woke up in slow motion - first looking for Sam to be in my lap on the bed. I heard Jim tell me she was on the floor… and then, horrified to think my little baby was on the floor; pure panic went through my veins like a cold chill. What was I going to see? Oh my God I couldn't look over the side of the bed on the floor. Oh my God! Was there going to be blood all over the floor? Was she going to have her skin ripped off and bloody from hitting the floor? Was the IV still in place? And, oh my goodness - what was the nurse going to think? Oh God… what if it is worse than that? Would the nurse condemn me? *And* hold me responsible for even more damage to my daughter? I mean, after all, you were not supposed to sleep in the bed with your child…. and for this very same reason. The nurse warned us and told us that we were not allowed to sleep with Samantha in her hospital bed. The nurse told us that the hospital bed was only made for one child - not one adult and a child - just *one* child. She also warned us that after I got out of the bed that I needed to make sure the bed guardrails were up on each side of the side so that Samantha would not fall out. Jim and I were both terrified. It was somber quiet in the room. We could hear each other breathing. Sam was on the floor, but she was still asleep... or was she unconscious? Maybe she hit her head?

We very slowly picked her up off the floor and put her back up in the bed in my lap. I held her so tight that I had to remember that I could make a boo-boo. The entire time from the moment I woke up when Jim touched my leg until right then, as we picked her up off the floor, seemed like maybe five seconds. I was praying and asking God to make everything ok... asking God to let this be ok... and please, God, let us get her back in bed before the nurse walks in. Please God, just let her be ok. I know Jim and I both felt like we had just been hit by some kind of shock. In reality our life, since the day she was born, was as if we were being shocked time and time again. Jim and I were whispering to each other as if we didn't want anyone to hear us. We were in a hospital room with the door closed so even if we talked with a normal voice no one would have been able to hear us. We quickly scanned her body for the blood or the blister or, yet worse, the wounds from her fall. But much to our surprise... nothing. There was nothing. Not a bump or a bruise, or a tear in her skin anywhere... nothing. We could not believe our eyes. We could not believe that Sam fell three feet out of a hospital bed where she was lying between my legs and she did not even get the slightest bruise. I guess she must have rolled over my legs and then fell on the floor. That would have been the only way she could have gotten out of the middle of my legs and then to the floor. I didn't feel her go over me. The whole thing was unexplainable. I didn't hear anything. How could that have been? I was the lightest sleeper on the planet. I would wake up if the door made the smallest sound. I had always been a very light sleeper. I am serious - I would wake up if her breathing changed patterns, so for her to have rolled over my legs and then off the bed and onto the floor was unthinkable!

Jim and I quickly looked over her body for any signs of injury, but still nothing, even the IV was still perfectly in place. Not a rip or a tear in her skin anywhere. Not even her IV line was moved or hurt one bit (which, by the way, was not even held on by tape, but merely held on just by a rolled gauze that was lightly rolled around her arm – you can't use items such as tape on an EB child so it was our only way to secure the IV in place). Yes, not even the IV moved even 1 centimeter - nothing. It was a miracle. But why? I was dazed and confused, but Jim appeared to be alert and awake. I must have fallen into a very deep sleep for her to have rolled right over my legs and then off the bed, and I felt nothing? Me -

the person who wakes up if the wind blows in a different direction. I started asking Jim all kinds of questions like, "What happened? You were sleeping in the chair, and I was holding Sam in my lap between my legs? How did this happen? And how did you wake up? And the nurse never came in? Like - how did that happen?" Jim looked so alert and awake, and something about his face told me that he was scared, he was white - like he saw a ghost or something, but yet he was so calm. For a second I started to panic, but he remained calm and steady. He was so quite, but I kept asking him, "What happened Jim? Why were you awake? Why doesn't she have any boo boos on her?"

Jim said very calmly but very matter of fact, "I heard a voice tell me to ... 'Get up'."

I said, "What? What voice? Who? What do you mean someone told you to get up?"

"Well I don't know Marybeth," he answered, "I was sleeping too. I thought I was dreaming or something... I am not sure. But I heard this man's voice telling me to get up... get up... He just said... GET UP! And when I opened my eyes I saw you there laying on the bed sleeping and Sam was on the floor. I thought I was still dreaming, but when I realized I was awake and she was on the floor I knew I had to wake you up and get her off the floor with out any of us panicking. I wasn't sure if Samantha was hurt or alive or anything... I was also confused."

And just like that, the nurse walked in the door to check on Samantha and get her vitals. I thought for sure I was going to have a heart attack. My pulse was racing and I knew my face must have been fifteen shades of red. I didn't know what to say first, or if should say anything at all. Should I tell her Sam fell out of bed? Should I just pretend that nothing ever happened? And, oh my goodness, was God talking to my husband? Can you imagine all of this happening within about a five-minute time frame? If my memory serves me correctly, we remained calm and composed and said nothing to the nurse. I do remember being very anxious for this nurse to leave our room so I could cross-examine my husband and try to make some sense out of what he had just told me. I thought I was confused that second my eyes opened and he was whispering for me to wake up because Samantha was on the floor, now after hearing that someone, or something, woke Jim up and maybe saved her life, and ours too for that matter, just sent my mind into orbit. Why would God talk to him? He was nowhere near as strong in his faith and belief in God as I was, so then why him? And why then... at that particular time?

The facts were clear: Sam did fall out of the hospital bed with an IV placed in her hand - being held on with a gauze bandage no less. She escaped any injury at all which, by all accounts, is a miracle. We had issues keeping that IV in place anyway. The way it was placed if she moved her hand the wrong way the IV would just slide right out. We could not use tape on her fragile skin. Mysteriously, a man's voice - presumably God - did speak to Jim and told him to wake up at that opportune time just before the nurse walked in the room. The nurse would have been the one to find that Sam had fallen out of the bed and presumably have been seriously hurt. Remember that any friction to her skin or bump will cause a blister, tear, or painful wound. A direct hit would simply just cause the skin to tear right off. It was a tiny hospital room we were in. There was only room for a single, small, hospital bed and a recliner chair. No one else was in the room with us. Jim and I continued to discuss the events that had just occurred for the next couple of hours. I was sure it was God. I think Jim was still in shock and thought, maybe, quite possibly, it could have been God! So then that would confirm that, in fact, God does exist. Maybe he is real. And maybe for the first time in Jim's life... he just heard His voice.

We were discharged a couple of days later with a prescription for Zantac and instructions for a bland diet for the next few days. Often at times with EB, things would happen such as this vomiting blood and such, and there would be no real reason why it happened. If the condition stopped it was like we just kept on moving forward. Most of the time we did not stop and ask why: Why did this happen, or why did that happen? Sometimes, just having whatever it was end was good enough for all of us... doctors included. EB did that to you. EB humbled you and made you thankful for anything and everything in life.

Apparently what was causing all of the vomiting and the blood was the constant blistering in her mouth, throat and esophagus. The doctors came to the conclusion that she would bleed from the blistering in her mouth, throat and/or esophagus, and the blood would then travel down to her stomach causing her to vomit. We had been having these issues for so long now, so it was just one more episode with EB that we had to get used to and work out. There was even talk of the possibility that strictures were forming down further in her GI tract causing damage. I had contacted some experienced GI doctors out of state who were familiar with EB who urged me not to let just any GI doctor go down her throat to look for such things. We had learned that the esophagus was one of the most fragile parts of their insides and it was also an area that was very easy to perforate. Then we had been warned of the consequences of a perforation with an EB child - and we listened. No one, except a well-trained EB – GI expert, was going to go down Samantha's throat - EVER!

That was the second course of training we received that your stomach can't hold blood in it. Your stomach doesn't like blood in there so it will just cause you to vomit it out as soon as it gets in there. If we give her the Zantac the moment she started throwing up blood she would eventually stop, because the Zantac will coat and sooth the stomach allowing the blood to stay down there.

Chapter 30.

"The Angels Are Here"

Shortly after that episode Sam started having so many more difficulties eating and swallowing anything. Her GI doctor at that time wanted to do an upper GI scope. This is where they take a thin tube-like instrument that looks like a long wire and has a camera on the end of it, and through the opening of her mouth they would insert this tube and go past the air way down into the esophagus and further. This was the same procedure that we had been warned about a few times to not do unless we had a well trained EB doctor.

This is how the doctor can get a better look and determine the best method of treatment for our current set of circumstances. This procedure is done under general anesthesia. We probably waited a year before having this done as we had heard that this is one of the worst and most dangerous procedures you can do on an EB child, so if you can wait to have it done, then hold out for as long as possible. We were not really in any position to just fly somewhere out of state and have one of the EB expert doctors do this procedure. Plus, then we would have had the issue of 'now who is going to follow her afterwards?' We couldn't just pick up and move somewhere. So we were trying to work with the GI experts here where we lived and even though they did not have EB experience we did trust them – to some degree.

Jim and I had researched this procedure, which is called an Upper Endoscopy, for a few months. We had been warned not to let "just anyone" do this procedure. We had spoken to many families and many doctors in the "EB World" (so to speak) that told us that if at any time the doctor feels like the area is to tight for their tiny, little, tube-like instrument to go through that the doctor must stop. Under no circumstances is the doctor to push it through, or force the tubing through at all, as this can cause a perforation in the esophagus and that can lead to more serious complications. Pretty much any tear in the skin in an EB child just results in serious problems. In fact we were told that if the doctor was at all aggressive, then to make sure there is a "GI Surgeon" present in the room at the time of the Endoscopy so that if such a complication should arise that there is someone qualified right then and there to repair it. Repairing a perforation anywhere can be difficult, let alone on an EB child, and the esophagus of all places can be very difficult to repair because the skin there is so fragile.

Since our GI doctor at this time agreed not to force anything through in any area that felt tight we felt comfortable letting her do the procedure. Basically, at that time, her esophagus needed to be looked at to determine the level of stricture involvement. Your esophagus is made up of the same tissue as the tissue on the outer part of your body that makes up your skin, so as you are blistering on the outside of your body from EB, you are also blistering in the esophagus as well. How much blistering in the esophagus usually depends on the severity of the subtype of the disease, and the only way to determine how severe the involvement is in this area is to go down there with a scope and look around. The other worry was that you did not want to get yourself in a place where the esophagus completely closed up because then that would bring on even more risky procedures.

I think that Jim and I had talked to our GI doctor so much about our fears with regards to forcing something through a tight area that we had instilled fear in our GI doctor, so she wasn't going to take any chances. She might have been feeling that "we," the parents, were more of a risk than the actual procedure itself, so she assured us that she would not take any chances and that she had no intentions of attempting to force even the slightest of narrowed area at all. I even went one step further and hand wrote those specific instructions on the consent form I had to sign prior to the surgery. It was always my feeling that if doctors did not comprehend laymen talk, then, for sure, they would understand legal talk. She was a fairly young GI doctor and we knew that she had no real EB experience and, maybe, that she had never done an EB child before ever.

Another condition for us was that I was to be allowed back in the OR (operating room) with Sam so that I could be there when she fell asleep, and also so that I could administer the eye gel in her eyes and, more importantly, I wanted to be in the operating room making sure that no one did anything unknowingly that would harm her. There are so many things you have to be careful of with an EB child before going into an operation room environment.

Usually when kids with EB go back into the OR the doctors will put some eye gel in their eyes to keep their eyes from drying out. When sedated, the eyes generally do not close all the way and EB children have eye dryness issues anyway as a complication due to their disease, but you don't want their eyes to get dry because that can cause a corneal abrasion, which is a whole new set of problems. You also don't want just anyone putting eye gel in your child's eyes that is not familiar with EB, because the slightest touch to the eyeball including the lid area can cause an eye blister. There is a particular way to open the eyes with putting one finger on the top of the eyebrow and one finger by the cheekbone area on the face, and then gently pulling the two sides apart opening the eye gently.

Also, you do not want to ever let anyone make the mistake of putting tape on an EB child's skin by accident either, because when they go to pull the tape off and you are not there the skin comes off with the tape. These are just simple things that can be avoided with some EB knowledge or the parent being allowed to be in the OR during the procedure.

So our trusty GI doctor agreed to let me go back and I did. The doctor was so sweet and you could tell that she clearly loved children. She even sang a child's lullaby to Sam to help calm her to fall asleep, and then I left.

I walked back to the waiting room to be with my husband where we both nervously waited for our GI doctor to come out and tell us of her findings. After about an hour or so she walked out and told us that she was unable to take the instrument below the airway level. She was able to see that Sam had extensive blistering at the top base of her throat and airway area, and that when she tried to put the tube down past that point it was very tight. Since we had asked her not to force anything through she then decided not to go past that area. That means that besides her mouth and throat area she could not see anything else. That was ok, though, because that was enough for us to know that we had big issues close to her airway area, and we needed to be extra careful when she was eating any foods that could cause her to choke easy if that area was at all constricted. It was just confirmation that her airway had been at risk since birth, and even though she did not have the Junctional subtype of extensive airway involvement, for whatever reason she did still have extensive airway involvement. We knew if her throat was tight, because there were times that she would not be able to swallow her own saliva, so it was at those times that we would keep her on a liquid or pureed food diet until the area improved. Our fear would be that if food were to get caught there, could that potentially cause her airway to close? At that point we knew certain foods could be risk factors when trying to swallow due to their nature of texture; like steak, potato chips, popcorn, hard candy, or any foods that are chewy and hard to dissolve.

So we waited an hour for Sam to get out of recovery so we could go home. All she had that day was a little bit of Versad, which is an oral sedation medication used frequently to mildly sedate children that need procedures but don't necessarily need to be under general anesthesia. So we got Samantha, who seemed to be semi-coherent and very responsive to us, but a little bit loopy at the same time, and we got in the car. Sam and I sat in the back seat and daddy drove. She lay on my lap on her side facing the front of the car, and I just wrapped the seat belt buckle around both of us. Samantha was awake and talking but still a little confused and dazed. She asked us all kinds of questions about her procedure and what the doctor found. She has always been very bright and very smart for her age. She has also been very curious about her disease and about the medical care she was getting. Samantha always liked to have all the details - even at a very young age she liked details. I always thought that was strange because I, on the other hand, would rather not know anything. I am sort of like, "Ok, put me out…do what you have to do… and that is all I want to know."

After a few minutes of her being quiet she raised her head from my lap as she was looking out the front of the car's front windshield and she said, "Mommy I can see the angels." A little startled and taken back by her statements, I said back to her, "Really honey? Well that is great, and yes, I do believe the angels are here with you sweetheart." "There are lots of them mommy and they are showing me the baby."

I thought for a moment she was talking about baby Jesus, but then she said, "I see the baby mommy, the baby is coming."

She got very excited as if she were going to be getting a present or something. She just kept repeating that until I told her that I acknowledged that what she was seeing was real. I just told her it was ok, and everything would be ok. How strange that after this procedure, and maybe partially still a bit fuzzy, Sam would actually see the angels and the baby? What baby?

About 4 months later I found out I was pregnant with my second child, my daughter Chloe.

Chapter 31.

Building the Fence

All in the same year, back in 1992,(before Sam was born) we bought our first house (which was also brand new construction), got married - and started a business. That's a hefty load to take on for two young people just starting out in life. Looking back I think it was boot camp for the future.

A few years after Samantha was born, around 1997 or so, we decided to move again and build our second new home. This home was different than our first because it was much bigger and it was in a more private area on a lake instead of a neighborhood. Since we were in a more secluded area and it was sort of out in the "boonies" (or more undeveloped areas surrounding the lakes) we wanted to put a fence up around our property with a private gate leading into the driveway. So Jim and I had decided we wanted solid, concrete brick columns, about 6 feet apart, with iron rod railings in-between the columns that would match the gate which would be electronic so I could buzz people in and out from the touch of a button of a remote control.

We soon learned that the company who made the iron rod railings would not make the concrete brick columns. So we had to look around for someone to build these 6-foot square, brick concrete columns. After a few weeks of looking and interviewing and price checking, we finally decided on this one concrete company. I distinctly remember it was very difficult to get a company to build the concrete columns because new construction was at an all time high so most of the concrete companies were already booked solid the entire year out, but there was this one man (family-owned business), who was able to build our columns at just that time.

I can't remember the name of the company or even the name of the man doing the work, but his testimony was profound and ever lasting. He would come every day and build brick by brick, and concrete pour by concrete pour, he slowly built each column. Those concrete columns took months to finish. Sam was about four or five years old. Every day

I would take her outside to play and get fresh air. We lived on a lake and we had a very large front yard with large beautiful, mature, Oak trees giving Sam lots of shady play area. We also had a very long driveway from the entrance of the property to the house. It was about five hundred feet long. Every day I would walk the long walk to get the mail. Samantha always trotted along side of me singing or playing. She was a happy child- always smiling and giggling. You would never have guessed anything at all was ever wrong with her if her bandages were not such a dead give away.

One day after about three weeks into this man building our concrete columns, Sam and I were making our usual walk to get the mail, and then play for a bit. Samantha had her little babies in the baby stroller and she was just as happy as she could be.

As I was walking towards the mailbox, and Sam was hobbling along side of me, I noticed this man stop working. He put his tools down and started to walk towards us. For some reason I had this feeling that he was going to talk to me on this day. He never really talked to me before unless to tell me he needed more supplies or more money, but usually he just came, worked all day, and then left. When he got about 10 feet in front of us he fell to his knees and folded his hands as if he was going to start praying. I thought, "Oh Good Lord what was this man doing?"

Samantha sort of stopped in her tracks and grabbed onto my leg. I wasn't quite sure what he was doing, but decided whatever it was, his hands were folded in prayer so whatever he was doing it appeared like it involves the Lord, so it must be ok. He looked straight into my eyes and he said, "Mrs. Sheridan I need to tell you about your daughter." He paused then said, "She has saved my life." I said, "Okay…."

He went on, "Your daughter she is special. She has this light around her and I think she has brought me back to the Lord. I can see God in her"

I thought to myself, "Oh my goodness, is this guy a nut or what?

But he stayed there on his knees and he was giving thanks to God for this job and the chance to be in the presence of such an angel. He was thanking God for sending him to our house to do this work. Which was another thing that I thought was strange considering at that time there was more work in the construction field than there were workers to actually do the work. Our job was small compared to the new home construction work that he could have choose to do, and our pay would not have been as much as the other.

So, not really sure what to say to him, or even what to think at that point, I simply said, "Thank you sir, and yes we also think she is very special."

The entire time Samantha said nothing, not a peep from her mouth, but she was taking every word and every action from the man in. I turned around and started to walk back to the house, and the man said, "No wait! Mrs. Sheridan, please wait, I need to tell you more." I turned back around to face the man who was still on his knees.

"She is an angel from God. You see when I started working here at your house I was not a follower of God. I have been in jail, and I have made a mess of my life. Then I see your daughter and I see her struggles with these wrappings on her body and how she cannot walk very well. I can see that her suffering must be great, but I see that she has a light around her and I feel that she has led me back to God."

He went on to tell me that a few days after he started working on our job he went back to church and has now finally started to get his life back on track. He told me that somehow he could feel her pain, and he knew that she was suffering. He said that her happiness led him back to God. I am not sure I got, or understood, all that he said to me. His English was broken and his first language, which was Spanish, was mixed in with his English making it difficult to really understand him. In my heart I knew what he meant. I had seen it before. I had noticed that some people were drawn to Samantha in some strange way. Others barely noticed her at all, but the ones who are drawn to her – the impact of their greeting - is usually unforgettable. This wasn't the first time someone had approached me about feeling some kind of connection between my daughter and God.

Shortly after that man finished that job we had another experience that would lead me to believe that people who were drawn to Sam - were also somehow drawn to God.

Chapter 32.

House Cleaning and Soul Cleaning
Go Hand in Hand

Now that we had built our dream home, and our hard work being self-employed finally started paying off, I decided that I wanted to be more involved in the non-profit organization DEBRA to volunteer my time and talents to help find a cure for this disease, EB. I also decided that it was time to get into the trenches with the other families and figure out a good survival mode for all of us to be in. In order to do this I needed to free up some other time, so I put the word out that I wanted to find a full-time housekeeper. I didn't like to put adds in the newspaper because I always found that if you throw the idea around that you were looking for some help, that help would come. It had always worked out best for me that way.

Around this time I decided not to have a nanny anymore. It served its purpose and time while I needed it, but I felt that I was not getting that time with Sam that I really wanted and just felt it best to stop having a nanny. Sam was getting older anyway now so really the need just wasn't there anymore. Same thing sort of happened with my personal assistant except she left for "personal reasons." Both my nanny and my personal assistant names were 'Carol' - ironic I know. The only thing I really needed at the time anyway was just some help with the house so that when I did have free time, that time could be spent having fun with Sam. We went to the park, the zoo and Busch Gardens any chance we got.

I will always remember the day this one girl walked through my door. She had confidence and she was very knowledgeable about cleaning. She was not up for negotiating on her pay. She was guarded and all business. She had a flat per-hour rate and I liked her. She had a certain sense of seriousness about her. When she worked, she worked hard, and rarely took breaks. I worked from home and Samantha was always with me. Her name was Maquida and she was from Brazil.

Maquida would come every day at the same time in the morning and leave at the same time at the end of the day around 5pm. Anything that I needed her to do, she would do - and more. Having her in my life allowed me to free up more time so that I could not only spend more time with Samantha, but also get more knowledgeable about being on the board of a not-for-profit organization. The ultimate goal was to become as knowledgeable about EB as I could, as I knew this would help us to give Samantha a better quality in her life.

I would try to make small talk with Maquida, but she always kept our conversations short. I felt like she had this wall up that said: I work for you so I can't be friends with you – kind of thing. I noticed that she rarely smiled and, for whatever reason, she seemed to always be in deep thought. I just assumed she was tense and stressed all the time; maybe something in her personal life wasn't going well. I almost felt like Maquida was angry with someone or something. I knew it had nothing to do with me since I had only just met her, and she was always pleasant with me. She did seem to like being at our house, and she really enjoyed her work. I could also tell that she took a special liking to Samantha the day she met her. Around Samantha, Maquida was all smiles and playful.

Since "Maq" was in our home the entire day every day she would be there when I had to do bandages. I know that she saw things - and heard things - that had to have shaken her up. I knew she could hear Samantha crying and at times - screaming from the pain because of her disease. Some days were worse then others for Samantha. Depending on how many wounds she had open at the time, or how poorly she was feeling, would determine how her bath and bandage changes would go.

I would imagine that to someone who didn't know us, who didn't know anything about EB, then seeing a child wrapped up like a mummy all the time, and then hearing that child's cries of pain and help to make it stop, might make someone really wonder what the heck was going on in our house. You could hear her saying things like: "Ouch, oh mommy it hurts so bad… please make it stop mommy… I can't do it mommy it hurts so bad… please don't make me." Followed by screaming and crying. Unimaginable. Unthinkable. Definitely not a normal household environment. Yes - I think that would be enough to freak out just about anyone.

When I hired Maquida I really didn't take into account that she might be uncomfortable with our daily home environment and medical routines. I never once gave it a thought until the day I saw Maquida's face for the first time after bath and bandage change. Maybe it was about a week into Maquida working for us, both Maquida and I had passed each other in the hallway. I was going back into the bathroom where I was getting Sam in the bath, and Maquida was walking past me headed for another room. Her face said it all. Maquida had horror and sadness all over her face. I realized at that moment that I had not prepared our housekeeper for the Hell that we were living and I really wasn't sure why. I just quickly went back into the bathroom. I couldn't just stand out in the hallway and try to explain EB to Maquida while Sam was waiting on me to get back in there. It was awkward and uncomfortable for me so I knew it had to be equally as awkward and uncomfortable for Maquida.

I was so emotional being the mom; falling apart inside trying to stay strong for my baby. After all, I was just a mom trying to make the best out of a really tough situation. I had no idea how to comfort this person I barely knew. I was completely at a loss for words. I prayed a lot. I asked God to help me. I prayed that Maquida wouldn't quit and leave me stranded, and I prayed that she would not be afraid. I needed someone to help me with the house chores and laundry. Even if I wasn't going to do volunteer work the bath and bandage changes took hours at a time, and sometimes we had to do them everyday.

Oh my goodness, the laundry was a nightmare. Samantha's bed sheets every day would be bloody and wet with blisters that had burst in the night, or wounds that some how just appeared and drained on the sheets. Sometimes Samantha would wake up and be stuck to her sheets. That was never any fun. We had to wash her sheets every day. The four or five towels that I would use for bandages had to be washed every day too. And her clothes had to be washed everyday as well. Every single day whatever she wore would have bloodstains or some kind of a wound stain on them. Usually her clothes had to be soaked then washed. EB gave laundry a whole new meaning.

As time passed Maquida and I would become friends. She would start to ask me a few questions here and there about Sam. Slowly it started off with, "What's wrong with her?" to "How do you take care of her?" The more we communicated the more comfortable I could sense Maquida being around us. Maquida and Samantha became friends as well. During the times of the day that we weren't doing EB care Samantha would play. Sometimes she would like to play with Maquida too. Samantha liked to mop the floors and play with the vacuum. I could see a slow change in Maquida. She didn't seem as distant anymore and I could feel a certain warmth towards her.

Finally, a few months after she had been working for us, she came to me and told me she had something to tell me. This was another one of those profound moments that I believe now was all a part of God's divine plan. I mean really we all have no idea what the plan is ever anyway - we can only assume that there is one, right? For me it was truth-telling moments like these that made me fully believe that there actually was a plan and it really wasn't for us to figure out - as long as we believed in God and trusted him.

Maquida was so happy this day. She came to me and she said, "Marybeth I want you to know that I have joined a church. I pray to God now. I know who God is now. I did not know who he was when I first came to your home, but I know him now, and I know him because of you and Samantha." Maquida wanted me to know that somehow our life - our painful EB life - had some kind of spiritual impact on her life. Enough to lead her into a solid, strong faith in God.

I would often wonder why my sweet baby girl had to suffer so horribly in that way in this life. I was starting to wonder now if it was because God was using her to somehow bring people to Him through her suffering. Somehow - in some strange way - when Maq would be in our house and be witness to the pain and suffering this sweet little girl endured on a daily basis, and then to see me, her mom, endure this hell as I prayed constantly for strength, somehow it changed something in Maquida's mind. I was not sure why or how I was thinking this, or even if it made any sense at all, but what I did know is that she did come to know the Lord, and for whatever the reason was she became close to God while being in our lives. Furthermore she was not the only person to reveal that to me.

Chapter 33.

DNA Testing

Dr. Save Me had given me the information on how to go about getting the DNA testing done. She wrote orders for the three of us (Jim, Sam and I) to go to the local hospital's lab and get all of our blood taken with detailed information about where to send this blood to and how. We did this early on - maybe when Samantha was about 6 months old. We thought we would go get our blood drawn and sent away and then in a week, or maybe two weeks, someone would call us with the DNA results. The DNA test was going to tell us if Samantha was a Dominate type of EB or a Recessive type of EB. It was also our understanding that the DNA test was used in conjunction with the Electron Microscopy (the 3-hole-bunch biopsy we had done when she was born) and clinical data (which just means the doctor's visual assessment of the child's and the families medical history combined together), which determines the actual subtype the EB child has. There are over 60 different subtypes of EB that range from very mild forms, consisting of a few blisters here and there occasionally on the hands and/or feet, to a form of EB that goes away as you get older (usually the Dowling Mera subtype), to - on the complete other end of the spectrum – two lethal or terminal subtypes that will have a life of horror and pain resulting in premature death. One of those two terminal subtypes is called Junctional EB which almost always involves the throat and air way resulting in death before age one, and the other is called Recessive Dystrophic where death occurs usually around the age of 20 or younger due to a variety of complications.

The DNA test was also vitally important if you were at all considering having more children. EB is genetic, which means it is passed down from either one or both of the parents at conception. I wasn't considering more children at the time, but I think my husband was, and even if he wasn't, the most important issue at hand was determining Samantha's exact subtype.

At the time we had our blood taken, there was only one place in the entire country that was doing DNA testing for EB that we knew of. That was at Dr. Joni Uitto's lab at Jefferson University in Philadelphia. Both of my parents and their entire families were from Philly, so that was a familiar place for me. After we had our blood taken and shipped up to Philly, Jim and I, along with my parents, went to Philadelphia to visit family and we also went to visit Dr. Uitto's lab. Dr. Ellen Fender was the doctor who was to investigate our results, but when we went to visit she was not there so we actually didn't get to meet her in person. I think she had the day off or she was on vacation or something. At that same time frame, there was another extremely talented researcher that was working at Dr. Uitto's lab and her name was Dr. Angela Christiano, PhD.

Dr. Christiano was not in when we went to visit the lab at that time, either. Being in the EB community there was a lot of talking and buzz around about "Angela." She was extremely smart and she was also very compassionate about our disease. Not to mention that she was young and very beautiful. I spoke to her a few times on the phone, as I would call into the lab to ask if they had our results completed. Mostly, I spoke to Dr. Fender; however, both Dr. Christiano and Dr. Fender explained to me that this DNA testing for EB was extremely difficult to read. They tried to explain the details to me but, honestly, that "DNA stuff" goes right over my head. What I did get was that if one of us (her parents) passed down the defective gene then her subtype would be dominant, and if both of us passed down the defective gene then it would be recessive. They also explained that because the DNA is so difficult to read that it could take a long time to get the results. Two weeks turned into two years.... Yes, that is right – it took 2 years to finally get our DNA test results back, and even then the results were still not clear.

I guess they found my husband's marker right away, but for some unknown reason my marker was harder to locate. When the test was finally concluded it was explained to me that they found the "Mickey Mouse ears" to my defect in my collagen number seven gene - but that they were unable to find "Mickey Mouse's whole head and body." Boy, did I laugh at that analogy. It worked, because I understood that definition. Anyway, the marker for the defect in my gene had to be there somewhere because if it were only in my husbands DNA then my husband would have to have signs or symptoms of the disease and he had neither. Also, we knew we might have been dealing with the Recessive EB and not Dominate EB by this time because of Samantha's symptoms. So we knew that their findings had to be somewhat accurate. This entire facility was working on little to no money, and it was my thought that most of their work was done out of a "labor or love" (for free) really, because at that time in our EB life it was clear that EB was a somewhat "rare" disease, and that funding for research and a cure for EB was also just as "rare." Nobody wanted to donate money to a disease that (primarily) they had never heard of, or affected them personally. That was another reason I wanted to bring awareness of EB out into the world. After visiting the lab at Jefferson it was clear that everyone there was familiar with EB and the devastating effects it had on the lives of the children it touched, but more importantly there was no money to help this lab with its research. We have to help this lab. These doctors and researchers here cared about our disease - and that was also a rare find. To know that they had been working on literally no funding made me feel horrible. There has got to be some way to get the word out that EB needs resources in order for the disease to be stopped!

Chapter 34.

The Facts: Real but Raw

The most painful times of the day for Samantha were during her bandage changes. Samantha's bandage changes had always been difficult for her due to the wounds being open and sore, and the blisters that would form all over her body for no apparent reason. I understood the blisters to form from friction to the skin, and because some of those anchoring fibrils that collagen produces were missing the slightest touch would cause a blister to form. What was confusing to me was that it seemed as though blisters would appear everywhere, and as if just wearing her clothes could cause blisters to form. Samantha would get 20 to upwards towards a hundred blisters a day. Those blisters would then need to be lanced with a sterile needle and the fluid drained from each blister. Have you ever had a blister anywhere on your body that you lanced and then pressed on the top layer of the skin of it to drain the fluid out? It really hurts. I know I have had a few on my feet more then a few times in my life. Imagine 50 of those on your body at one time. Ok - how about everyday?

Sometimes draining the blisters would cause the top layer of the skin to slough off causing an open wound. Those wounds would sort of look like third-degree burns. I don't have to tell you how painful blisters are. Most of us have had a blister on our feet or somewhere on our body at least one time in our life; it is just that normally we do not lance those blisters we just let them go away on their own and heal. With EB children you have to lance the blisters because there are no anchoring fibrils below the dermis layer there to hold the skin together so the fluid in the blister will keep filling causing the blister to get larger and larger until bursting on its own. These kinds of blisters most always end up being very large, open wounds that are slow to heal. So for EB kids - if you can lance the blisters at the very onset, or as soon as you see it, or the child can feel it form when they are still small, then the body does not have to work so hard to heal that area.

This is what EB is. The defect at birth is that a child is born without the proper amount of anchoring fibrils and collegian cells to hold the skin together. Therefore, any friction to the skin causes the skin to either tear and come off or a blister to form. The fluid that fills in the blisters is protein from the body. Most EB children spend their lives being malnourished because there is so much involvement with the mouth, throat, and esophagus it becomes difficult for EB children to eat the necessary amount of food and/or protein required to keep their bodies healthy - which is why most kids end up with a permanent G-Tube placed usually before they get into the double digits in age. The nutrition issues become a priority because wounds will not heal if the body is not properly nourished. Also, when the body is losing protein fluids as quickly as EB kids lose those fluids from their 50 to 100 blisters a day, somehow they need to get that protein back in their bodies - if they can't swallow liquids the only option left is a feeding tube.

So now on top of popping blisters and bandaging wounds all day, they have be to hooked up to a machine at bedtime that will pump nutrition into their bodies through out the night. Those are called G-Tube feeds and they usually last eight to ten hours. Eating foods is a pleasure that most of us take for granted. It is one of those pleasures in life that you would never give a second thought to unless you or your child were unable to do it. Most EB kids resort to soft foods and liquid supplements. Foods like potato chips, bacon, and popcorn are foods that every EB parent learns to stay away from. Most EB children will attempt to continue to eat foods and some will do okay with small amounts and chewing their food for a longer period of time. That is what most EB kids do. They are afraid of choking or gagging, which is a common occurrence when an EB child is eating pretty much anything - depending on how their throat is doing. Some EB children, along with having a permanent feeding tube placed, will also have repeat esophageal dilatations done to try and keep their esophagus's open.

Samantha can have blisters form while she is sleeping due to tossing and turning. Sometimes the blisters will form and fill during her sleep and then burst before she wakes up. Then in the morning, when she wakes up, sometimes her clothes will be stuck to the wound, and/or the sheets. There have been plenty of times we have had to take an hour or longer just to get her un-stuck from her clothes or her bed; I think the bed had to be one of the worst memories of being stuck to something I can recall. We would have to find creative solutions to getting her "un-stuck" from those things. We tried everything from covering everything in water and letting it sit there for hours, to using an entire 20-ounce jar of Aquaphor, which is an ointment similar to Vaseline, and rubbing that everywhere until whatever it was that was sticking slid off, and then, yes - there were times that I had to cut clothes off and sheets too.

Imagine having an open sore on your leg and not covering it with a bandage, then falling asleep in your bed and waking up only to find that your bed sheet somehow became embedded into the wound or the pants you were wearing. The pain is excruciating. The ordeal of un-sticking it can be a nightmare.

Samantha's daily routine consisted of taking off her existing bandages, which would take at least an hour. I would cut all of the bandages and she would sometimes slowly (and sometimes not) pull them off. Then, after the bandages were off, we had to get her body into a tub full of water that, when she sat down in the tub, the water would be to about her chest. We had to fill the bathtub that full so we could soak as much of her body as we could. She has wounds everywhere and keeping those wounds clean was a huge challenge. As she would get into the tub and the water would hit a place where there was an open wound, it would be the most intense sort of pain I would ever see my child feel. I felt like it was a form of torture, and as her mom I was the one inflicting it upon her. Watching Samantha suffer in such tremendous amounts of pain was beyond anything I thought could be real. I prayed so hard that God would turn me into stone. I prayed for strength constantly; because I just knew that I was not strong enough as a person, or as a mother, to witness my child suffer in this way. The alternative of not getting in the bath was even worse. If we choose not to do her bath then we would be inviting secondary infection to occur in the wounds thus frequently leading to premature death - and that was not an option.

After she would get into the bath and succumb to the pain, she would then soak in this bath for about 30 to 45 minutes. Over the years I would become numb to the emotional pain. Every time I would hear her cry, or see her body turn shades of red from the pain, it would rip my heart to shreds. I cried and I cried. When I would cry, it would just make the whole experience worse for both of us. My tears would increase her tears and if she did not see the strength in my eyes it was all over. I then became the "nurse." I had to dig deep inside my soul for the will power to wake up the next day only to have to repeat the same methods of torture and treatments to my precious baby girl. I found myself praying everyday and throughout the day - many, many times throughout the day - I would ask God, "Please, God, give me the strength to give Samantha the best quality of care that I can as a mother. Help me to be strong because I feel so weak oh Lord."

Taking her bandages off was hard enough because most of the time they would be sticking to the wounds that were healing, and although I would be gentle, Samantha herself would just rip them off. I never fully understood why she would do that (other then she was just plain angry, which I found to be a common emotion amongst EB children), and I would try to discourage her from doing that. But our battles became more than I could bare, and sometimes I would just let her do what she wanted to when taking off her bandages - just because. There would be blood everywhere and tears flowing not only from her but from me, too. Being subjected to having to watch my child suffer in this way was unbearable, unthinkable, and unimaginable. Then there was the battle of getting her into the bath. Oh, boy, that was a whole new ball game. I had to convince her to get in and soak her poor ragged, beaten and battered body in this bath that just by the water touching her wounds would send this raging pain so intense through her body that she would shake from the pain. Her body literally, at times, would turn red. I guess it would be like having a lot of cuts on your skin and then getting them wet, deep cuts. She would scream in pain, and then she would cry. I tried everything; we tried aromatherapy, we tried all different kinds of music, happy music, hip hop and even classical music therapies, there are too many to mention, but you get what I am saying. If someone suggested it, we tried it. We tried the whole "distraction game." We tried to make a game out of getting in. We tried to be happy and make it fun. All those things would work once, maybe twice if we were lucky, but nonetheless it just became a struggle.

As the years would pass, the struggles turned into fights. I struggled with, "Should I keep making her suffer in this way? Or should I just let her wounds get bad?' But I felt it was my duty, my responsibility, to do whatever was in my power to care for her broken body - no matter what the cost to both of us or anyone else for that matter. Anyway, after each bath and bandage change, she would be happy and you could tell that even though our struggle was intense and horrific, when we were finished she was feeling fresh and new... and the next day or so her bad wounds would heal... and that is what kept me going.

Then, on the flip side of all that I just said, sometimes no matter what we did, her wounds would just get bad, and then the fevers would come, and then she would require oral antibiotics. So at the end of the day, no matter how hard I tried or how diligent we were about her wound care and doing dressing changes, we found ourselves battling secondary infection anyway.

Chapter 35.

The Apligraf Adventure

Just like that it was a National Media attention getter: "Child with a fatal skin disease is cured!" is what I recall reading in the USA Today newspaper. Then there was a story of the same family on CNN news a couple of nights after. The story was about a mother who had just given birth to a baby with EB. The baby was born with nearly 60 percent of her skin denuded or completely missing and was diagnosed with the fatal disease EB. I remember stopping dead in my tracks and breathing every word of the details in like the first ray of sunshine since our daughter had been born.

The newborn baby immediately after birth was given a very new product technology called "Bio-engineered Skin" made by a company called Apligraf. The news made it sound so real so Jim and I started researching every doctor and family member involved. We learned that this new Bio-engineered skin was made in a lab and grown in a dish in a lab to replicate human skin. It was being publicized that this new product was put all over the new born baby's body where the skin was missing and attached itself to the baby's own skin and cured the child's EB.

We found out that a well-known reputable dermatology center in Miami were the ones responsible for this find as well as cure. We wasted no time about getting on the phone and pushing our way through for an appointment. This was the first thing that had come along since we had heard about the gene therapy gun that ended up not working. We went to Miami and we participated in what is now known as the "Apligraf Trials." I can't say that I wasn't warned - but we were warned by the same doctor who told us that a cure would not be found in his life time but we were desperate for something - anything.

We would travel from our home in Tampa to Miami at least three or four times. The drive was long and tiresome and it would take us six hours to get there, and six hours to get back. The doctor involved told us that he would have to take an existing blister on Samantha's body, take the top layer of the blister off, scrape away at the wound, and then apply this three-inch by three-inch patch of Bio-engineered skin. The hope is that this new skin would adhere to Samantha's own skin thus growing more of this new lab grown skin, and where the patch was placed would no longer blister in that spot. They first wanted to do trials on 12 or more patients and with the use of photographs and biopsies determine if in fact this new lab grown skin would act as a cure.

What we didn't realize, or research enough, was the information about the medical aspects of our skin. Everybody's skin sloughs off after 12 weeks, and regenerates new skin under the old sloughed-off skin. That throws the whole Appligraf theory right out the window. Still we had hope. The procedure was painful for Samantha even though they would numb the area it just wasn't enough and it was also very traumatic for her as well. In the end her own skin grew back and it was all for nothing. I bet you're asking yourself, "Well what about the new born baby that the news media went crazy over saying that the Appligraf saved her life?" Oh yes, let me tell you about that. Well first of all that EB baby had a very rare subtype called Dowling Mera Simplex and this particular subtype (most of the time) gets better with age and then eventually goes away. At birth this subtype can be more lethal because being born with that much loss of skin can cause secondary infection to occur rapidly and a new born baby does not yet have the mature enough immune system to fight such massive infection. This particular baby was "cured" or "life saved" because when they applied the artificial skin it allowed the babies body to not have to work as hard to close the area's where there was no skin and also prevented secondary infections from developing. That subtype is the only one rare subtype of EB that actually heals itself with age and time. And at about age four or five the child is no longer in bandages at all, or seldom blisters. Differentiating these subtypes at birth can very difficult and sometimes almost impossible. Sometimes the only way to know if you were lucky enough to have this subtype is to wait and let time tell. With that particular family though they knew from the beginning what they had I think.

That whole experience for Samantha was emotionally wrecking and a huge waste of our time.

That family became close personal friends of ours. Lorriane Camerron is the mom of the baby who was all over the news. Lorraine's time in our EB community was well served. She was the originator of many wonderful new plans, ideas, and concepts that would be forever cemented into our EB family. To this day those benefits have improved an EB child's life. Some of these benefits include the EB baby newborn baby baskets that were to be delivered to a new first time EB parent either at the hospital or their home. She was also the founder of "Have A Heart For EB Disney," or some may know that as just plain EB Disney. She also served time on the DEBRA organizations board of directors. All of her time was strictly as a volunteer. I am privileged to call her my friend.

Chapter 36.

It's Not Just the Bandages
That Makes it Hard

Through the years, as people would come and go in and out of our lives, I would often see how being around our child affected different people in different ways. This horrible disease would move people. By this time Sam's sister, Chloe, was born and we were still living in our dream house on Lake Osceola. I had been working from home since Sam was born. My husband Jim took over the day-to-day operations of our business, and I managed the finance end of things from the house. I only ended up having a nanny for about one year and then decided that, for me, having a nanny complicated things too much. It was nice while it lasted, but I think mentally I was so afraid of losing Sam that the thought of not being with her every second of every day haunted me like a bad dream. I just didn't ever want to look back and say to myself, "Well I shouldn't have had someone else watching her for those hours, or I should have been the one to do that." Plain and simple: I didn't want to have regrets.

I was determined to be the nurse and the mommy. I was still traveling back and forth from Florida to New York for the Board meetings of the non-profit organization DEBRA that I was on the board of Trustees for. I liked learning more and more about the inner workings of the non-profit world, and in my mind I was starting to think of ways to help bring more awareness about EB to our local community and to the world. DEBRA had changed their logo from a stick person to a real live child with EB -that was my child, Sam. It was a picture of her just before she turned two. The picture was of her in nothing but bandages and a diaper. A local photographer, who had been doing some family photos of us, gave me the picture as a gift with the hope that maybe someday I would be able to use it to accomplish our goals of bringing awareness of this disease EB out into the world. That picture became my inspiration behind my desire to work as hard as I could to give Sam the best quality in her life as we possibly could. I think for us, bringing awareness out into the public meant so many things. In my mind I thought, "Well if I can let people know about EB then maybe people won't stare at us all the time. Maybe if our own local community knew that our daughter has a disease like this… and what our life is like they just might be a little more accepting of us and her." Maybe the awareness will lead to money for research. Maybe that doctor who is the EB expert is wrong and they will find a cure for this disease in HIS lifetime. If nothing else, all of the work I did for EB was therapeutic for me.

Samantha was wrapped in these gauze bandages from her neck down to her feet. Even her fingers and toes were wrapped. She had wounds and or blisters pretty much all over her body pretty much all of the time. When she was an infant we would dress her in little boys T-shirts. We had to put the T-shirts on her inside out, so that the seams on the inside of the shirt did not rub against her skin and cause a blister. Her beautiful, long, brown hair with curls at the very end, and her big blue eyes were enough to stop and make you take a second glance… but the bandages she lived in were also a huge attention getter. We live in Florida where the weather is always 100 degrees so it wasn't like I could bundle her up in blankets all the time to hide the bandages, either. Believe me, I thought about doing that a few times. Some days, and especially if it was after we both cried for hours, or if she was doing bad, I really didn't feel like having to explain EB to anyone… or answer questions. Sometimes I just wanted us to be left alone. But no one knew that, and the bandages were like an open invitation to ask questions.

As it was - going to the grocery store became a big deal. I started to dread leaving the house at all for any reason. People were always staring at us. Sometimes they would follow us around and ask us crazy questions like, "Did your husband do that to her? Does he beat you too?" or, "Was she is in a fire?" The really bad thing is that EB is not one of those diseases that is a one-line answer. I would say, "Oh she has EB," and then they would say, "What is that? I have never heard of that before," and then I would find myself in this 30-minute conversation and most of the time the person asking REALLY didn't want to know in the first place. As I would start telling them about it they would let me know that they wished us well, but that they were in a hurry, or thank you anyway but they really just thought she had been in a fire. What no one ever realized is the amount of pain we were in as a family was horrendous, and that even having to talk about EB was heartbreaking for me as her mother.

Most of the time, people thought that somehow I inflicted this on her like, "Did you burn her with boiling water?" I would hear stuff like that and just give them a look right in the eyes and walk away. I really have always disliked confrontation. In general I would avoid a confrontation at all cost, but suddenly at that time in my life I found myself in awkward situations all the time. I wanted to be confrontational after the hurtful words were said, or the hurtful stares. People would say negative things and I would want to give them back a negative response. I didn't want to become a negative person, nor did I want to be angry, so I found myself thinking of ways to help people understand EB better. I prayed a lot about that too. My prayers were becoming more specific and I would ask God to help me be a better person: please to let me have love and peace in my heart, and find a way to communicate with the public... even when I didn't want to.

I had to go to the grocery store. I had to be out in public. But most of the time I really didn't feel like talking about her disease, or what it was like to live with it. I mean, who can care for a child who is in the most intense excruciating pain and the only method of treatment is a process in which you have to pop 20 to 100 blisters a day on this poor, tiny, little baby, and then bandage up her bloody, battered body knowing all along the pain she is in you just made worse by cleaning and caring for her wounds? Because you have to do it. And while you are doing it, you are feeling like all you want to do yourself is crawl in a corner and cry, no - sob - for hours, because the pain you feel inside your heart, watching your baby suffer, is more than words, more then any feeling or emotion you have ever felt before. It is more then anything you can possibly describe to someone... especially someone you don't even know.

How can you function normally? How do you get up and go to the grocery store? Or church? How do interact with people? It really puts a whole new spin on making friends... and then keeping them. My mood swings were like the wind: always changing and always blowing. Life with EB was extremely hard for everyone in my home to live with. The organization DEBRA had done a really good job of creating literature about EB in handy little booklets, so I ordered a whole bunch and I would carry them with me anywhere I went.

A few times in my travels, I would meet celebrities and I would go up to them and hand them a brochure and ask them if they would consider helping our charity DEBRA raise awareness about EB. Over time, I would realize that what our disease really needed was a celebrity to speak out on our behalf. If we only had a Julia Roberts or an Angelina Jolie to talk about EB - wow! - Then the whole world would know what EB was. Then not only could I go to the grocery store in peace, but we might actually be able to raise some money to find a cure for this disease. That would be dreamy. It was painstakingly noticeable that I wasn't really making any progress with awareness or money for research, and if anything at all I was barley functioning as a human.

Chapter 37.

The Perfectly Fitted Suit

One year, I had no idea what to get my husband for his birthday. It was sometime around 1999, because I remember Samantha was around three or four at the time. A friend of mine had told me about a clothing man who would come to your house and measure your husband for "The Perfectly Fitted Suit." I thought, "Wow - that would be the coolest gift! What a great idea!" I had never done anything like that before for my husband. What a nice change from the normal cologne and clothes from the Mall stores. So my friend, her name was Ping, gave me this man's name and number and I called him up and set up an appointment for him to come to our home and measure Jim for a suit. It was the perfect idea because Jim needed some new suits. I don't think he really had any at the time, anyway. My friend Ping had been one of my sister's dearest friends for the past 10 years and I knew she had impeccable taste. Ping lived in a completely different part of town, and she rarely socialized on our part of town, so I assumed that this man would also be coming form the Clearwater side of town as well.

At that time, I knew I wanted to advocate about EB for all EB families - not just my family. Not only was it therapeutic in a way for me emotionally, but I have always found that by helping other people it helps your soul, too. I wanted to raise money and awareness for EB, but I didn't want to go one-on-one with the public. I prayed a lot about direction and would always ask God to help me with my passionate need to bring EB to the world's attention.

In my mind I was convinced we needed some awareness and media attention. I always thought a celebrity would be good since celebrities are always the focus of media and always in the public's eyes. I would talk to anyone who wanted to help me or anyone who would listen. I had met people who got me involved with local Community Health Conventions, and local events happening in the area that I could participate in from time to time.

On a few occasions a few friends of mine and I would get all of the EB literature we could find, go to Kinko's and print up a few hundred copies, set up a couple of 6 foot tables and, oh, of course, my photo of Sam (who was my sole inspiration behind my mission), so we could show people what a child with EB looks like, and we would sit at the table all day long (at these Health Fairs) handing out literature and trying to educate and inform the public. I was pretty excited when those opportunities presented themselves to me because I really thought it was going to be a chance to educate the public about EB and actually do some good.

After a few of those local Health shows I realized we were making absolutely no progress. After sitting at the table for 10 to 12 hours a day for the entire weekend and handing out literally hundred's of copies of literature on EB, it just didn't feel like we were even scratching the surface of what needed to be done. Nothing had ever come from it, and well it just sort of felt like a waste of time and energy.

I was still traveling back and forth from New York to Tampa for the Board meetings at The Debra Organization, which generally occurred every three months. So, just by jumping on a plane every three months, I was getting to meet some really neat people and talk about EB and get ideas on how to go about ways to get more awareness.

I had met a half a dozen celebrities by now, but to no avail - no one was interested in EB. I just couldn't process why someone - especially someone in the National Media's eye - wouldn't jump at the chance to be a hero for thousands of children affected by one of the worlds most horrific diseases. One time I was on a flight to New York and Lisa Marie Presley was on the same flight as I was. I happened to be sitting in first class on this particular flight. I was sitting in the first row closest to the pilot, and she was sitting in the very back row closet to the economy section. She was the last one to board the plane with her two children in tow and another man I did not recognize. She had sunglasses on, so I wasn't totally sure it was she, so I asked one of the flight attendants and sure enough the flight attendant confirmed it was. I thought to myself, "Oh this would be a great time to hand her a piece of literature and ask for her help. She is really famous, and I knew if she were to (at the very least) mutter the letters EB to anyone, then that would be a fine way to get EB out in the public's eyes." So I pulled out of my purse a tri-folded piece of literature about EB and I handwrote a brief letter to her. I can't remember exactly what the note said, but I remember it went something like this: Dear Lisa, I can see that you are traveling with your children. I also have a child. However, my daughter is afflicted with this horrible illness called "EB" that I have given you a brochure on here for you to read whenever you have time. I am asking that you please consider helping our organization. We so desperately need a celebrity to help us bring some awareness about EB out into the public so that we may hopefully find a cure for this disease someday. Thank you.

Then I listed all of my contact information. First I checked with the stewardess and asked her what she thought and if she thought it would be ok for me to get up and hand it to her, and she said, "Sure, go for it!"

After the plane took off and we were up in the air and able to unbuckle and get up, I got up and turned around and looked at Lisa in the eyes and said, "Hi.... Lisa Presley?" and she answered, "Yes."

I had the brochure in my hand. I was sort of leaning on the seat that I was sitting in facing the row behind me so I could talk to her. I went to hand her the brochure, and I was about to tell her what it was, but at that moment her eyes went from me to the brochure (she had a pen in her hand) and I thought by watching her looking at the brochure that she thought I was going to ask for her autograph, so I quickly said, "Oh... uh, sorry... I just wanted to ask you to read something when you get time. I know you must be very busy, so please just when you have a chance. It is about a disease my daughter has and this organization that desperately needs help."

So she took the paper and thanked me and I turned around and sat back in my seat. She seemed very sweet, but I was worried that she might have thought I was just some crazy person trying to get her involved in something weird. Matter of fact I know that was exactly what she thought by her reaction when the flight ended. Which, by the way, Samantha stayed home and I was traveling alone at the time.

For the rest of the flight I kept myself busy with my work, and I said a few prayers too in hopes that this could be the one person, maybe the one celebrity, who might actually want to help us. When the flight ended I got up to get my things to exit from the plane, and as I looked over at her, her entire entourage of people had her surrounded as if I were going to approach her again. She was guarded by all the people she was with and clearly they did not want me to approach her again. So I just sort smiled at her and left. That was it. I never heard from her, so I assumed she didn't read the note or the brochure about EB. I understood that celebrities get bombarded with stuff all the time. I guess I was just hopeful that one of the ones I met would help. I would talk to anyone who would listen to me, figuring at some point I would get lucky.

So Jim's birthday came and inside a card I put the gift certificate for the custom fitted suit. He was so excited and the gift idea was a huge win for me. Well, the clothing man finally came to the house to measure Jim for his new suit. His name was Robert. We were both so excited about getting a custom fitted suit. I mean, how cool was that? And the person comes to your home. We were all giggly about being so pampered... or at least daddy was going to be. Samantha thought it was pretty cool, too. Robert came right on time, as promised. He was a very nice man: soft spoken, dressed impeccably professional. He was dressed in a suit that looked like it was worth a thousand dollars. It turns out that he sold lots of different kinds of clothes, not just suits, but formal button-down shirts, casual shirts, ties, belts, pants - pretty much anything for men. All of his clothes were custom to fit your particular size. So he explained to us that after he took Jim's measurements and Jim picked out the clothes and suits he wanted, that he would come back to our home after the clothes had been tailored to perfection and Jim could try everything on and make sure that everything fit perfectly. Robert told us that sometimes the clothes may need an adjustment or two, but it was his job to make sure that everyone he sold clothes to was completely satisfied. Now, granted the clothes that Robert sold were a bit pricey, but it made sense that perfect tailored suits in the comfort of your own home would be more expensive than clothes you would pick up off the rack at a department store.

On the first visit when Robert came to measure Jim, he ended up being at our home for two to three hours. He brought all his different assortments of clothes and accessories, which took about 45 minutes just to get his things in the house and set up. Then Jim would go and try on different clothes and Robert would measure his waist and height. After all that, it was three or four hours. Sam and I would just be hanging out and playing in the TV room. Like any other four year-old she was curious, maybe even more so. She was always looking and trying to get his attention while still playing with me, she was so cute. Besides having EB everything was completely normal about her. EB did not affect her mind. If anything, Samantha was extremely bright and very smart. Sometimes she and I would just hang out and watch.

Well, something happened on one of Robert's visit to our house that I do not fully recall. There were so many incidences with Samantha getting hurt and having bad boo-boos that after a while it becomes blurry. If she tripped over a toy and fell, whatever part of her body she fell on was sure to be something that would need immediate attention. If she picked up a toy the wrong way it would rip the skin right off her finger, and by the age of four, her fingers were slowly webbing together anyway. Sometimes she would be drinking juice and just start choking and gagging and I would rush to her and just pat her on the back gently or try to fix whatever was wrong and comfort her. Blood dripping from a freshly open spot on her body, tears and pain, were something Jim and I had become immune to after four years of EB. We had no choice - we had to make it part of our normal life simply because it was our life with EB as we knew it.

All of these alarming, disturbing situations had become second nature to us and I think because EB had already taken all the shock jolts on us for so many years nothing seemed to really faze us anymore. When people came into our home that I did not know, or that I knew did not know EB, then I would usually prompt them with a little bit of 411 on EB before they got there just so they didn't have to experience some kind of awkwardness. Plus, I always tried to head off questions about her disease with someone before they were to meet her in our home because I wanted to make her home as normal and as comfortable as we could. After all - it was her home. If someone were to have walked through our door staring and asking questions, then I was worried it would make Samantha feel awkward. Being out at the grocery store is one thing. Being in your familiar surrounds of home is something completely different.

All I remember is that Samantha got hurt when Robert was in our home. Whatever it was that happened, it got to him… because from that moment on he would always ask how she was doing.

We would just handle situations very calmly and very matter fact. That didn't mean that we didn't care about her, or that it didn't break our hearts, because it always broke our hearts, but we knew what needed to be done, and to keep Samantha healthy, we had to just fix the blisters and wounds and keep going. Really, we didn't have time to worry about what someone might see or how they might feel, which is why I would give a little EB introductory on the phone prior to anyone's visit.

We kept bandages handy all over the house. Our house was a mixture of medical supplies, comfy cushy pillows, beautifully decorated walls and décor, and lots of toys.

Without even giving a second thought to this man being in our home, or (who did not know us at all) being witness to our daughter and her disease EB, I started to bandage up the wound that she had just somehow made; cleaning up the blood and drying Samantha's tears giving her love and trying to make her feel better. I think she fell on one of her toys or something like that, but I know we had blood, and a painful open wound, that I had to clean up and wrap, while the tears started flowing from the pain it had caused Samantha. With an EB child in your home you can have emotions shift gears in a matter of seconds. What I didn't realize is just how much the whole ordeal had affected this man as well. Human suffering affects all of us differently. Watching little children suffer can be one of the most difficult experiences a person can be witness to or process. It just didn't seem fair, so that made it all the more difficult to wrap your mind around what was happening. I understood that because I was living through it.

In our home we never hid EB, maybe out in public we would try to dress her in a way that would be hard to see bandages on the days we could, and we made our life *look easy* and simple, but in our home, EB was real and present and extremely difficult to tolerate all of the time.

Robert never really said anything about that incident to me except that he was sorry she got hurt and wanted to know if she was going to be okay. I told him about EB and I think I may have just said that I was sorry that he happened to be there when she was hurt, and I apologized for not being more empathetic to his emotions. I thanked him for his concern and assured him she had the best nurse on the planet. We were all giggling at my snide remarks and then that was that. Someone changed the subject and the conversation was over.

I became like a machine just going through the motions. I would fix the wounds and the blisters all day long and just matter-of-fact, keep going. I used to cry and get upset, but when I realized how upset it got Sam I very quickly learned how to be strong and suffer through it. Praying for strength and courage were constant and daily for me. After a while, I would pray and ask God to make me numb to the pain; seeing Samantha in the kind of pain that is un-describable in words was enough to kill me. I knew I had to care for her, and I couldn't care for her very well if all I did was cry and weep all the time. That just didn't do anyone any good. A week would pass and Robert would call to see when the next best day and time would be to come over for Jim to try on some of his new clothes. When I was talking with him on the phone he would ask me how Samantha was doing again, and how I was doing. He seemed to be very interested in EB. Whenever someone started to show a tiny bit of interest I would focus in on that right away and to me that was an invitation to talking, and telling everything about my thoughts on EB and my grand plans to change the EB world. For this man Robert, the more I talked the more he wanted to know. Not everyone wanted to know. He seemed to be really interested in my awareness campaign efforts, which, at this point, had been zero. I told him just as I would tell anyone else, "Hey if you have any ideas or if you know someone who can help me, or if you yourself want to help me, please feel free to give me their number and I will call them. Or you can give out my number and have them call me." That was my famous line to everyone all the time. I figured out of all of the people I would meet in my life time, surely someone would have to want to help me raise awareness about EB right? That is what I have always been taught anyway. It is a numbers game isn't it? If you ask 100 people then you are bound to get one "YES!!!" That's what I was hoping for anyway.

So that was it. We set up another date and time for Robert to come and bring the clothes that were done and ready to be tried on.

A few weeks went by and Robert returned to have Jim try on his new clothes. You could tell Robert had a special place in his heart for Sam and she knew it too. I could always tell the difference between genuine and fake… he was definitely the real deal. He would also continue to get updates from me on how my awareness efforts were going. I would tell him how I met a couple of celebrities and how I tried to get them to help us. The celebrity thing really bothered me. I never did understand why someone who was constantly in the spotlight with the media would not want to use that attention to do some good for thousands of children. I mean I have always read that most celebrities felt invaded and that their privacy rights had been violated. Why not turn that around and use the media to help others? It felt like every story I told him ended with, "Well I guess it is just the disease. It must be so horrible that no one wants to help us."

By the third or fourth visit (because we had purchased quite a bit of clothing from him), after asking me his routine of questions, he told me that he knew someone who might want to help me with my awareness efforts. I said, "Wow - that would be a dream… feel free to pass my number along and have the person call me, or I will call them either way. It is ok with me." At the time he seemed a little bit nervous at even mentioning that "someone" to me, even though he never said a name I got the feeling that "that someone" must have been someone worth talking to. There was a spark of excitement inside of me that I was using much constraint to keep down. He never told me who it was, or if it was a man or a woman, only that he knew someone who might be able to help get the word out about EB and help me with bringing awareness of EB out into the community and the nation. He also told me that I could not contact this person, that the person would be contacting me. I thought that was a little strange, but after knocking on a million doors and talking to anyone who would listen to me - I really didn't care. I figured if someone called me, great, if the person decided not to, well, that was ok too. I had nothing to lose at that time anyway.

A few weeks later Samantha and I were driving in the car somewhere and I got the call. His name was Tom Shannon. Turns out Tom would be the beginning of another chapter in our life. We spoke on the phone for a few minutes as he introduced himself to me, and then he told me why he was calling. Our mutual friend Robert had told Tom about our family and especially about Samantha and this little known disease EB she had, and how I (me, the mom) had been desperately trying to raise awareness about EB at the same time having very little success. Tom asked me a few question about my intentions and then he suggested I go to his office so that I could tell him about EB and tell him how he might be able to help our campaign. Usually I never would have taken Samantha with me to meet anyone that I would have been trying to solicit into helping our cause just because you never know how those meets will end up. Plus, I never wanted to make anyone - most of all Sam - feel awkward or uncomfortable. On the day I was to have met Tom, at the last minute my baby sitter cancelled and couldn't watch Sam. I didn't want to cancel the meeting at the last minute so I thought, "Ok - oh well - I will just take her and explain when I get there." I always thought in my mind that if for some reason it got uncomfortable, or he was freaked out because of her bandages, then we could always just leave. I was nervous about bringing her but he seemed like a nice enough man to me. I just prayed about it. I was always praying before everything: "God... ok... please help this meeting to go ok, and please fill this man's heart with the peace and love he will need to help our EB world." I would talk to God as if He were sitting in the front seat of my car... all the time. I was trying very hard to practice what my mom had taught me. And in doing that, I was slowly learning how to trust in God.

Sam in tow, we went to Tom's office. His office was big and beautiful. Tom owned lots of Outback Steakhouse Restaurants in

California. He said he traveled quite a bit - back and forth - from his home here in Florida to his restaurants in California. He told me after talking with me and hearing our cry for help he wanted to help us (DEBRA and I) raise awareness about EB. He said he wasn't sure why, because the whole thing was kind of crazy, but he just had this feeling that he should meet with me and at least hear me out. Boy, did I feel pressure! I wasn't really sure who he was at that point, but I got the feeling that he must have been someone very important and I had better not get to nervous and mumble goofy words out of my mouth. Sometimes when I was nervous I would just completely forget what the heck I was supposed to be saying or doing and fudge things up.

Remember I had Samantha with too, so I immediately tensed up for fear she would break something in his office. She was such a nosey, curious, little girl; always touching things and just being a little snooper so-to-speak. The first thing she spotted was the huge, stuffed kangaroo he had sitting there against his door as you walked in. Tom noticed that Samantha liked his kangaroo and right away he asked her if she wanted to take it home with her. I was so embarrassed, "No that's ok really... she doesn't need anymore stuffed animals, I promise you. Thank you, anyway, you are so kind, but really I just came to tell you about our organization DEBRA and how we need some help." Well, the kangaroo had a little pouch in the front of it with a little baby kangaroo stuffed in there. Samantha just loved that kangaroo and she wouldn't stop playing with it. Tom got up and walked over to her and he started talking to Samantha asking her if she liked the kangaroo and then he told her she could have it and take it home. What was I supposed to do then? Ok... so I just thanked him a hundred times. Gosh, I didn't want him to think we were needy in any way because certainly we were far from needy. As it was, Samantha was plain spoiled rotten. I mean, we celebrated her birthday just about every month of her life for the first five years or so. When Samantha pointed her finger at a toy - and believe me, that was all she had to do - she would go home with that toy that day.

As we were talking, I noticed pictures of his family around the office. I got the feeling that family was something this man held very close to his heart. There were pictures of children that I assumed were his and, also, I noticed a few plaques around his office - and they weren't all about golf, either. One of the plaques was from an organization honoring him for a "Gratitude & Love Award" of which there were only five of those awards ever given in the world and he was one recipient.

Princess Diana was another, as was Nancy Regan. Just as I noticed that award in my mind I was thinking, "Wow! God is so good. He put me in this man's office and I am so thankful."

You could just tell that Tom had genuine concern for helping people, and I could tell he sincerely wanted to help us. Tom was very thorough. He asked me questions that I myself hadn't even thought of. He was also full of tons of ideas in which I had never thought of either.

The picture on his coffee table of his wife (which, at that moment, I only assumed she was his wife, or maybe some famous movie star) was strikingly beautiful. I asked him if that was his wife and he answered 'yes.' He shared a few moments with me about his children and his wife. I felt very blessed to have had the opportunity to be in this man's office, and now to know that he was willing to step into our world and help us. I was so excited… finally a person who wanted to help EB. Someone who actually cared enough to listen to me and then say, "Ok I will help." How cool was that? Someone who was willing to help a disease - who had absolutely no personal reason to do so - amazing. I have to admit I was nervous about meeting him. After all, the only people I ever asked to help were people I met through business, or through friends or celebrities. I hadn't actually gone to someone's office before for the sole purpose of asking for help with EB. I had started a business pretty much on my own without help and that turned out to be a success, so asking for help on a personal level with a little known disease was a little uncomfortable, differt.

Tom said he knew a few people in town and he was willing to organize a breakfast or lunch with these friends so that I could share my story with them, and then from there we would see what kind of community interest we could stir up. While still in his office we conference called Faith Daniels (who was the President of DEBRA) so that he could talk with her and get her ideas on the best way to get things started in terms of ways to get EB's name out there. Faith thought that maybe a goal of getting an EB Awareness video done would be one good way of starting this new venture and I think Tom also thought that was a good place to start as well. A video would be an easy tool to share with not only the public but the medical community as well.

So I thanked him - and Sam and I went home. I felt so energized with hope that all kinds of wonderful ideas were swarming around in my head. I was immediately on the phone with my husband telling him all about this great man I just had the honor of meeting with. What a great feeling to have a person in our own home town community agree to help us get a plan together to bring awareness of this horrific disease out there with the goal in mind to result in fundraising efforts to eventually lead to a cure one day for EB. I was bouncing around on clouds all day and for days later.

The strangest of all things followed that meeting later on. I think it was maybe one or two days later I was in the grocery store getting ready to go through the checkout line. This woman walked past me and her face looked so familiar to me, but it was taking me a minute to realize where I had seen her before. I knew I had not met her personally, but she looked so familiar to me. Then, just like that, it dawned on me that the woman was the person in the picture in Tom's office that day I had the meeting with him. In my mind I was thinking, "No way… that can't be his wife. What are the odds of that happening?" Running into Tom's wife in the grocery store just a couple of days after sitting in his office and seeing a picture of her… really? I had no idea they lived near me, but I guess they must have because why else would she be in there?

I think that is called "God's odds," right? Certain people just end up in certain places at just the right time for whatever reason and that is certainly not an accident. I walked right up to her and I said, "Is your name Kathy?"

"Why yes, yes it is, do I know you?" she asked.

"Well not exactly," I replied. "But I met your husband a couple of days ago and I recognized your photo from his office, and you really are as pretty in person as you are in the photo."

We both laughed for a few minutes at the sheer coincidences of our chance meeting and then she went on to tell me that Tom had just told her about my family and our need for their help. She further explained that she was excited about helping us, and what a worthy cause we had.

I thought that was the coolest thing meeting Kathy in the grocery store just a few days after meeting her husband who had agreed to help our cause. In the few years that we lived on that lake out in the middle of nowhere I had never before seen either Tom or Kathy at that grocery store or anywhere in that area ever. It turns out that Tom and Kathy just lived a mile or two down the road from me on a different lake. We were practically neighbors.

Tom and Kathy did organize meetings and gatherings and they brought forth pretty much an entire town that I had no idea even existed. Our first gathering was at a private club in town that I had no idea existed either. A beautiful, elaborate facility that was exclusive only for men. The first meeting consisted of just women who were the wives of all of their friends. They were all friendly and most of them were eager to help us develop a plan. The next meeting Kathy and Tom had held at a local restaurant and I invited some EB families that I knew to come and help me talk about EB. One friend in particular, Denise, was the mom of a little boy named Hunter who also had EB. They lived about an hour north of us. Denise was very technical and very well educated on EB and all of the intricate details of the how's and why's - more so then me. I thought it was important to also rally in the EB mom's who wanted to join forces as well because after all it was not just about my child we were doing this for.

Then Kathy and Tom would become involved in the DEBRA organization's fundraising efforts as well. They gave generously and always without thinking about it. Eventually we had a small, informal fundraiser and got to the point where we were able to pay for a video to be made. The truth was that we didn't actually raise enough money to have a professional video made about EB, but Tom and Kathy made it happen anyway. That is just the kind of people they were.

It is because of them that my efforts to bring awareness ever even got off the ground at all where we live. The video of course was geared around our family and raising money for research. A local TV news station also helped us by producing the video for half the actual cost, and a pretty well-known news anchor volunteered to do the interviewing and managing of the film. Irene Mayer was the local news reporter and she was amazing. I got to spend quite a bit of time with her as we collaborated efforts to get the video done. We even had Faith fly down from New York to represent DEBRA in the video, and Tom and Kathy got a sports celebrity friend of theirs, Vinny Testiverde, to participate as well. I brought in a few EB families and we made the day of filming just one big day of fun. The EB kids were so excited to get to meet Vinny and thrilled that we had a clown and balloons. Everyone had so much fun on film that day. The video was a huge success and a well needed item for DEBRA. It had been at least twenty years since the last DEBRA video had been made so it was time to update our materials. We shipped that video everywhere and to anyone who wanted one. I used it to solicit wound care companies to help us with programs at DEBRA. When I joined the board at DEBRA the wound care companies were not fully participating in any of our programs. I knew that every EB family had to be spending thousands of dollars on wound care supplies, and if they were not actually spending their own personal money then they were spending their insurance company's dollars. Either way it was my thought that the wound care companies were obligated to give back. Chasing wound care companies for money from their budgets to help our disease became a personal passion for me and I was good at it, too.

Then the video became yet even another tool to educate the medical community as well. A friend named Joanne that I met yet again through Tom and Kathy had developed a way to get nurses to watch the video, learn about EB, and get credit hours for their continuing education. Joanne, who is with Children's Medical Services, incorporated that video into the nurses program so that if a nurse needed continuing education hours they could watch the video and then take a quick test about EB and the video and they would receive a credit for that course. So now we were also educating the medical field about EB as well. We got miles and miles of use out of that video and it was all because of this incredibly generous family, The Shannon's, that made that possible for EB and for DEBRA.

One of the famous EB stars on that video was a beautiful, young woman named Jennifer Deprezio. Jennifer was 19 years old at the time the video was filmed, but looking at her you would have thought she was maybe about 13. That is what EB does to its victims. EB gets worse with age and as a child ages, especially with the recessive subtype, it radically changes their appearance. Their bodies shrink, their hands and feet web together and also shrink, and they appear to be much younger than their actual age. Anyway, we all became very close to Jennifer. After meeting Jennifer and hearing her story of how her own mother, who could not care for her, literally dropped her off on the side of a street one day only to have had Jennifer's Grammy (Shirley Jones) rescue her was heart breaking to say the least. Shirley was Jennifer's father's mother, who had been taking care of Jennifer since she was about eight years-old. Shirley was a miracle and a blessing for Jennifer as both of Jennifer's parents were incapable of taking care of her. As a recessive Dystrophic EB child grows older they lose the use of their hands, making it impossible to do anything or care for their own needs. I mean, the simplest of things like opening a door, or putting clothes on, or holding a pencil, or opening the refrigerator and getting a drink - those were just a smidgen of the things a RDEB child either had difficulty doing or was unable to do at all on their own. Think about it: If you don't have fingers or hands, but yet a rounded sort of fist, what things do you think you can do for yourself with two round fists that got sore a lot and most of the time were bandaged and had wounds on them? I can tell you the answer... not too much.

Jennifer even with her disability and all of her daily challenges, rose above all of the adversities in her life and she was one of the most loving and caring young ladies I had ever met. She was the star of that video and she told the viewer in her own words what living with EB was like. Jennifer died a few years after we made that video and it broke all of our hearts. The reality of what EB will do to your child and your life was an ice-cold bucket of water in your face when someone like Jennifer dies. She fought so hard for a normal life and she put her brave face on many times for the sake of others who suffered from EB to help at fundraisers and EB events around the country. Jennifer was a great speaker and her heart was made of gold.

Years would go by and Tom and Kathy would still be supporting EB from awareness to fundraising to simply being supportive of all EB families, including ours. Many doors were opened because of their generous gift of time and love. I met some of my very best friends because of them. Their entire family became involved in our EB campaign and our EB community. They brought the entire town into our EB world, and because of them many people today now know and have learned about EB. The knowledge I gained from knowing Kathy & Tom was far more than any school that could have taught me. Life lessons were part of the learning and growing. Eventually the fast pace life of fundraising and awareness campaigning would slowly taper down for me. This was about the time I started to be aware that I was on a "Spiritual Journey." People like Tom and Kathy do not just come into your life by accident. EB did not come into our life by accident either, and the chance to have a beautiful butterfly like Jennifer fly into our world and then leave was also not by accident. I knew these chance meetings were all part of God's Divine Plan, and that my purpose in life was fulfilling the journey I began when I was carrying Samantha in my womb.

Losing EB friends that we made along the way was the most difficult part for me to recuperate from. Two horrible realities would hit me in the face every time a EB friend would die: Losing the friend, and knowing that at any point, without notice or warning, Samantha would be leaving me too.

With every year that Samantha grew another year older we would celebrate her birthday as if the cure for EB had been found. There was just that much excitement and enthusiasm in planning and celebrating her birthday parties, and along side of those happy days her disease EB would hit us with new set backs, and beat us down with the harsh realities of what was lurking around the corner.

Chapter 38.

Food On the Table Or Bandages To Heal

I spent the next six or seven years being on the Board for DEBRA, helping my husband with our business and caring for Samantha. The non-profit world could be an entirely separate book all by itself because there was that much information to tell about. I became very involved with wound care companies and distributors of wound care supplies. Early on I realized that the amount of money our family alone would spend on bandages (that our daughter would be in every single day of her life) was astronomical: $30, $40, $50 thousand dollars a year. In most cases insurance companies would not pay for these supplies. Insurance companies would discriminate against diseases because, at that time - they could. They deemed the medical supplies EB children were using, as "over the counter items," so they would refuse to pay for them. It was just their way of getting out of having to pay for the huge cost of supplies needed to keep our kids alive. Everyone knew that you couldn't get your insurance company to pay for "over-the-counter" items, such as Tylenol or a box of band-aids, and maybe, in their defense, they thought that was what we were buying. The problem was that the bandages we needed to use for EB most grocery stores and or drug stores did not carry. We couldn't use a band-aid or anything that had tape on it on our EB kids. Remember we were dealing with wounds, and all different kinds of wounds, but mostly wounds that looked and acted like third degree burns. No, in all honesty the only place you could get the supplies EB families really needed were from either a wound care company or a bandage distributor of some sorts. These were very specific specialty wound care supplies that the average drug store did not keep on their shelves. Sure, you could get some things at the drug store, but not enough to provide the level of care an EB child needs.

Insurance really became an issue for EB families all over the world. Being on the board at DEBRA gave me the opportunity to mingle with EB families at different functions and learn what issues they were having and how they coped with those issues. Always, families would tell me about their struggles with EB and with insurance. Was it not bad enough that this disease EB was emotionally devastating, family wrecking and financially devastating, but now families who had insurance couldn't even get their bandages paid for? The stress EB inflicted on the family unit alone was enough to break the family apart, now throw a financial struggle on top of that and almost always a single parent emerged from the battlefield alone to fight a disease that has no boundaries... no rules... no how-to book... and is ruthless and relentless until the brutal end. A single parent trying to work, pay the bills and care for their EB child - who has to pretty much have round the clock care depending on the age and severity of the disease. Sometimes, most often than not, that single parent at some point will have to choose between putting food on the table or bandages on their child. It just didn't seem fair. It wasn't fair at all. No one cared about that - no one but another EB family that is, but most of the EB families I had met were all struggling to keep their own heads above the water: financially, mentally, emotionally, spiritually (because that is what EB does to the family) – let alone to try and take on some other EB families battles.

Sometime around that time frame, Debra's National Director, Miriam, and the Academy of Dermatology's Representative, Cheryl Hayden, created what is now known as the "Bandage Bill." I believe this was created sometime in 1999. I became involved with its birth after it had already been created, but I was able to add some verbiage that I believed would be helpful to the voice that "Bill" needed to have.

I briefly touched on the insurance issues here just a little bit, however the issues surrounding insurance companies and EB were so large they were almost too big to think about. The whole reality of the life we were living with EB (and the medical supplies and nutritional supplements needed to give our daughter quality in her life) was all too overwhelming for me. It was overwhelming for every EB family. When I would sit and think of how other families would manage their financial burden of EB it weighed heavy on my heart and my mind. The whole issue of insurance and EB and families having to choose between food and bandages nagged at my heart constantly. All of the sudden awareness and raising money to find the so called "cure" just didn't feel as earth shattering important to me anymore as it used to. After I had spent some time in the trenches with other EB families and heard their cry for help every goal I had changed. Plus, as every year passed the "cure" for EB seemed to be less and less of a reality than when I had first started volunteering for EB. It was plain and clear that the cure would have to involve gene therapy and all of the gene therapy expert researchers and doctors all over the world were all saying the same thing: That any kind of gene therapy was light years away from being a reality for any cure for any disease, no matter which one it was. So, to me, focusing on research and the cure became less important then the current needs that all EB families shared, which was: How do we give our child quality in our child's life and still put food on our table?

Although I enjoyed being on the board for DEBRA and volunteering my time in that organization, I was starting to feel that the core problem for EB families was financial and somehow I wanted to find a way to fix that and find the solution to their problem. Chasing a cure seemed pointless as all the research coming out gave me no hope. The door for hope in my mind was closing and it seemed to me that the most immediate need was to our fellow EB families who were starving for solutions just so they could live.

As Samantha grew older everything became more and more difficult. We had to find shoes that would work, because her feet were always bandaged because remember I told you *any* friction to her skin would cause painful blisters and open wounds. Well, then you can imagine what her feet would look like after a day of walking on them. We have always had to buy her shoes that are soft, but sturdy enough to handle being outside of our home, and that fit one size bigger then she actually needed so there was room for the bandages that were always on her feet. There were times when we just couldn't find a shoe that fit so she would have to wear slippers. She wore slippers to school for probably about two or three years before we could actually get a shoe that fit okay enough for her to walk in. Everything became a challenge.

Another memorable EB tale was at our home on the lake. Samantha and I had just come back from being away from home for one reason or another. Our neighbor walked over to say hi. I welcomed the company. I never really chatted with my neighbors much as there was just never the time for that. We had only been talking for a few minutes when Sam had tripped over her own feet from the awkwardness of the shoes she had on that day and fell face down on the driveway. As she got up to her feet the first thing you noticed was that the skin hanging off from her nose to the bottom of her cheek. The second noticeable image was the pain her face told you she was in. I looked at the neighbor in a way to sort of calm her, but the fear on her face was not for me to calm. My priority was tending to Samantha's new wound. The neighbor very quickly left and I don't recall her coming to visit again after that. EB had a tendency to scare people....

I think because of EB I was trying to become a hermit - never wanting to leave the house. After five or six years of EB and the daily challenges it puts in front of you, your emotions can become rigid to say the least. We went from "What's wrong with her?" or "What happened to your little girl?" to people that we did not know just walking right up to Samantha and asking her, "Oh my goodness honey what happened to you?" It really depended on which day you got me on which person inside of me you would get. I really - and I mean I really - tried to be nice all of the time. I actually would pray about it and ask God to help me to just be nice. My prayers would go something like this: Please God put the words in my mouth to the ignorant people who will approach us today. Help us to use every person's curiosity as a time to make them understand EB, so that the next time they will pass us by and just say... Hi.

If you happened to catch me on a day that I had just spent four or five hours doing bandages, then God help you, but mostly we learned to walk around with brochures on us and if anyone approached us we would just hand them a brochure. I will tell you that probably about 75% of the people we would hand a brochure to never read it, and sometimes they would hand them back to us and just say, "never mind." By this time our EB video was completed and quite a few people around town had previewed it. Tom and Kathy got the news station that produced the video to also do a local story on Samantha and EB as well. Then word starting getting out around town about EB. A couple of more local news stations did stories on her disease and our family too.

The local media helped a lot. From the front page photo in The Tampa Tribune, of me holding Sam back in October of 1995 when we went before our County Commissioners regarding a local EB awareness day, to the awareness that now Tom and Kathy have helped us generate, we were starting to ease into our society of our own local town a bit more easily.

It did become easier to go to the grocery store. Our church was becoming a place we could pray instead of a place to be stared at. More people were getting to know us either by our consistency of shopping at one particular store or by the media attention locally that we were creating.

Although our community was becoming more accepting of who we were, Samantha's life was getting harder. The older she got the more she realized how different she was. So many fun things she wanted to do she couldn't do. I mean, we lived in Florida for goodness sakes - the beach was a natural element of joy for anyone who lives there, but going to the beach was not fun for her unless it was one of the coldest days of winter. In Florida our winters were short so there weren't very many days to go to the beach. The sunshine was not even the issue at the beach either; the real issue was the heat and the sand. Heat would cause her to be so uncomfortable. Being wrapped in bandages from her neck down all of the time, and then with her clothes over her bandages she was always sweating and ten degrees hotter then we were... all the time. When it was 90 degrees outside, for Sam it was more like 110 degrees. I noticed that when she would sweat she would get more blisters and the sand was no fun at all when it managed to sneak its way into all her layers of bandages, so at some point we just stopped going to the beach. Most of the fun things to do in Florida required you to be outside and with the weather consistently so hot most of the time that pretty much eliminated Samantha's ability to enjoy them.

She did manage to learn how to ride a bike without training wheels, and she managed to do that without ever falling once. Samantha was always very determined and when she would put her mind to something she would master whatever it was she was trying to do.

Chapter 39.

Do Not Lay Down Your Sword

This chapter especially is for my EB family out there! *I wrote this for you because I feel empowered to share this experience with you in the hope that after you read it you will gain a better understanding of what "fighting for your child" is really all about. When not to give in or give up, and even when you feel weak you still have to pick up your sword. We EB parents need to share these experiences and we need to gather on the same field all the time to benefit others.*

Back when Sam was still an infant I wrote about how our insurance company at the time had terminated our policy abruptly and without warning saying that due to the exorbitant charges of bandages that they deemed "over-the-counter-items" and had paid into unknowingly, they were not only going to terminate our policy, but they were not going to pay that particular bandage supply house the remaining fourteen thousand dollars in charges. And if we tried to fight them they would come after us for all of the supplies they had paid for Samantha since the day she was born that were "over-the-counter-items," and according to their contract they were not liable to pay. In the next chapter of this book I will tell you that my assistant Carol had, upon my instruction, called around to a variety of wound care suppliers and made the astounding discovery that the wound care supplier we were using at the time was grossly over-charging us on bandages. Where one bandage was running around ten dollars, the company that we were using was charging my insurance company $100 dollars for that very same product. Instead of our supplies being ten thousand dollars, they were coming out to fifty thousand dollars.

Well, the letter from the insurance company was just a scare tactic that I would later learn is typical of insurance companies. They do that to intimidate you so you won't fight their unjustly decisions. Instead, I went to the supplier, walked right in his office and told him he should be ashamed of himself for taking advantage of my daughter's illness as a means to steal from the insurance company and all he did was get my policy terminated.

Later on (and several different insurance companies later) we ran into another snafu with insurance companies and our bandage supplies, but this time we were smarter and more aware of what was coming as opposed to getting hit blind-sided.

The issue has always remained that EB families have to fight for what they NEED not what they want. Bandages are a life necessity for our children. They cannot live with out them because they have open wounds all over their bodies. They cannot wash bandages and re-use them either because that will only lead to pre-mature death and other horrible consequences... but some families are forced into doing just that. In a perfect world these bandages need to get changed everyday. That is not always possible for the caretaker due to the plain and simple fact that working 40 hours a week and doing bandages 45 hours a week is just not humanly possible: the laundry still needs to get done, the house still needs to get cleaned, and food still needs to be prepared and served. Oh - and let's not forget sleep. And how about general hygiene care for the caretaker, which does not even include a mental break or time off?

The point I want to draw attention to is if you have health insurance you have benefits and you should take advantage of every benefit you have.

That brings me to a little story I want to share. I, too, at one time in Sam's life, had to pay cash for all of our supplies. We were self employed and we had private health insurance from the time she was born. For a period of time we were paying anywhere from $20 to $50 thousand dollars a year for our bandages but then we changed insurance companies. This time when Jane Perdigon called to tell me our insurance was up for renewal and she had some new companies to look at and go over the details of the benefits – I was listening. Honestly I am not sure how Jane ever put up with me. I was always in a hurry: rush this, rush that, so it wasn't like she didn't get an A for effort. But it took a bee sting to slow me down a couple of notches and the bee sting was one insurance company terminating us and the sudden realization that we can be terminated basically for no reason. And insurance companies CAN and DO discriminate!

We were so lucky to have Jane. She took really good care of us, and despite my efforts to go one hundred miles an hour without stopping to examine our benefits – she always did!

We did have to fight for our bandages to be paid for through our insurance company. The whole issue about bandages being an over-the-counter item is just a bunch of crap. You can't buy Monlylcke Wound

Care Products "over-the-counter." They cannot be purchased at a drug store or grocery store or anywhere like that. The only place you could buy the types of products we used to take care of our children was through some kind of wound care supplier or distributor. They may have been over-the-counter per se, but not easy for the common consumer to get their hands on. In my mind that made our kind of products much different than buying a band-aid from the drug store. Plus these wound care products were what our kids lived in. Our kids were no different than a child who was trying to heal third degree burns in the burn care unit at a hospital. Ok – well - the only difference is that our EB children live like that all day, every single day of their entire lives.

Then Aetna became our insurance. In the beginning everything was ok. Then a year or so into our policy Aetna started to examine us a bit closer. Before I knew it we had a case manager and my boxing gloves went back on. I really felt like some of the people I was dealing with there were not of our human race. They were questioning our benefits and the bandages. I almost felt like I was being harassed at times. The fact that we were living, eating, and breathing wound care was the hardcore reality of my broken world. When I was done fighting EB there just wasn't much energy or will power to take on any other battles. Since I had lived through some insurance struggles already I was well aware that a battle needed to be fought, because if I caved in then we would have never survived financially and as it was we were paying not only really high premiums, but we were also forced to pay the bulk of our employees insurance in order to keep our insurance. It was this nasty little catch-22 deal. Our premiums were high and so were our employees' premiums. Our premiums were high because we had a child with a catastrophic illness, which just exasperating everything.

The battle began with one case manager who, after a few rounds, tossed us onto another case manager. This went on for I think two or three case managers. Next on the opposing side was Dianne. She took me off-guard. I started my 'hello' screaming at her because by now screaming was all I could do. No one would listen to me. She was very different from any case manager I had ever met with ANY insurance company ever in my life. Dianne cared about us and I never got that feeling from any one at an Insurance company before ever. She heard my pain and she listened to my story. The most amazing thing ever that happened to us was that, in a weird twist of fate, Dianne would become the sole reason for which my views on insurance changed forever.

Dianne fought for us. She went to levels above her to plead our case, and there were times that I feared she would lose her job. Right around the same time Dianne came into the picture, ironically my partner Silvia and I were working hard to get our famous EB Bandage Bill some much needed attention in Washington. I wanted to finally put an end to discrimination and termination and constant, unwanted battles for EB families and insurance companies. It was the leading cause of financial stress. I mean, heck, everything an EB child needs to provide any kind of quality in their life costs money and all of it, every single bit day-by-day, was either already over-the-counter or becoming over-the-counter items: I mean the nutritional supplements, the medicines, drugs, and all of the antacid drugs were no longer prescription. So as fast as we were fighting for the Bill to be on the Hill everything that we used to get prescriptions for was becoming a non-prescription item. Lets not forget the eye gels and lubrication drops, which were running us twelve to thirteen hundred dollars a month (which insurance was not paying for), and the special clothes - all of it. If it was overwhelming for me (and I was financially ok), then I could not imagine how an average American family making one hundred thousand dollars a year (and let's be honest that was a high number for the average) was holding on. When I did the math to calculate what we spent in just one year - between co–pays, medicines, and wound care supplies, we spent more than $87 thousand dollars. In one year! Imagine that.

By the time Dianne came onto the scene, my boxing gloves went on and my swords were drawn - only to be blindsided completely by her courage and determination to HELP US. She took the beast on and after months of doing endless battle she won our ability to have our bandages covered by the very insurance company she worked for – because she cared.

The reason I wanted so much to share that with you is to give you hope. I want to let you know that sometimes you just don't know what or who is coming around the corner to help you. God sends angels in disguise at every turn. You just have to keep your eyes open for them. God sends us help when we ask for it, and more importantly if you are willing to trust and have faith and really and truly believe – and Lord knows – DO THE TIME: Good things will come.

Don't ever give up. Don't ever give in. Fight for what your child needs to survive in this world. Stay positive at all costs and know that the good Lord above is listening.

The other important note I wanted to share is nursing. Take the benefit. Every EB mom needs a break. Take the break. Take the nursing. If you have nursing benefits then take advantage of them. When you get a break in the bandage change action your mind and body get a break leaving you refreshed. You will no doubt have a much better relationship with your child if you let a nurse come in once a week to help with your dressing changes. Take the benefit.

Chapter 40.

Bandages

After a few years of battling Insurance for bandages we did manage to find not one but two amazing wound care suppliers. After I blew it out with that one supplier who overcharged us, we were forced into finding another supplier pronto. Samantha required daily bandage changes; therefore I quickly learned that our bandage supply cabinet (or at least the one I didn't have yet) was going to need to be stocked as frequently as our kitchen pantry.

The first amazing supplier came onto the scene soon after that incident occurred. Their name was Direct Medical. Not only did I start buying all of our bandages from that company, but also I quickly learned who the owner was: Ed Brown. My motives were always front and center and I made sure everyone in the wound care industry knew exactly what was on my agenda. If I was purchasing bandages from you then for sure it would be a matter of time before I would be asking you to give some money back for DEBRA. I had two goals in mind. One goal was to get these wound care companies and the manufactures of the supplies they sold to donate bandages to families in need. Next was to ask then to donate dollars to our DEBRA Patient Education Program that I was raising the money for to host. I also wanted them front and center at the conference to supply our EB families with free goodies of the newest latest and greatest wound care supplies on the market. What a great opportunity for manufacture of these supplies to educate their constituent base as well as Hero a great cause. Ed Brown and I became fast friends and as a result of our friendship he introduced me to many wound care companies that would soon become the anchoring fibers to the ongoing patient education and support programs through The Debra Organization today..

Not to long after I met Ed, we ended up getting new insurance and winning the battle of us not having to fork out cash anymore to pay for our supplies. I am a huge advocate that families of a child with disabilities should not have to spend their life savings to keep their child alive. The disease itself is punishment enough having to choose between food or your child is purely unfair. After all - this is why we have insurance right? We still had a large population of families without health care insurance so I was always soliciting free bandages for them. Direct Medical became a huge supporter of DEBRA and has remained a HUGE supporter to EB to this day.

Next on the scene was National Rehab. Now they were only next on the scene with me, but they had been participating in the EB community for some time. When National Rehab came into my life I had already had Chloe and my fundraising efforts slowed way down. My first experience with a wound care supplier (that was and still is located right here in my hometown) was a nightmare. They grossly over charged me on supplies, which I believe was the cause for our insurance terminating our policy. We went from that extreme to the complete other end of the spectrum, National Rehab. I have never met another human being in my life who gives as freely and as generously as Tim Weibe from National Rehab does. I have literally witnessed this man write a check for fifty thousand dollars to a family in need with out ever asking why. His kindness is the example of how we should all be living. I am not saying that it is all about money but rather it is about what we can do to help, the sick, and the needy. National Rehab not only provides the largest variety of wound care supplies and bandages but they also support every single EB event known to man. If they don't take your insurance they will find a way to help you. No EB child gets left behind in their minds. In all of the years of getting our supplies through National Rehab we never once had a situation where we did not get exactly what we wanted or needed and we never had to wait. Every single EB family in the world should be buying from this company. The impact they have had in our community has been profound and truly stunning. If it was important to us, than it was just as important to them. Bill Cornman who is the representative that takes all of the EB orders. He willingly gets personally involved with all of the families. He learns your needs and more importantly he learns the manufactures and always keeps his eyes and ears open for new products that will help too. This is crucial for EB caregivers because as an EB Care Giver it is impossible for you to have the time needed to investigate new products and their benefits at all. Having someone that you can depend on is life saving. EB will consume so much of you that keeping track of simple things becomes a real challenge. Keeping track of our wound care supplies in terms of how many we will need for the next week was a daunting and exhausting chore for me. Bill on the other hand was a huge help in that regard. I cannot say enough about Bill Cornman, Tim Wiebe and Ed Brown. I am sure there are other humans in the world who also provide excellent quality of care for wound care supplies but in my 14 years these are who I know. I have a reference page in the back of this book with all of their contact information in it if you are interested in contacting them. I just had to tell who they are and what kind of impact they had on me as an EB mom. I told you about the company who cost me my insurance at the time and then stuck me for the remaining bill, so I wanted to also let you know that this is how God works. Just as that chapter ended in our lives along came Direct Medical and then National Rehab, at which point my outlook on wound care companies changed dramatically.

I no longer had to go find the Monlylcke Health Care products on my own, and I no longer had to search for new wound care products because strangely these companies that sort of fell into my lap did all that work for me. Their guidance and wisdom was monumental in our efforts to fight to good fight.

These bandage supply companies taught us the core wound care classes. There are many different kinds of EB wounds: Wet wounds, dry wound, deep wounds, and so on. With the help from both of these great companies and their manufactures we were taught the best way to bandage these wounds keeping the main goal in mind – to heal them.

The care and compassion they provide is priceless. Both companies have amazing web sites that offer the most up to date information possible.

Chapter 41.

In the Bleachers at The Horse Show

My nieces were riding horses at this time. Samantha was around five years-old. My sister-in-law, Brenda, invited us to go and watch Samantha's cousins in a big horse show they were both going to be in. We thought this would be fun for Sam. It was a hot day, though, so we were worried about that, but we thought we would at least give it a try, and by now we had learned that the heat was not Samantha's friend. Heat would make her sweat and more importantly sweating would cause blisters.

We arrived at the horse show early in the morning and we found a great spot on the bleachers for all of us to sit and get a great view. We figured since it was still early enough in the day the heat might not be that bad, and if it did get bad then we could always leave. Samantha was little so Jim and I had to explain to her how these horse shows worked. She had never been to one before and she was very excited to be there. Samantha always liked horses and whenever she had the chance she would ask to ride one if we were at a place where you could do that. I only knew how the horse shows worked because when I was little I showed horses myself. Horse shows are very serious, and when a rider is being judged in the arena the entire area surrounding the rider is extremely quiet. People do this out of respect to the rider so that he or she can concentrate on the course they are riding. People do the same exact thing for golfers when it is their turn to hit the ball. It is the same kind of atmosphere at a horse show as it is at a golf tournament.

The show had begun and we were only maybe 30 minutes into the beginning. My nieces had not yet gone through their turns in the arena yet, when the unthinkable had happened. Samantha was sitting in between Jim and I on the bleacher seat, and she was trying to get comfortable (or at least this is what I assume she was doing). The bleachers we were on were very high up - about 10 feet or higher. Typical with bleacher-style steps, with each step up to the next step there was an opening in between. So as you were walking up the steps you could put your foot through the hole of the next step if you weren't paying attention. If you wanted to, you could throw something in that hole and it would fall to the ground. The bleacher seats were exactly the same way. You could sit on the bench but you could dangle your legs off back behind the step your feet rested on.

To this day Jim and are not 100 percent sure exactly what happened. All we knew is that somehow by Samantha standing up and turning around to get comfortable on the bleacher bench (or at least that's what I thought), when she lost her balance and fell through the hole under the step our feet rested on directly below our seats. I know for sure God saved her life through Jim, because neither of us recalls how or why but Jim managed to catch her just in time. But he did! He reached for her arm and caught her just before she would have fallen to her death (I am pretty sure a little child would not do to well with that kind of fall) about 10 feet below.

The entire bleacher area was packed with people who, by the way, were all silent as they were focused in on the show and their children in this horse show. A few people sitting around us got a glimpse of her fall and his rescue, and they made that sound of, "Oh … oh good thing he caught her," but no one knew she had EB… and no one knew how bad it was actually going to be for her. Jim and I somehow managed to stay calm, all the while imagining in our minds the horror we were about to be faced with: What were we going to see when she got back up? Instantly, Samantha started to scream from the pain. I was whispering in her ear to stay calm, and to try as hard as she could not to be loud. I still have no idea why I even cared about that. People around us had no idea at all what was going on. Some people seemed to be annoyed that we were making any noise at all and creating commotion. I could not tell anyone what I knew was going on. I could barley breath.

As Jim pulled her up we both knew, without even talking to each other, that we had a severely damaged arm, and a leg that must be very bad from the way she slid down through the bleacher hole. It was a tight hole – you could see her pants that she had on crinkle up and squeeze against her leg as she slid down. As she fell through the hole, we both saw her leg smash up against the edge of the step as she went down. As we got her lifted back up to the bench we were sitting on which, I forgot to tell you, was the next to the highest bleacher just before the highest bench, blood started to drip from under her pant leg. Jim and I were both zoned in on her pants and her leg. A huge, red blood stain started forming on her pants as if someone dropped some red paint on her pants - it just got bigger and bigger. Jim and I were both horrified at the thought of what was under that pant leg, and at what these people (who were now asking us to be quiet) were going to think when they saw the blood.

She was wearing thick, pink, corduroy overalls; you know - the kind that is all one piece and has straps that came around from the back to the front and hook onto two buttons on either side of her chest. They were pant overalls, not shorts. Samantha liked to hide her bandages even if it was steamy hot out side. She would rather sweat then be stared at. Jim and I quickly and quietly schemed how we were going to get her down the bleachers very quickly (without drawing too much attention to ourselves), and to the car so we could see just how bad things were. She was trying very hard to hold back her tears. She was in excruciating pain. Samantha was so brave and so strong even at her little age. It felt like God stopped time, and somehow we got from the bleachers to the car in a matter of seconds. We remained calm even though our hearts had fallen to our knees and we both knew it was going to be brutally bad. We franticly opened the back doors to Jim's car, which was a sedan, and we laid her down. She was just moaning from the intense pain. The safe familiar place in back of her daddy's car allowed her to release her tears. By this time, blood had soaked her entire leg of the pants. Her whole pant leg that was smashed sliding down that hole was stuck to the wound underneath, which looked massive from the stain of blood on the pants. Strangely, her arm that Jim grabbed onto just as she fell that saved her from a 10 foot drop to a hard surface had nothing - not even a blister. This was an arm that would blister at the slightest of touches so for whatever the reason her arm was spared, but her leg was bad.

We couldn't even see the wound still because we couldn't figure out how to get her pants off. These were her favorite pink overalls and we really didn't want to cut them like we had to do many times before with other favorite clothes and other situations. But we knew we had to stop the bleeding and examine the wound right away, so we quickly located the bandage scissors. I was keeping a bandage bag of supplies in both of our cars just for emergency situations like this one. We cut the pant leg off of her and then we couldn't get the pant material off of her leg where the deep wound was, so we had to rush her home and get her in the tub so we could soak it off. The wound was deep and the fall through that step just ripped about an eight-inch section right off her upper thigh. Can you imagine the pain this poor child was in? And then, when her raw open leg had to hit the water.... Oh, man, even telling that story hurts me still... but it was the only way. Eventually we got the pant leg off of her, and we bandaged up the leg, and in a couple of weeks it did heal. The whole ordeal was so painful for all of us that we never really spoke of it after it happened. The mention of "Bleachers" ever around us just sends shivers up our spines instantly.

Some things are just better left where they belong. In the past!

All my nieces really knew was that we left. I am not even sure if I ever fully explained what had happened that day and why we had to leave before we could see their performance. If that had happened to a child who did not have EB then, for sure and without one doubt in my mind, someone would have called 911. This was our life with EB: A 911 call that *we* would have to take and be the medical team to provide her care - whenever we were called upon to do so. Those kinds of tragic, heart pounding, intense moments were so damaging to us emotionally that it would take weeks for us to rebound from. And years for me to finally write about.

Even bringing the subject up about the Bleachers and that horse show and Samantha that day will stop us dead in our tracks and make both of us gasp for a breath. I am not sure if you ever really recover from that kind of emotional trauma.

Chapter 42.

DANA

On one of my travels to New York for a DEBRA Board Meeting I was able to be a part of a fundraiser there that DEBRA had organized to rally some support for the organization to help EB. The fundraiser was in the upper, "nice" side of Manhattan. This was sometime in 1999 before I was pregnant with Chloe. I think it was also in the wintertime because I remember the weather being cold and wearing a jacket, which is something I rarely got to do in Florida. Anyway, the apartment building the cocktail reception was in really wasn't much to look at from the outside, but on the inside it was plush and elaborate. Very rich dark wood decorated the walls and made the gathering room we were in feel comfy and cozy and rich, at the same time making you feel that you might be mingling with some of New York's upper class executives and well-to-do's. I believe the gathering room we were in was actually a "club" of some sorts that one of our fellow Board of Trustees belonged to. He donated it just for DEBRA and just for that nights' fundraising event.

I arrived a few minutes early to see if there was anything I could do to help get ready for the big night. Miriam (the executive director of DEBRA at that time) was scurrying around getting everything prepared and set up. I went to her and asked her if I could help. She told me, "Yes as a matter of fact you can help. There is a beautiful young woman coming tonight who is going to speak about EB for a few minutes and her name is Dana." She went on to tell me that Dana had EB too, and she had just won an award for a paper she wrote and DEBRA was going to recognize her achievements that night at that event. The paper Dana wrote was called, "Public Views, Private Thoughts" by Dana Marquardt. Miriam also told me that Dana was a 28 year-old woman who has the exact same subtype as my daughter Samantha, which is Recessive Dystrophic. I knew RDEB was usually terminal before the age of 20 and this woman was 28 so, hmm… that was odd. I thought, "Wow I had never met anyone with RDEB that was 28 years old before… or any kind of EB for that matter." That was weird for me because I had met plenty of other children with EB and even some young teenagers but never any adults.

I was very excited to meet Dana. Miriam told me that Dana would be arriving in a black, stretch limo. She said that she wanted to have Dana arrive in style because she was being honored and she really felt that all EB children and adults should be arriving in a limo for anything in life. Considering all they have to contend with in life, a ride in a stretch limo was the least anyone could do for her. She went on to describe Dana as a very gifted and unique, beautiful woman. You could tell Miriam had strong admiration for Dana and held her way up there on a pedestal. She told me that when Dana arrived that I should go outside and help her up the stairs. I asked Miriam why? And she replied, "Well because Dana uses a wheelchair and because the event at this building does not have an elevator to get to the front door. From the street to the front door were five or six stairs up to get to the door with no wheel chair entrance." Miriam paused for a moment and then said, "Dana will need help getting up the stairs, and I figured that since you are an EB mom yourself, you would be the best person to help her so that you can make sure she does not get hurt. Someone else may not know that they have to be so gentle holding her hand." So I agreed and didn't give it another thought. I was happy to meet Dana and now that Miriam had so many wonderful, encouraging things to say about her I could hardly wait for her to arrive.

About 30 minutes later, someone came to tell me that the limo was out front and Dana was waiting for me to come out and help her in. As I was walking down the steps of the front entrance Dana was getting out of the limo. It was cold and dark outside. I reached for her hand to help her up as I greeted her at the same time. She was only about four feet tall (if that) and she had short, straight, dark brown hair. She wore glasses and they looked like pretty thick lenses, so I assumed she must have had vision issues. Dana was as skinny as a nine year-old, and her body was frail and badly disfigured. She had no hands, so when I reached for her hand it was actually balled up like a fist. For a split second I was about to gasp, but then I caught myself and was able to remain calm and act normal. So many emotions were going through my mind at that time. Dana was beautiful, but for some reason I just didn't expect EB to look this way at that age. Samantha did not have any of those changes to her body or face, so at first sight it was difficult for me.

Here I was looking at a 28 year-old, young woman who was suffering from the very same exact disease and subtype of that disease that my own four year-old daughter had. In my mind I thought, "Oh God please tell me that this is not what Samantha is going to look like. Is this what EB and adulthood looks like when you have RD-EB? Stunted growth, legs that looked like they did not bend too good, arms bent in one position, no hands, and her face was distinctly different in an EB sort of way." The face I had seen before: The EB characteristics with the tight, pulled skin and the eyes sort-of big, as if the lids were smaller then the actual eye. Dana's face looked very similar to other, older EB children that I had seen in photos before. Their mouths were all very small in comparison to their head size and age – same thing with their noses too. There is definitely a very common distinguished look EB children have with their faces that almost makes all EB kids look similar in a strange sort of way. More so when they get older.

I am not sure if I am describing the EB characteristics accurately, but my point is that all older EB kids seem to grow into some common changes with their faces. Somehow, with age, something happens to their skin causing this common tight, almost distressed, look. I also noticed with a few EB teenagers that they did not seem to have facial expressions either - even a smile was difficult to detect and not because they didn't want to smile, but because their faces were pulled so tight, or maybe their mouths had shrunk and were smaller (I am not sure exactly), that it was very difficult to see if they were smiling or not.

Just as those crazy thoughts started to plow through my mind, Dana started talking to me. We had already gotten up the stairs and had safely entered the event. Dana took me totally by surprise by just the first few words that came from her mouth. As we got to the place from where we were to stand I made sure I was standing next to her so that if she needed anything I could be the one to help her. I felt like I could see my Sam standing there one day - and at that moment I felt honored to be the one helping Dana and hoping that when my daughter is there one day, and on her own standing somewhere, that there will be someone who feels honored to stand next to her the way I was feeling at that very moment.

Well, when Dana started talking, I nearly passed out from the sheer shock of her wit. I found myself lost in her words and, for a moment, I was dumb founded standing there staring at her - like it was just me and her in that room, and I was trying to process that this person I was standing next to was quite possibly the smartest, coolest person I had ever met in my life. Dana giggled at me. She knew I was confused. She knew I was like every other fool there that judged her on her looks, and then when she spoke, the fool staring realized what a complete idiot she (me) was. Admittedly I was taken for a moment from her disease and then I humbly confessed I was having thoughts of my own child who has EB when she gets older. Dana knew. She told me she knew. She said it was ok as she gently let me off the hook. She was brilliant, amazing, and extremely smart. I think she was so smart she could read your thoughts, or at least she was really good at reading mine.

This woman who looked like she could not possibly be a day over 13, but in reality she was 28, was using words I didn't even know how to pronounce - let alone repeat or comprehend their meaning. I knew Dana was happily amused at my expense as she should have been. I was the one with the issues. I stared in disbelief and I couldn't get past her physical body to process her intelligence, which she was well aware of. I was standing next to a 13 year-old, but having conversation with a triple PHD who had to explain and define almost every word that came out of her mouth so I could understand! I was drawn to her instantly and I knew that night that I had just met one of the best friends I would have ever made in my life.

Dana was very witty and quick with her thoughts. Sometimes I had difficulty having a conversation with her because it would take me a few minutes to figure out what a word she had used meant. After a while, I just gave up and started asking *her* what the words she just said meant. She would laugh at me and that would make me happy inside… that she was laughing at all. I knew what her life was like without ever having to tell me anything. I had a little, bitty, miniature Dana at home, and I knew what living with EB was like. I had HUGE admiration for Dana and her parents. Dana was courageous and brave. Courageous does not even do her justice, but the mere fact that she would boldly stand before an audience of people and talk about this disease that had robbed her of every thing in her life, and speak with such grace and strength, was powerful. Most of us, including myself, have difficulty speaking in front of a large audience - or even a small room full. We worry about how we look and if we sound ok, and if our words will sound like our lips are quivering. Dana was better then anyone I knew. She spoke clear and with confidence and intelligence. Her thoughts about EB made you question whether you were doing your part to help this disease. Her story made you want to stand beside her on the same battlefield as she and fight for her and for every single EB child in the world. And her character made you self-examine your own intentions as a child of God, and question whether your own character was deserving of the life you were living and, on an even higher level, could you be half the person Dana was if your entire life existed of pain and suffering? Most of the people I knew were popping pills at night to fall asleep and their biggest problem in life was what outfit they would wear to their next big party or, better yet, would they even get invited to The Jones's next big party?

Along with Dana's quick wit she also had an incredible sense of humor. Oh, how I love someone with a great sense of humor. One thing my mom always told me is that this world we live in does not laugh enough and everyone's real issues were all because they needed to laugh a little bit more, and she would always tell me that if you can laugh at yourself, then you're doing good!

Dana and I became very close friends instantly. Her friendship was as familiar to me as if I had known her all my life, or maybe in some other life even, who really knows anyway? The speech she gave that night about EB was fabulous. When Dana spoke, the people listening took her thoughts in like a breath of fresh air. Her brain and her body confused me. Maybe that is because the life we are living has created these stereotype images of how people are supposed to look. What really bothered me more than anything was that - if I was thinking and feeling this way, then so was everybody else, and furthermore - this is going to be my own daughter later on in life - and that wasn't making me feel very good.

It was then that I had the realization that all those people who curiously stare at Sam all of the time, and approach us in public, and ask us strange questions, that they, too, are just as confused and innocent as I was at that very moment with Dana. For the most part, I was just like them – no better or worse, but just the same. I think I was starting to learn that really and truly when people see someone who is wrapped up in bandages like a mummy they are just curious. Maybe they're even startled at first sight because, after all, it is not like you see a kid wrapped up in bandages all the time. I was really starting to learn how to be more accepting of strangers and their stares. In my mind I would start to figure out how to explain EB, as opposed to just getting angry with people. I used to just get angry and say stuff like, "I can't believe that person just asked me that, who do they think they are?" Now, though, as Samantha was getting older I wanted to be more of a role model for her of how to stay positive and use those awkward moments as an opportunity to educate people on EB. Especially after meeting Dana and finding myself in the position of the stranger looking at an EB person for the first time. I, too, was guilty as charged.

The way I would handle the general public from now on in my life had all changed for me the night I met Dana. She gave me a whole new outlook on life, EB, and myself. If we, as people, really wanted to make a change in our world to be a better place, then we must first make the change within ourselves. We have to be the person that we expect everyone else to be to us and, most importantly, love should be the one emotion we use to make all decisions... no matter what the solution is.

Dana and I had so much fun that night at the fundraiser. We had many things to talk about and laugh about and it seemed as though our views on life were quite similar.

Getting to know and share in Dana's life was monumental for me. I look back on that time we shared together and I give thanks to God because I know it was a time that was meant to happen in my life, and in hers. The sweetest gift life had to offer was getting to become best friends with one of the smartest, most talented and kindest human beings I had ever imagined existed on this earth. And I got to be friends with her.

Dana and I talked every day - sometimes two or three times a day. She gave me a better understanding of EB, and life. She educated me on the bone-chilling facts that would lie before us as our sweet Samantha would grow older with EB. We researched things together. Of course she lived in New York and I in Florida, so all of our communications were either over the phone or via the computer. Dana self-educated herself after high school. Going to school was hard for her with EB and the hardest part was the pain she would endure just getting up and out of bed in the morning. The agonizing bathtub soaks followed by the painful de-breading of wounds and lancing of blisters all over her body, then bandaging was pure torture. She went on to tell me that high school was tough on her too, but she liked to read and she read her way to most of all that she knew. She liked to tell me stories about things she had learned or adventurous things she did. We shared the same love of music and the same artist as well. Our favorite of all was Sarah McLaughlin, and every song she sang we both agreed was the best. I still have the bag she bought for me when she went to the "Lilith Fair" concert with her dad that year.

She knew that people stared at her and she knew exactly how to handle them. The story she wrote called, "Public Views, Private Thoughts" was a story about just that – people staring and how it made her feel and how she knew they felt. A very compelling story coming from someone who had years of experience with people staring at her. That story won her a Gold Triangle Award, which is presented by the American Academy of Dermatology, and one of the most prestigious awards given for writing.

As soon as Samantha turned four years of age, her bath and bandage changes became more and more challenging. Sam would remember the pain she had at the last bathtub soak and she started resisting the idea of the next one. That would lead into fighting and arguing because she just did not want to get a bath. That's right - by four years of age she was telling me that she wasn't going to get in the bath. As it was, we were not doing the bath tub soaks as frequently as our dermatologist, Dr. Save Me, would have liked for us to, so when it was time to do them we really had to get them done. It was a constant struggle and fight but there was no other choice. If Sam didn't get her wounds clean, then she would be more susceptible to secondary infection and from everything I had read up on about her subtype of EB, the alternative of not keeping her wounds clean would only lead to death at an early age due to secondary infection.

On many occasions that I remember, Dana would (via the phone) talk to Samantha and try to help us. She would tell Sam how important it was for her to get in the bath and get it over with. Dana shared with Sam how hard it was for her (Dana) to endure the pain as well, but as soon as it was done she felt brand new, and so would Sam. Dana was a great friend that way, always ready to help and always eager especially to help another EB child.

Dana was selfless and loving and she would do anything for anyone - anytime. She was a real friend, someone you could trust, believe in and count on for anything. She was involved with the EB community and she also tried to stay involved with the DEBRA organization as well. When Miriam picked up the phone for a favor from Dana she was always willing to help. Miriam absolutely adored Dana and I know Dana felt the same way about Miriam. Dana enjoyed feeling useful and she really enjoyed helping other people. By looking at Dana you would instinctively want to help her, but by talking with Dana you would instinctively want to go and get some help for yourself.

By the time summer came it was time for our family to go on vacation. Dana had been having some bouts with cancer here and there, but at that time everything seemed to be under control. Most EB children/adults usually die from some kind of cancer, or some kind of complication with secondary infection at Dana's age if not earlier. I had already learned so much about EB that, looking back now, I think too much information too fast was not always a good idea.

Jim, Sam and I were headed to the mountains for our summer vacation. We were going to Tennessee. This had been a favorite place of ours since our honeymoon back in 1992. I had this gut feeling that I shouldn't go. I felt like something was going to happen to Dana and I should just stay in Florida in case I needed to go to New York. Dana was currently being treated for a couple of areas on her body that she had just gotten squamis cancer cells on. Squamis cell cancer on EB people can be very aggressive - largely in part due to chemotherapy - and radiation not being a method of treatment for an EB person because of their already obvious skin issues, so the cancer just runs rampant and spreads like wild fire.

She was telling me everything was okay and that they were waiting for more test results and going to weekly doctor's appointments to keep a close watch on her areas of concern. I couldn't keep up with all of the medical jargon she was sharing with me because it all just felt so "over my head" and out of my league at that time. Dana was a brilliant writer and consequently writing had always been a secret passion of mine too. Writing was just one more "thing" that both of us had a common interest in. I grew up and became a businesswoman, wife, mother/nurse, but writing was a something that I loved to do even as a child.

When we left I decided to take my computer with me because I told Dana that if I couldn't take her with us physically, then I was going to write her with me and write about every detail of our trip; including the beauty of the mountains. I knew that I would be able to make her feel like she was with us in the mountains even though she would be at her home in New York. She liked that plan.

Dana loved that I took her on vacation with us via my emails and stories, and we laughed about the fun things we did on vacation. When we returned home Dana had told me that the cancer had spread and it was beyond any kind of small removal of skin or treatment at that point. She told me that her only chance of survival was to have a three-quarter amputation. The cancer had spread so fast. I wasn't sure what a three-quarter amputation was and I was afraid to ask her. She was devastated and sad. We cried together on the phone for a while. She told me she wanted to live so bad that she would do anything to beat this cancer. Later, I called and asked someone in her family what a three-quarter amputation was. The removal of her shoulder halfway down to her pelvis area and maybe more. The chance for survival was roughly 10 percent. I may not be totally accurate on the details of that amputation - the words seems to fold together as my mind was processing the news. I was stunned as the details of the surgery were being told to me. All of the sudden I was having trouble breathing.

As soon as I could compose myself, I called Dana and told her I did not want her to do that. I begged her not to have the surgery. Dana was determined to live. We told each other often that we loved one another, and on this particular day saying 'I love you' to Dana was so much more emotional than ever before. She told me that she was doing it and nobody was going to talk her out of it. I will never forget that phone call until the day I die. I was standing outside of my lake house leaning up against the backside of the house. Our house was brick and our back yard looked like a green, lush forest. You could see the lake off in the distance, as it was a good 100 feet down the back yard. The view was breathtaking and serene. I just remember sliding down the wall and crying for what seemed like hours. My heart was melting into the view of the wilderness that I was facing. I felt like I was going to lose my new best friend and there wasn't a darn thing I could do about it. Everything happened so quickly. A few days later the surgery would begin, and now we were talking on the phone five or six times a day now. Time stopped for me as if I was right there in New York going through every step with Dana. She even called me as they were wheeling her down the hall into the operating room and she was telling *me* it was going to be okay. I was still begging and pleading with her to reconsider this decision and not to do the amputation.

As she went in, I went back to my serene spot outside at the back of my house again and waited. I cried, prayed, cried, waited, and prayed some more. Next thing I know Dana calls me to tell me that the doctor had decided at the eleventh hour not to do the operation. He felt it was too risky for Dana and that she would not live through it. We both knew what this meant. Now Dana's days were numbered. I was so angry with God for letting my new best friend suffer in this way. I was so angry with God for not making her better. Surely He was capable - was He not?

My mom was always telling me to believe in miracles, to trust in the Lord, and to stay strong in my faith. Where was God now?

A few short weeks later, Dana's mom called to tell me that if I wanted to see Dana alive that I had better come now. Things were rapidly declining and Dana did not have much longer to live. I literally booked the very next flight to New York. I had packed some paper work of projects for DEBRA that I was working on in my "stay in the plane with me" bag so I could keep myself busy during the flight. I felt like my faith had been shaken. Not only was I mad at God, but I was starting to wonder if there really was a God? I mean really – how could our God allow such suffering to exist? How could God allow such a good person like Dana to have lived her entire life with the most horrible disease that I had ever heard of? And if that wasn't bad enough - now she has to die this way. Why, God? Why do you allow such things to exist? Why does my friend have to die now? Why aren't you answering my prayers and making her better? I was really struggling with my faith. Even then I would get a quick flashback of my friend Kelly telling me, "Keep your faith Marybeth - Just keep your faith." I dismissed the memory of Kelly saying those words to me and I replaced that thought with anger and doubt. I was in a bad mood getting on that plane. I was so angry with God - I was angry with everyone.

As I was boarding the plane, the strangest thing happened: I noticed almost every single person getting on the plane had a bible in their hands, was older than I and were all African-Americans dressed as if they were going somewhere fancy. I thought that was odd. Then I took my seat. As soon as the plane departed the runway I took my DEBRA work out and started working on some projects I had in mind for their next big Patient Care Conference. There was this rather large black man sitting next to me and every now and then, out of the corner of my eye, I could see him looking at my papers and then at me. I knew he was trying to get my attention, but I didn't want to talk to anyone. My new best friend was dying a horrible death and it wasn't fair, it wasn't right and I was angry. The last thing I wanted to do was to tell someone about it, of course, because talking about Dana dying hurt my heart.

The next thing I knew this man started talking to me. He asked me what I was doing. I kept my answers short. Clearly I was being rude. He said that he noticed that I looked like I was very busy with my work, but that he couldn't help but notice that my work looked interesting to him. He wanted to know what DEBRA was and what the word DEBRA meant. He asked me if it was someone's name. He just kept coming at me with more and more questions. He was so nice that I felt bad for ignoring him with my short answers. He told me that he could tell something was wrong with me and that he wasn't trying to mettle in my business, but he just wanted to offer a prayer for me and an ear if I wanted one. I thanked him of course, and said 'no' - but then somehow the whole story about EB and Dana just sort of rolled off my tongue and out of my mouth. He listened closely and was quiet. I told him how mad I was at God, and as soon as I said that he started to chuckle. I didn't see anything funny about it, so I asked him, "Why is that funny?"

"Well my friend," he replied, "You picked the right day to be mad at God seeing is how you are on an entire plane filled with the National Baptist Convention, Praise God."

Then he asked me if he could pray for my friend, and I said of course. All of the sudden the entire plane was chanting prayers for me and Dana, praising God, and giving thanks to the Lord for bringing me in their presence. Some of the elderly woman got out of their seats and they came up to where I was sitting. They were dressed very prettily with floral dresses and beautiful, large, over-sized floral hats that had large, colorful ribbons circling the top of the hats making a bow. They were singing and dancing and, really, you couldn't help but just adore them. It was so loud on the plane that the stewardess had to ask them to quiet down, and she walked up to me and asked me if I wanted to move my seat. I laughed at her kindness because *really* there was nowhere to move my seat. "Honestly, I liked my seat though and the Baptist Minister sitting next to me."

We talked the entire way there. I felt honored to have been seated next to such a wonderful man. He talked about his faith, and he was an example of his words. I was thinking to myself, "Wow - how lucky am I, or how good is God, to have placed me here on this plane today, seated next to a Baptist Minister, who would somehow take my anger and re-route it to an understanding of God and love that somehow made the anger seem like only a memory soon to be forgotten."

I smiled the rest of the way to New York. I knew in my heart that it was God's way of telling me, "Hey! I am here. I am in your life, and you have to trust me, Keep your Faith Marybeth." My friend Kelly's words were still ringing in my ears like an old song. It is funny how the smallest, simplest things people can say to you can have such profound impact on your life in an ever-lasting meant-to-be sort of way.

When I arrived at the hospital to see my friend it was already too late to talk with her. Dana was in a semi-unconscious state and she looked as though it could be hours before she passed. I just sat next to her bed holding her hand (fist), and praying that God not make her suffer. The day had ended and I went with Dana's grandmother and aunt to their room at the Ronald McDonald House and spent the night there. The next morning, when we arrived at the hospital, as I walked into Dana's room I noticed that she noticed me. Her eyes followed me as I walked into the room, and then at that very moment the nurse walked into the room and she had noticed that the morphine pump was not on. For a split second Dana was semi-alert and it was enough for me to know that she knew I was there. As soon as the morphine pump kicked on, her eyes closed slightly and rolled away from mine. I was, and still am, so thankful for that moment in time. I wanted Dana to know that I came there to be with her, to hold her hand, and to tell her I love her.

I left New York the next day and a few days later she passed away. I couldn't attend her funeral because of issues with Samantha, but what was most important to me was seeing my friend alive, and having a chance to say good-bye. Being Dana's friend was one of the best things to ever happen to me and Dana being my friend was a gift.

Chapter 43.

Most Holy Redeemer

It was time for Samantha to start school. Jim and I both agonized that going to a school was only going to lead to more injuries and more ways to get injured. In addition to the physical pain we would now have to endure the pain of being accepted or not being accepted with the other children. We initially intended on having her enrolled in public school. We both felt that by being in public school there would be more resources to help us manage her care while at school.

As it turned out public school seemed to be a tougher battle than we had anticipated. I made all the calls, set up the meetings, got all of Samantha's doctors involved and made sure to have all of my EB literature together. At one point I went to a meeting where there were about 10 public school administrators and officials in one meeting sitting at a very large table. My general feeling about it was that they saw her disease EB as a threat to their school environment. It was the first time that I felt as though anyone might be thinking this disease could be contagious or a threat to the other children in some way. Nothing could have been further from the truth. EB was not contagious. Well, I guess it could be if the child was not properly bandaged and there were wounds exposed, then, yes, you could potentially spread a staph infection around pretty quickly I would imagine. However, with Sam no one has ever been able to see any kind of deep open wounds on her when we are in public. Once in a while she might get a blister on her face or neck in an area that we could not wrap and then, yes, you could see that wound, but there was nothing that would touch anything or anyone for that matter. I even went to the trouble of asking her dermatologist and pediatrician to write a letter to the school board explaining that EB was not contagious and in no way shape or form was she or her disease a threat to anyone.

Either they saw us as a threat to the other children or a liability to the school and it was quite clear that as much as they said they wanted to help us - the fact was that they really wanted us to just go away. We had a few meetings and after full discussion of our daughter and her illness their idea of school for her was to put her into a physically impaired classroom where six out of the seven children were non-verbal. Jim and I both said 'forget it.' What I didn't know at that time was that we could have fought their decision to put her in a physically impaired classroom – and had her mainstreamed into the general population of students like we would have wanted – but that was only if we wanted to appeal their decision and fight. That was just God's way of closing one door and leading us towards the next. I didn't want to fight with them. I was too busy fighting with EB everyday.

Again I prayed for God to lead us to the right place. My mom, who was my rock, was constantly by my side encouraging me to leave it to God. I wasn't fully leaving it to God all the time, but I was slowly learning more about prayer and how to pray. Praying would frustrate the heck out of me at times because I always felt like I would pray for something and then … nothing. Some prayers I prayed for, the answers would stare me in the face, and then some prayers didn't hit me until much later on and then there was always the prayers for her healing and a cure that seemed to be unheard… but I still prayed for a miracle everyday. I continued to pray for strength and courage. I could feel myself getting stronger and somehow I was managing our life with EB fairly well at that point in our lives.

We, for one reason or another, were led to an amazing little piece of safe haven called Most Holy Redeemer Interparochial School (MHR). It was a long haul from our dream house on the lake. I really didn't care for the area it was located in, but everything else was sort of falling into place for Sam to attend that school. First of all, it was a Christian school and in the same faith we practiced (Catholic), so it was working out to be the best fit for a variety of reasons. I realized that the best place of all for Sam to be would be in an environment where they not only learned academics, but were taught by a school that was led by Christian values. Looking back I understand more clearly now that when one door closes there is always another door that is waiting to be opened, and if God wants it to work out He usually lets you find your way to that door. Getting her in wasn't completely easy, we did have to wait in line just like everyone else did and then wait to see if she was accepted. That part was a little nerve racking but in the end it all worked out.

The first year we attended MHR they (the powers that BE at the school) insisted that we have an aide accompany Samantha the entire school day, as the school really didn't officially have a nurse. I also think they were afraid of her disease. I was afraid of her disease at times myself so I completely understood that feeling. EB makes everyone afraid... everyone.

I remember like it was yesterday having a private meeting with the teachers and the staff regarding Samantha's illness. August in Florida can be as brutally hot as May is - it just depends on the day. This particular day it was hot outside and the sun was beaming without a cloud in the sky. The Principal, Mr. Coffaro, is the one who actually came up with the idea of having a meeting with the teachers and staff to sort of get everyone acquainted with Sam's disease EB.

We were so blessed to have such a caring and understanding principal like Fred Coffaro at Most Holy Redeemer (MHR). Every decision he made was always strictly by the book. He wasn't the kind of person who "ever went into the grey area," so at first I was worried that we were going to have problems arise as I felt EB was always in the "grey area," The more I came to know this man, the more I would learn that he would take this "grey area" and find a mutual resolution within the rules of the school. I also learned that he had lost a child of his own a few years earlier, so that explained his compassion for our struggle.

Samantha needed social stimulation - not isolation - so somehow we needed to make school work for her. The hours it took just to manage her EB care could very easily result in isolation from the world outside, but Jim and I both did not want that for her. We worked hard to keep her life as normal as we possibly could given the circumstances. As parents we worked even harder to make our life look *easy*, and we wanted to believe that our life was easy - when in fact it was nothing like that at all.

I think that when you have something that is emotionally painful in your life you either choose to show it or you choose to hide it and want to be treated like everyone else. We chose the latter.

Now that school was about to start for her we had to figure out how to 'create easy,' and roll it over into a social–academic school life, while at the same time living a life with EB and that was hard. At that time Jim was running our computer business so I was full time in charge of Samantha's care. I thought of everything anyone should know about EB and put it down on paper. I got help from the DEBRA organization's nurse, and help from our pediatrician, Dr. Yee, and Dr. Save Me, as well as other EB parents. I put all that information into a summary of needs for school for an EB child and presented my findings to the staff. From that meeting we designed a plan specific to Samantha's needs, her disease and her education. This plan we designed was one that would require frequent revisiting and yearly tweaking. Most Holy Redeemer (MHR) was eager to make it work and so were we. We were thankful for their acceptance.

I knew that because of Samantha's special needs the school was going to have to break some of their rules and make special exceptions for Sam. We knew that Sam would not be on time every day due to her rigorous schedule of bath and bandages. Her bath and bandage changes were every other day after school, and some days, if her wounds were really bad, we would have to miss school and just do wound care. Sometimes these bath and bandage changes would take four to six hours a day. In-between those days she would need bandage changes, and every morning before school required wound care from the night of sleep prior. In addition to the tight schedule, Sam required a minimum 10 to 11 hours of sleep a night. Being an EB mom for about five years I knew that sleep was a huge component of the healing element for her survival. When she didn't get enough sleep and we tried to push her, or she tried to push herself at school, her skin would break down more and be slower to heal.

Another issue we were having was corneal abrasions to her eyes. We began to notice that if she got less sleep then she was more at risk to get a corneal abrasion. Those were so painful for her. She would wake up and literally not be able to open her eyelid because of the pain. A corneal abrasion is where she would get a scratch or a blister on her eyeball in the cornea. Usually when someone gets one of these they tape their eye shut for a few days until it heals and they are fine, but on an EB child you can't use tape of any kind so we used to have to keep her in a dark room and have her keep her eyes closed so the abrasion would heal. Light to the eye was bad when an abrasion was present and if she opened and closed her lid it would only get worse. The eye is one of those parts of our bodies that can heal itself. Later, through the help of an amazing Corneal Specialist here in the Tampa area, we learned how to slow these abrasions down. Sam started to get corneal abrasions so frequently that our regular eye doctor (Dr. Williams at the Guggino Family Eye Center) referred us to Dr. Steven Maskin. He did a thorough evaluation - and I mean thorough. After he examined her eyes with every machine you can possibly imagine and did his clinical evaluation he found the solution. Having a doctor find a solution to an EB problem was rare. Dr. Maskin discovered that due to the scar tissue, her skin in areas was tightening so, for example, her eyes did not close all the way when she closed them at night to sleep, so that when she was sleeping the air would hit the eye drying it out, and then when she opened her eye lids in the morning the eye lid would scratch the cornea because the eye was so dry. So all we had to do was keep her eyes lubricated. We had to put lubricant drops in her eyes through out the day, and then at night we would use one tube of eye gel in each eye at bedtime. That became very expensive. One tube of eye gel alone was around thirteen dollars and we would require at least 50 tubes a month, and that was separate from the lubricant drops. A box of lubricant drops was about twenty dollars and we would need at least two of those a month, so now we were looking at an additional $700 hundred dollars a month just to keep her eyes from blistering. Insurance wouldn't pay for the eye products either because those items were over-the-counter medications.

Everyone at the school seemed perfectly comfortable with the information I gave them, and it was not too long after that, that I got a sense of understanding from everyone there. The more we educated people about EB, the more comfortable they were with the whole idea of being around it. The teachers we had throughout the years at MHR were all a blessing to us. They all had to make special exceptions to just about everything in their daily classroom activities just for Sam. We were late to school more than we were on time, and I know the constant classroom disruptions had to be hard for the teachers but never once did anyone complain.

From the moment she started school she thrived in the classroom environment. The first day of school is one I will never forget. I was nine months pregnant with Chloe and, well, let's just say that Samantha had to be gently pulled off of me, as she was screaming bloody murder and holding on for dear life. It was the first time in her life she had ever been away from me for anything - ever - and then going into a new environment without me standing right there next to her must have been a complete shock. It was torture for both of us, probably more for me then her. She cried a river of tears, as did I. Soon after that she couldn't wait to get to school every day. She made friends quickly and her teacher simply adored her. Her teacher for Kindergarten was Mrs. Martha Shepherd. Later on in our life the irony of her last name "Shepherd" would come to unfold to us in ways that only God could have known about. This teacher was the perfect teacher for Samantha in kindergarten, hand picked from God and the angels.

We were blessed to find the most amazing aid. Her name was Mary. Not only was Mary fluent in child behavior matters, but she was kind and caring, and her faith beamed from her smile. Mary had a strong Christian faith and she was proud of showing it. She was a good woman who always had a smile on her face. Mary talked about God all the time. She would praise Him for the success of anything and thank Him for anything else publicly. All the children liked Mary and Mary had a way of getting all the children liking each other too. Mary had lost a child of her own a few years earlier and I think being with Samantha made her feel good.

At Sam's school every Wednesday they would have something called "Flag Ceremony." That was a time when the entire school body, students, and facility, would honor our American flag, sing the National Anthem, and say prayers. Then Principal Coffaro would hand out awards for various achievements, honor volunteers, and acknowledge birthdays. The students would each take turns standing in front of the crowd speaking into the microphone, quoting scriptures from the bible, and reciting prayers. I remember when it was Samantha's turn to be a part of flag ceremony. Samantha's teacher, Mrs. Shepherd, gave each of her students a chance to recite a scripture at flag ceremony. On that day. Mrs. Shepherd had picked out scriptures for each child to memorize the week before for this day. When Samantha came home from school the week before and showed me the scripture that she would have to recite, I had one of those slow motion deep thought moments as I read, *"I was pushed to falling but the Lord gave me help. My heart, my song is the Lord, who has become my savior." (Psalm 118:13-14).*

I knew at that very moment that scripture was going to have substantial value to our lives from then on. I felt like it was some kind of sign from God - like some kind of a rope being thrown to us. Maybe God was letting me know that the road ahead was going to get bumpy and this was some kind of gift - a tool that maybe we were going to need. So maybe I should keep these words handy or close by, and ponder the meaning of its words in my mind.

Samantha had to study that verse and prepare for the morning that she would have to get up in front of the other students and read it. So everyday for a week on the way to school, on the way home from school, and just anytime we thought about doing it, we would say it. That psalm really had so much meaning and depth for me. Every time we read it I felt a deep connection to its words and I would go into deep thought of its meaning. Much later on in Samantha's life this scripture would have invaluable meaning to all of us. The scripture itself would become words we would live by… breathe with.

Getting her to school was a huge challenge. She would wake up in the morning with new wounds, or new blisters, and sometimes both. Sometimes her pajamas would be sticking to a wound that came about though her nights sleep. Just by tossing and turning in her bed blisters would form and burst and then open up. She would wake up in pain, and then the wounds that needed to be tended to would again cause more pain. Our goal was to give her as much normalcy as we possibly could while maintaining optimal health, and *that* was the real challenge. Sometimes it would take one hour to bandage up her wounds before school, and sometimes it would take three or four hours depending on the situation. Even on some occasions I would have to do wound care when she came home from school as well. Her feet would blister all the time, and the more she was on them the more they would get blisters. There have been a few occasions when I picked her up from school she would be limping. I would ask her, "What is wrong honey, do you have a blister?" She would be so excited to tell me about her day and all the fun things she did and learned, that she would just answer with, "It is okay, mom, we can fix it when we get home." Then we would get home and I would take her shoes off to find blood soaked socks and wounds on her feet that hurt me just to look at them. Samantha never complained. School was definitely her happy place.

By the end of kindergarten, she was losing her hands. One characteristics of the EB Samantha had, which was the recessive (RDEB) kind, is that the finger and toes web from constant scaring and breakdown of the skin. So when I say she was losing her hands, then what I mean by that is that her fingers were webbing together and shrinking into her hand in a sort of cone or fist shape. It was becoming difficult for her to hold a pencil or even carry her books. We did try to have the hand surgery to save her hands but after two surgeries we all felt that the surgery not only did not work, but may have made the hands web faster because we did the surgery. Plus, we had met lots of families at this point who also had the hand surgery (syndactaly release) and we did not meet anyone with the same subtype as Sam who had the hand surgery and had fingers afterwards. So after two attempts to save her hands, her hands would web right back into the same position, and then even worse with in six months of the surgery. We decided to stop with the hand surgeries. The surgery itself was extremely hard on Samantha as well, so all around there was no real benefit to doing it. The drugs they used for general anesthesia just never really agreed with her. Sometimes after surgery when she would wake up in recovery she would have these episodes doctors called "emergents." They would last for hours, one time I remember an episode lasted for 12 hours. Finally, some doctor figured out a good drug combination of Benadryl and Haldol given together at the same time while still in recovery and before she woke up would eliminate those emergents.

Samantha wouldn't remember being in those episodes, but they were awful for Jim and I to have to see. She would be screaming, and she would say really bad things to us, like she hates us - mostly her anger was always directed at me. The doctors said that was because I was her full-time caregiver so that was the obvious reasons why. She would just be so mean and horrible and it was like she had some kind of split personality or something, anyway we got through it. I cried through most of them. Seeing her behave that way just after coming out of a surgery was bordering too much for me to contend with. So the operating room experiences were just too difficult to deal with when really the hand surgery didn't work for us anyway.

We were so thankful to have someone like Mary with her all day long while at school. Someone who could carry her books and open doors for her was a blessing. The little things we do with our fingers and hands that we all don't even give a second thought to, Samantha was starting to really struggle with. It gave me peace of mind and I think it gave Samantha peace of mind as well to know that she had someone there to help her and be an extra set of hands for her. Kindergarten seemed to fly by and I will say it was one of the better years of school for Samantha in terms of her health.

Chloe, who is Samantha's younger sister, was born that year as well. School started in early August and Chloe arrived in late August. I had really slowed my pace back with work and with my volunteering at DEBRA. I was exhausted from being pregnant and Samantha's care was becoming more challenging. When I was pregnant with Chloe we found a wonderful high risk OBGYN who was able to do a test called a CVS – stands for Corius Villas Sampling. If you have had a child with EB before (and/or any disease, I think this test may also be available) then at or around 12 to 14 weeks an experienced OBGYN can do this test if you choose to. They go in through the belly button and actually take a sample from the placenta to test the DNA to determine if the baby you are carrying has EB. The CVS can also be a test for other birth defects as well, and it can tell you what the sex of the baby is too. Actually the CVS test can tell if any of the chromosomes are abnormal, which would indicate some kind of birth defect. I think the CVS is probably more detailed and accurate than an amniocentesis. Because we had our DNA testing done, and they were able to identify the paternal marker and a tiny piece of the maternal marker, they were able to take the CVS sample and tell us if the baby I was going to deliver was going to have EB or not.

We found out that our baby was not going to have EB, nor was she going to be a carrier for the defective gene either. What a relief that was. I prayed about that from the moment I found out I was pregnant. I told God all the time that one child with a disability I could handle, but two children with the same disease might just do me in. The day we got the DNA test results was an answered prayer to God that I prayed all the time. There were friends in my life who knew that Chloe would grow to be something special. My one friend Denise told me after Chloe was born that she felt deep in her heart that Chloe was coming here for a higher purpose. Denise felt really strongly about the fact that Chloe was born in the year 2000 and that it was no coincidence that it was a millennium year. Denise even gave me a silver engraved baby set with the year 2000 engraved on it, and when she gave it to me she told me that she just knew this baby was going to be special. I thought to myself, "Yes - she is going to be Samantha's sister. She will be someone who will love her unconditionally. Chloe will be someone who will not see her bandages and boo-boos, she will only see that she is her sister and love her." That is what the word "special" meant to me - later on in life we would learn how incredibly special Chloe would actually prove to be.

Chapter 44.

The Millennium Year and Chloe

Samantha was five years old when Chloe was born. She wanted to have a little sister so badly. Samantha prayed for one. I would hear her ask God to send her a little sister, not a little brother – mind you, but a sister. She was so cute when she said her prayers. I have always thought that little children have a special "hot line" to God. There were times that Samantha would tell me she was talking to God and that He was talking back to her. If anyone heard her saying this they would laugh and think it was cute, but I always believed it was real. The doctor that managed my pregnancy care was Dr. Jeff Angel. We met Dr. Angel when I was just 10 weeks pregnant. The wonderful Tom and his wife Kathy that I talked about in the "Perfectly Fitted Suit" chapter (and then throughout this book, really) had taken Jim and me to a local fundraiser. Tom and Kathy were trying to raise awareness about our daughter's disease and they were also getting us out in our local community more so that we could meet people who might be able to help us. When we went to that local fundraiser Jim and I already knew we were going to be using Dr. Angel for my OB care as I had to have a high risk OB doctor, and he came highly recommended to us from a few friends at this point. We had not actually met him in person yet, so Tom and Kathy were giving us the chance to do that at that fundraiser. Consequently that fundraiser happened to be for Dr. Angel's groups Fetal Program.

Dr. Angel was one of only two high-risk OB doctors in town, and he was also the most experienced doctor to do CVS tests. His OB group was known as the "best" anywhere. When anyone spoke of him it was always with very high regard and respect. I knew people who used him as their High Risk OB doctor for the delivery of their babies, and they all had wonderful things to say about him. After we became his patients I understood clearly why everyone adored him. He was one of those doctors who *really* cared about his patients. He listened to you. He was a perfectionist and he paid very close attention to even the smallest of details. Samantha would often accompany me to my OB visits and his office and staff always made her feel welcomed and accepted.

He always liked Samantha, and I could tell that somewhere inside of him he has always had a special place in his heart for her. Somehow her pain and suffering touched him and he was always very supportive of anything we had going on for Samantha in terms of fundraisers or awareness benefits. When I say fundraiser for Samantha what I really mean is 'fundraiser for DEBRA,' the organization that will give the money for research that will ultimately find the 'cure' for Samantha. Before Chloe was born, Dr. Angel made arrangements for Samantha to be able to be one of the first people to see her sister. He also made arrangements for Samantha to be able to give Chloe her first bath. By five years of age Samantha's EB was quite visible. She was bandaged from her neck down all the time. Her arms and legs were bandaged as well. Sometimes she had little boo-boos on her face and neck area, so if you didn't know her, or know that she had EB, you would definitely wonder what was wrong with her. I know that it was important to her daddy that she be allowed to see her sister after she was delivered, so Dr. Angel must have pulled some pretty tight strings to make that happen. Hospitals have rules, and I am pretty sure that just by Samantha's appearance they would have been arguing about letting her anywhere near the neo natal unit for fear that Samantha could have some kind of contagious medical condition. I went into the hospital that early morning in August 2000 to deliver Chloe with the peace of knowing that Dr. Angel was going to make every effort possible to have Samantha be as much involved in the arrival of her sister as he could.

It was going to be my second C-section, so I was a little bit nervous because I knew what was going to happen. The whole idea of being cut wide open and then pulling my tiny precious baby out was just scary. So many 'what ifs?' go through my mind. The comfort of knowing that you are being taken care of by the best OB in town made everything seem ok. Plus I also had a tiny bit of worry about EB. I mean I knew we had the CVS and all the test results came back negative for EB, but I guess for me seeing my baby healthy and holding her was going to be the real proof. I longed for this day, to deliver a healthy baby and then to actually get to enjoy the moments after delivery that you always hear about when you are pregnant. I felt robbed of all those precious mommy moments when I delivered Samantha. So although I knew everything was going to be ok, I still had this tinge of fear that lingered inside of me from my first pregnancy.

This delivery was a planned C-section, so the atmosphere was lighter, smoother, and easier. The minute the epidural was done I started to say my usual "Our Father" prayers and "Hail Mary's." I would repeat those two prayers over and over until the delivery was complete, until I knew my little baby was healthy and EB free. I am not sure why, but the second C-section felt worse then the first one. I didn't like knowing what was going to happen next. I know that doctors like to tell you step-by-step what they are doing because they want you to be aware and stay calm, but for me having someone say, "Ok, Marybeth we are making the incision now," was just terrifying. I tried to keep my mind focused on prayers, but every few minutes I would drift off into the fear of the moment, and the 'what ifs?'.

Again, Jim was sitting next to me by my head on my left side. I got the shakes again from the anesthesia drugs they give you, but I had a really wonderful anesthesiologist who was present through the whole delivery that monitored everything. I already knew the questions I was going to ask the doctor the minute I knew she was out. The second he told me she was out I was going to ask him, "Does she have EB? Does her skin look ok, normal, healthy? Are you positive?"

Finally she was out. I could hear her crying and Dr. Angel, before I could ask, told me, "She is ok Marybeth. She looks good, her skin looks normal and healthy."

Tears were rolling out from my eyes - tears of joy. Dr. Angel then asked Jim to come around and cut the umbilical cord. Jim was spilling with happiness at the sight of our baby girl, Chloe. Jim held her and then they brought her to me to see and hold for a few seconds before having to sew me back up. I couldn't wait to breast feed her. I couldn't wait to see her little body naked and touch her skin. I was chomping at the bit to have mommy moments with Samantha and her new sister. So the usual steps followed: Dr. Angel put me back together and then off to recovery I went. Oh, how I hated the recovery room. I would forever think of the recovery room as a dark and lonely place. When Samantha was born it was like a prison cell, only worse because as much as I wanted to get off the table and run to see my baby, my entire body was numb so I couldn't move it even if I wanted to.

Here I was, waiting to go see Chloe. I was watching the clock. I knew from my past delivery that usually you are in recovery for one hour, but how strange it was that one hour had passed and now we were getting close to two hours. This recovery room experience was not so lonely this time. No - this time I had one nurse sort of in and out of my area the whole time. She didn't really say too much, just that she was monitoring me and making sure I was ready to go to the labor and delivery unit to my room. I noticed that every time she looked down towards the incision area where Dr. Angel had taken Chloe out that this worried, almost panicked look came over her face. As the clock was now two hours past, I started to ask her, "Hey when are we going to my room? I really want to see my baby. It has been two hours now! Why am I still here in recovery?" The nurse answered me with, "You seem to be bleeding to much right now so I am just making sure that your bleeding slows down before we take you to your room," then she would go out of my little area and be gone for a few minutes. She kept coming back in and checking my vaginal area and since I couldn't see down there I could only tell she seemed to be wiping something and throwing whatever it was away. Then she came back and told me that she was giving me a shot of some medicine that would slow down the bleeding, so we needed to wait and see if that was going to work. Then three hours passed, then four, and then I started to get worried. I could hear her talking to someone. She was talking about how much blood I was losing. Then suddenly Dr. Angel walked into my area and it was written all over his face... fear. I could see the worry on his face. I was like, "What is wrong?" and he told me that I was hemorrhaging and he wasn't sure why. He said they were giving me some medicine to help stop the bleeding so we needed to sit tight and wait and see if it works. I thought to myself, "Oh this is just great... I finally deliver a healthy baby and I don't even get to hold her, or be with her or anything, dammit! What about my special mommy moments?"

There I was in the recovery room waiting, again, to get to my baby. Six hours had passed now and the nurse was still coming in and out of my area in the recovery room checking for the amount of blood that seemed to be pouring out of me. I could hear her telling Dr. Angel that he had better take me back to the OR now. I couldn't make out what he was saying too well because he was not as loud as her. I thought, "Oh My God – take me back to the OR... no way!!! This can't be happening." Dr. Angel once again came around the corner and again his face said everything. He explained that my bleeding had not let up and the drugs they use to stop hemorrhaging were not working on me. He went on to tell me that he wanted to wait a little while longer, but he wanted to prepare me that he might have to take me back into the OR and open me back up and see if he can find the reason why I am hemorrhaging and fix it. He told me that he really didn't want to do that, as that could very well cause him to have to take out some of my female organs - or that is what I think he said anyway. Suddenly I felt really scared; it occurred to me that I might die. Then Dr. Angel asked me if there was anyone I wanted to see before he had to take me back to the OR, and without hesitation I said, "Yes, I want to see my husband first, and then I need to see my mom."

I had been in the recovery room now for about 10 hours. It was so strange because it didn't feel like 10 hours it felt shorter, more like a couple of hours. So many thoughts were racing through my mind: "Who was going to take care of Samantha if I died? Chloe was never going to know me? And, ok God, are you serious? Is this it for me? No way - I couldn't believe that God had led me here to this perfect day – in this time in my life - for my life to suddenly be over." Just then Jim walked around the corner into my little area in recovery. My little area was just me on this bed, in a space that two white sheets from the ceiling to the floor hung on either side of me. So all I could see was a clock on the wall and two white sheets that hung on each side of my bed. Jim's face looked so tense. I knew my husband for eleven years now, and through all these years I have never seen this look on his face. He looked at me as if someone told him I was dying, or that I might die. He was terrified. In my mind I was like, "Oh shit I am in trouble now. Something big is going down and this might be the last time I see my husband, or my children." He came next to my side and he was trying to tell me everything was going to be ok. But his voice was cracking and tears were rolling down his face, and who the heck did he think he was kidding anyway? I was like, "Jim I need to see my mom. I need to tell her I love her, and I need to see Samantha. Promise me that you will bring her here before I go back to the OR please… I love you Jim, we did it - we gave Samantha the sister she wanted and she doesn't have EB."

Dr. Angel walked back in and Jim had to leave. I wanted him to be with the girls. He shared with me how tender it was for Samantha to give Chloe her first bath, and how the nurses let Samantha hold her and feed her. Jim told me it was the most beautiful moment in his life and how I would be so happy to see the bonding of love between these two sisters. Jim left and Dr. Angel proceeded to tell me that my hemoglobin had dropped to a dangerously low number and that I needed a blood transfusion. "Oh no… no-no-no - I am not having a blood transfusion, no way. I have heard all about those things giving people diseases nope I am not doing it. I am going to get something bad from a blood transfusion and you know it Dr. Angel I am not doing it".

Twelve hours had passed now and I was still in recovery and still losing a lot of blood. Dr. Angel was waiting patiently for me to stop bleeding and trying his hardest not to take me back to the OR. He was, however, extremely mad at me for refusing the blood transfusion. He came back in to my area several times trying to convince me to take the blood. Each time I stood firm on "No." On his final attempt to get me to do the blood transfusion, he told me that he was not going to be my doctor anymore if I didn't do it. I think he was supposed to leave on a cruise with his wife for some kind of vacation, and he hadn't left yet because of my situation. I didn't care, I was scared to death of a blood transfusion and I was convinced I was going to be fine, so I just kept refusing. Then I started to feel really sick, and very weak. Anyone who came into the room told me that I looked as white as a ghost. Mary, Samantha's aid from school, came in and she said, "Honey you better take that blood, you look like someone has sucked every drop out of ya, take the blood woman." I was so weak I couldn't even respond to her. Then I think I heard someone say that they were going to get my husband to over ride my decision, or I dreamed it... to this day I have never asked about that.

Then, like a ray of beaming hope, in walked Kathy Shannon. Kathy and Tom had become such huge supporters of EB, and of Samantha and of us, period. The arrival of Chloe was just as important to them as it was to us. I felt so weak by that time, like even talking was too much work. Speaking words made me tired. I had never experienced anything like this before, but then again I had never lost so much blood that my hemoglobin had dropped to a five and was still falling. Just before Kathy walked in, they had typed my blood and told me I was "B – positive" blood type, and Dr. Angel told me that if my hemoglobin fell to a four - I could start to have organ failure amongst other things and die.

Kathy was so happy and cheerful when she came in. You could see the joy in her smile of the news that Chloe was here and healthy and most important EB free. I told Kathy that I didn't want to do the blood transfusion. I told her I was scared. She said, "What is your blood type?" and I told her, "it is B-positive" and very enthusiastically she responded, "B-positive – Marybeth... Be positive and take the blood. You have a brand new baby to care for and what about Samantha she needs you.

Come on BE POSITIVE Marybeth, think positively about this and take the blood."

She was right - I needed to take that blood. The only thing I remember after that is holding my arm out off the bed and looking at someone and saying, "Ok, I will do it... give me the paper I will sign it... give me the blood." I can't remember how many units I had to have, and I have very little memory of anything that happened after that transfusion, all though I do remember feeling better after the transfusion was over. To this day I still have a small lump in the arm where the transfusion was given. They had to stick a needle in me like every hour to check my hemoglobin. I never had a fear of needles and my pain tolerance has always been high, so none of that bothered me. The lump in my arm is a constant reminder that getting a blood transfusion the day Chloe was born saved my life, and in a split second, life can stop, and, while in this life, I need to always be... Positive.

A couple of years after Chloe was born I went back to work. I was self-employed and what I was really good at was creating and starting businesses. I wasn't too good at managing them or people for that matter, but lucky for me my husband had strengths in my areas of weaknesses. By this time our computer business was shut down due to the fall of the whole tech industry. I had started a jewelry bead business that Jim took over and grew. I tried to volunteer as much time at Samantha's school as I could, while taking care of little Miss Chloe.

By the end of first grade Samantha had decided that she no longer wanted an aid to follow her around at school all day. The school's staff also agreed that they felt no need for Samantha to continue on with her aid. Everyone at MHR had really gotten to know Samantha and they all knew she was capable of being independent. All Samantha really needed was a friend to open a door for her on occasion, or a friend to help her get her books out of her back pack, but basically small things like that. Samantha's best friend from kindergarten, Meghan, was always the first one to volunteer to help Samantha with anything. Meghan and Sam were like two peas in a pod, they did everything together. They ate lunch together, went to recess together and, since Sam couldn't go to PE, sometimes the teachers, and of course with Meghan's parents permission, they would let Meghan hang out with Sam in the office at MHR while the other kids went to PE.

Her teachers were always impressed with her courage and determination. Samantha was also very bright and she would catch on to things really quickly. So we said goodbye to her aid, Mary, and Samantha started out on her own in school. By the end of second grade Samantha would celebrate her first communion. Second grade is when battle with secondary infections really started. Up until this stage in her life, her team of doctors consisted of Dr. Save Me and Dr. Yee, her dermatologist and her pediatrician. First go-to-doctor was always Dr. Save Me, until colds and flu's started, than our first go-to was Dr. Yee.

Samantha started to get this funny-color green drainage on her dressings and she started having frequent accompanying fevers. Dr. Yee referred us to an Infectious Disease (ID) doctor who started to lead our care. At some point, near the end of second grade, Samantha started with high fevers around 102, and our new ID doctor, Dr. Pompusious gave us a free pass to a direct admit into the hospital. The secondary infection we were battling was pseudomonas. Dr. Pompusious was very thorough in explaining this bacteria. He would come into the hospital and watch me do bandages, and he would become a teacher of sorts to us. He wasn't all that familiar with EB, but when it came to secondary infections he was brilliant, and what really mattered to me was that he was confident in his ability to treat and protect against them. He taught us so much. He taught us how to tell what certain bacteria's look like, smell like, and signs and symptoms on when to call him, or not call him. I told him that with EB I had learned that the over-use of antibiotics can cause an EB child to get immune to drugs, which can lead to bigger problems down the road. He taught us how to be proactive with pseudomonas, and what wound care would work and what wouldn't. Samantha's first IV drug was used during this period as well. We were sure we had acquired this infection because we lived in Florida due to the fact that the bug pseudomonas is a bug that likes moisture. So I had to learn how to bandage up her wounds that were infected with this type of bacteria with a dry bandage and figure out how to keep the bandage from sticking to the wounds at the same time.

When the secondary infection with her wounds started, her pain levels went off the charts. I would call Dr. Yee up and tell him that the wounds were too painful to get wet. That was a real problem because, especially with infected wounds, you had to keep them clean. Our ID doctor explained very clearly to us that keeping the wound bed clean and free from dead skin and drainage was extremely relevant to the way the wound would heal. The blood needs to get to the surface of the wound in order for a wound to heal and it couldn't do that if the surface of the wound was dirty and full of gunk. Samantha would scream when her wounds would hit the water, and when she had infections going on it was nearly impossible for her to get in the bath. We started trying everything from Tylenol to Tylenol with Codeine to morphine. The Tylenol and Motrin were no help. The Morphine helped the first few times we used it, but with each time used we would have to keep increasing the dosage because the she would get immune to the normal dose and it just wouldn't work. That only lasted a little bit, because you can't just keep increasing morphine… not unless you want to stop breathing, that is.

Pretty much her entire First Communion was spent in and out of the hospital that year. We had to have one of her favorite Priest come to the house just to do her confession because she was so sick. We started to live in fear of every infection. Samantha seemed to just get so sick that she would become listless and lifeless. Part of her celebrating her First Communion (which was a Holy Sacrament in our Catholic faith), was that she would have to have Confession before the actual ceremony. So one her favorite priests from our school, MHR, came to the house to do it, his name was Father Al. Father Bob, who was our parish priest from the church we regularly attended, drove Father Al over as Father AL was sick and elderly. Samantha was terrified to have Confession and, really, after all I don't think the child had one thing to confess. She only had two friends. One friend, Gina Rae, she made while in kindergarten and they became best friends fast. Gina Rae's parents moved her out of MHR by the end of 1st grade, so with the passing years their friendship faded. Samantha had also become close to another little girl in Kindergarten, Meghan Crawford. How they managed to stay so close through the years was hard to believe.

Samantha missed out on so much of her school years. Once the wound infections started, even though we would get a handle on them and clear them up, it would just be a matter of weeks before the next battle with an infection would start again. Samantha's skin started to look so bad that it became hard for me to tell what was an infection… and what was just a normal EB wound. Our guide was fevers. Dr. Pompusious gave us parameters to be with in. If Samantha got a fever higher than 101, then we were to call him. Samantha would almost always run low-grade temperatures daily. Matter of fact, even when Mary was still her aid in first grade she would keep a journal of temps for Sam. Samantha ran anywhere from 99.0 to 99.9 every day at the same time, and her fevers would fluctuate through out the day. We learned not to treat the fever until it was higher then 101, and then at that point not only were we to treat it, but also call our doctors.

By this time our real "primary care" doctor was our Infectious Disease doctor, Dr. Pompusious. We had a great relationship with him. I felt we had built a team of doctors that not only cared about Samantha, and doing their best to help her feel good, but who also cared about our entire family as a whole. Shortly after 2001 and the World Trade Center devastation, many things would change for us. First of all, the DEBRA organizations funding for research from the government came to a screeching halt due to budget cuts from 911. Many of our friends and family were being shipped over to Iraq for the War that had just begun because of 911, and in that group of service men and women was our trusted ID doctor, Dr. Pompusious. As doors closed in that year, we would soon find that new doors were opening.

We ended up moving from our lake house to a community named Avila that was actually closer to Sam's school. The drive from the lake house to MHR began to be an issue, as it would take up too much time we just didn't have. Our new house was only ten minutes from MHR, where the lake house was a good 30 to 40 minute drive. With every year, Samantha seemed to have new challenges with her health and we found ourselves always trying to find a solution to a new problem. Third, fourth and fifth grade Samantha was pretty much not there. We were constantly in and out of the hospital due to infections with her skin that we couldn't get a handle on. We started having issues with her hemoglobin always being too low, and with each year her nutrition became more of a concern. Samantha had always had esophageal problems. Sometimes she couldn't swallow foods, because her throat and esophagus were so tight, and then sometimes she could not swallow her own saliva. I can remember on plenty of occasions her walking around the house holding a cup that she would spit in because nothing was going down. Somehow Samantha managed to do what schoolwork her teachers would give her. Her ability to learn with out too much instruction was really unbelievable. Sometimes, Sam would miss an entire week and go in to school and ace whatever tests were given.

As a family, we started living for the day instead of for tomorrow. We were never sure what tomorrow was going to bring, so we tried very hard to stay in the current moment.

The pain Samantha had to live with day in and day out was becoming more and more of a concern. Finally, one of our doctors recommended we go to a different hospital this time to maybe help with the pain issues. They wanted us to go to All Children's Hospital in St. Petersburg, which was about one hour from our home. This particular hospital was really designed for children, and they had a variety of specialty doctors there to help with any kind of problem you might be having. At that time we were also having secondary infection issues again, and when she had infections in her wounds, the pain in her wounds would multiply. Going to this different hospital was a good idea. We spent two weeks there. Two weeks I will never forget.

The hospital was amazing and their care was even better. We consulted with a variety of doctors on all the issues Samantha was having; infection, pain, wound care options, and nutrition. The Doctors decided we should try to get on top of the pain issue first. So they brought in their pediatric pain management team. Dr. Susan Senical and Dr. Rice. These are still some of my favorite people to this day. We started out with drugs in the versed family. Samantha did not seem to do so well with those drugs. Instead of making her sleepy, they made her irritated and agitated, and had actually the opposite reaction. Then we tried Vicodin, Lorratab, and the list goes on and on. Samantha would have these "paradoxil" reactions (as the doctors would say) to all of these drugs. I remember one day we went into a special room where they had the oxygen tanks ready incase we needed them. The doctors had tried so many drugs and nothing seemed to either make her pain go away, or make her sleepy, or do anything the drugs would normally do. So on this one day they wanted to go beyond the normal dose limits of the drug Kettamine to see if they could just get her calm and mildly sedated. We had to sign a paper saying that the doctors had explained that we were going beyond the normal dose limits, and that she could go to sleep - in which case she could need oxygen. There were about three or four doctors in the room with us and they were all talking amongst themselves that this should do it, that this dose will probably knock her out. So they gave it to her... we waited. Nothing. The increased dose of Kettamine did nothing. The doctors were shocked. We were just confused. It didn't seem right that there wasn't a pain medication that we could give Sam to pre-medicate her before her wounds have to hit the water. We ended up having to have anesthesia completely put her to sleep in the operating room just so we could do her dressing changes. The hospitalist at that time's name was Dr. Heather Stevens. She was so wonderful, she would arrange everything so that Sam could be safely sedated in the OR, and then I could go in and do her dressing changes and Heather would sit in there with me. That was all fine and good, but we couldn't just take her into the OR every time we needed to do her dressing changes while she had an infection present.

Dr. Stevens and all of the other doctors involved met with Jim and I again to conclude that they had exhausted every drug known to man to attempt to either mildly sedate her, or help with her pain, and to no avail. Samantha either had some kind of allergic reaction, or she would have a paradoxil reaction to each and every drug. Dr. Stevens told us that their hospital computer systems was set up so that if there was some kind of issue the doctors were having that they could not resolve, they could create an email and send it to participating doctors around the country. Dr. Stevens told us that as soon as she got any information she would make sure we were the first to know, and that she felt very badly that they were not able to help us with this pain problem we have been having. We knew they tried everything, and we knew they really cared about Samantha. Those doctors saw the kind of pain Samantha was in - they could see her wounds all over her body. They knew, yet there was nothing they could suggest, or provide, that could fix our problem.

Once the secondary infection cleared up, and we just had normal blisters occurring and normal wounds on her body, the pain did not seem to be as severe, but she still had pain.

That night Dr. Stevens sent the email out to their fellow physicians around the country. Dr. Stevens would call us back into the conference room to read on her computer the one response… the only response she had gotten. First, Dr. Stevens initiated an email that said: Who she was (Dr. Stevens), what hospital she was working out of, and where we were located. Then her email went on to state that she had a seven year-old female child (I am not sure if Samantha was seven or eight, but close enough) with Recessive Dystrophic Epidermolysis Bullosa that was having re-occurring secondary infection with pseudomonas, as well as heavy growth staph, and her team of physicians were unable to sedate her, or adequately relieve her pain, in order to do her necessary bath and bandage routine." The shocking part of all of it for me, was that in the entire country only one doctor responded… Wow. I was happy, however, to see that the one response was from a well-known physician named Dr. Gary Bellus, whose name I had heard on several different occasions as being one of the EB friendly doctors in our EB world, and families seemed to like Dr. Bellus very much, so this was a relief. Dr.

Bellus' response said something like this: "Dear Dr. Stevens, my name is Dr. Gary Bellus and I currently have an EB clinic in Colorado. This type of situation you are describing is not common amongst the EB population, and in fact I have only known of one other case. This person is being seen at our clinic. We actually have to have that EB child sedated in the OR on every bandage change because the pain is so intense and this is the only solution. This particular child has the same type of allergies and paradoxical reactions to all oral pain medicine and sedation medication." We read that, and as we finished, the room was just quiet. Dr. Stevens sat in her chair just looking at us. "Well it is an option for Samantha. We understand the level of pain she is in and we are here to help."

Dr. Stevens went on to explain; the other risk was to the Propaphal drug they use in the OR to sedate her with could also cause similar results.

Somehow putting Samantha completely asleep with general anesthesia just didn't feel right. Neither Jim nor I felt good about the whole OR thing. We had every reason under the sun to not feel good about the OR since our experiences in the OR had been a little scary. There were a couple of times that when they used the Propaphal to sedate her (and I am not sure why this happened, not even sure I really want to know), but she would go so deeply in a sleep state that they almost had to intebate her, and one time she coded while I was in the room. So, no, the OR was not something I wanted to become familiar with... ever! We left that hospital after two weeks of trying absolutely everything they had in terms of oral sedation medications and pain medications. We explained everything to Samantha and she understood. From the time she was very little, there had always been highly technical medical conversations going on around her, so at around seven or eight she was well-versed on her medical care.

It was so hard for me to comprehend that not only did my baby have the most horrible disease I had ever heard of in my life, but also the suffering aspect of EB was relentless. There wasn't anything anyone could do to ease her pain.

Shortly after that hospital stay we had met a neighbor who, at that time, lived across the street from us. Our neighbor was a local anesthesiologist who worked at a local community hospital for adults. After meeting us and Samantha he asked us if he could review her medical records and see if there wasn't something he might be able to come up with to help with her pain. When we told him our story and how we spent two weeks at the Children's Hospital in St. Petersburg. He said he had some vacation time coming and he would read over her records and let us know. So I got the medical records from the hospital. I had to go down there physically and pick them up. Much to my surprise, the medical records were around eight inches deep. I thought, "Oh my goodness... it will take that poor doctor months to review these records." Well, about one month later, he came over to our house and sat down at our kitchen table and basically told us that he was a little surprised himself as he discovered that every option had already been tried. He said in all of his years he had never ran across someone - especially a child - who has a disease in where there is so much pain - that there is no help or relief for the pain. He did suggest that maybe we try laughing gas (like from our dentist). We did try the laughing gas, but it didn't relieve any pain and Samantha said she didn't like the way it made her feel.

Chapter 45.

The Pompusious Training Camp
Before He Went to War

Samantha was old enough at that time in her life to understand that her bath was not an option. She very bravely forced herself to get in the tub of water that would come up to her neck and soak for 30 to 40 minutes. I think she was about seven years old, and maybe in the second grade, when we had our first hospital stay for pseudomonas. Yea... we did the same thing: pseu... do... mon... us - what? Yes... it is one of EB's worst nightmares. Again, we were so lucky to have been given an Infectious Disease doctor who would help us to become educated on this new bacteria that wanted to find a permanent residence inside Samantha's wounds. His name was Dr. Pompusious. Upon first meeting him I was weary of his ability to communicate with me. He always seemed so stern and astute.

For the past seven years of being involved in the medical community, I guess you could say that I was spoiled. I wanted to know that with each doctor we had the best, most experienced in that field, and I also wanted to have the personal relationship as well. Communication is half the battle. If you can't communicate with your doctor, and this is a person who is either going to help your child and dig their grave, then you had better go out and find a doctor who has blood running through their veins. Dr. Pompusious was very much on high demand. I think he was probably one of the few Infectious Disease doctors in town who handled children.

After I got to know him and he got to know us, I feel like he took his suit and necktie off and became more comfortable with us. When we were admitted into the hospital my first question was always, "What floor are we going to be on?"

Then the next thing was, "I am not going through the ER so I want a direct admit, and nobody touches her without my knowledge. And I will do all of her wound care and give her all of her medications."

Then I would hang signs up that said "DO NOT USE TAPE ON THIS CHILD FOR ANY REASON" and, "Wash your hands before entering and when leaving this room, and you must always have gloves on when touching her!"

I was super paranoid of being on the Infectious Disease unit floor, and even more paranoid a nurse would make an innocent mistake that could cost us dearly.

Dr. Pompusious was gracious with our request and he always accommodated us. He agreed going through the ER was not only a waste of time, but not the best idea for Sam, and he was able to bypass that entry. He also liked the idea that I would be doing all of her bandage changes and overseeing her care. The first day in, and after we were settled in our room, he asked me to take off all of her bandages so that he could get a good look at her wounds. It was then that I started to take pictures of her wounds. I could not keep up with every wound on her body and that was important so that we would know how long each wound was taking to heal and close up. So I would take a photo with a paper next to the wound with the date and where the wound was located. Actually, that was the only way to keep track of the wounds she had, the wounds that were new and the wounds that had closed up and went away.

After we had all her dressings off, Dr. Pompusious pulled up a chair next to her bed and he began to exam each wound separately. He was incredibly smart and taught both Samantha and I so much about wound care, and in particular wound care with a secondary infection present such as pseudomonas. He taught us what pseudomonas looked like and even what it smelled like. Ok, so wounds are not something I recommend anyone have to smell, but when your child lives with wounds, then you are forced into learning about the different colors and smells of them. Each bacteria, such as staph or pseudomonas, etc., has a different smell, and the drainage that seeps onto the bandages has a distinct color. Those things help to determine what kind of bacteria you are dealing with because almost all bacteria have to be bandaged a different way, and are also treated with different regimens of antibiotics. For example: pseudomonas is one of the most difficult bacteria's to get rid of, and actually most times you never really do get rid of the bug, but what happens is it travels from wound to wound and sometimes it hides and then re-appears with a vengeance. So staying on top of that one can be very tricky. Unlike most bacteria, pseudomonas does not have a large variety of topical antibiotics, or oral, or IV for that matter, that will kill it. Usually you start with the topical antibiotic ointments first, then you move into the oral medication, and if that is not working then you go to the IV drugs.

For Samantha, she instantly ran high fevers, and because she was so colonized with the pseudomonas we have to resort to the IV drugs right off the bat. Our biggest problem living in Florida was that the climate was more moist than dry and, because of the heat, she would constantly sweat so her wounds would always be on the moist side. Well, pseudomonas was the kind of bacteria that like to live in a moist environment, which made it extremely hard to get a handle on since that was our environment. I learned that it could live in our water system, our showerheads, and our swimming pools. Although Samantha does not take showers, it could still get to the bath water and penetrate a wound.

Dr. Pompusious did not have a crystal ball and could not predict our future, but the training and education he gave me and Sam about bacteria, and more importantly pseudomonas, was the foundation of life-saving situations in the years to come. He was also the doctor who taught me that if we could care for her at home with an IV in place instead of the hospital, then we should always push for that if, for some reason, he was not around to do that for us. He told me the very worst place for Samantha to ever be, due to her skin always being open with wounds and was more susceptible to airborne bacteria and infections that spread rampantly through, were hospitals. He especially warned of staph infections. There was a new kind of staph infection that we worried about the most called MRSA –Methicillin Resistant Staphylococcus Aureus. He made sure that I understood what MRSA was and how easily she could come in contact with it unknowingly. The very most important information of all was that at its origination of becoming known there were not any drugs at that time that could kill it, and for someone like Samantha it could most definitely cause her death. That was why the word "resistant" was part of its name. He instilled fear in me about infections and diseases, and EB, but at the same time, he was very thorough about teaching me how to be suspect to secondary infection and how to respond quickly at the onset so we could control, contain it and hopefully eradicate it before it caused Samantha any real harm.

Then Dr. Pompusious left for the War and he never came home. It was weird. We waited for his return, and in the interim Dr. Yee and Dr. Save Me would handle everything. We had guidelines in place because of

Dr. Pompusious and we had a plan. The weeks turned into months and then finally Dr. Yee broke the news to us. The war in Iraq must have been just too much for our trusted ID doctor because he went straight from the War to (I think) Ohio. All I remember is Dr. Yee telling us that Dr. Pompusious had moved out of state and that he wanted us to know that if we wanted him to follow our care from out of state that he would be more then happy too.

I knew there would be no way for him to follow our care from out of state That was crazy.... a crazy thought. So what we did was find a new Infectious Disease doctor. One of the most important learning experiences with EB for me was not to find the best EB doctor in the USA, but to find the best doctors in our own town and build a team out of them that we could learn from them and they us. That was probably the most important component to making our life somewhat normal. Saying goodbye to the man who by all accounts became our teacher, but also our lifeline whenever secondary infection wanted to rear its mean ugly head, was extremely hard.

Chapter 46.

I Am Closing This Chapter –It Is All Up To You, God

Sometime around November 2002 things were still hectic but somewhat steady, so I started thinking it was time to get my "tubes tied" or a Tubal Ligation done. Dr. Angel told me that it would not be a wise decision for me to have another C-section, and he also told me that since I hemorrhaged after my last C-section that he really wasn't in favor of me chancing a third. Frankly I was too afraid anyway. In my heart I knew I always wanted to have a big family with lots of little people running around, but my mind was way too nervous about our 25 percent chance of EB hovering overhead.

Anyway I would have tied my tubes when Chloe was born had I not hemorrhaged so badly, but God had different plans for me. Since Dr. Angel was a High Risk OB and one of only two groups in town that did that sort of practice I decided right away that I would just go to a regular OB/GYN to have a consultation for my Tubal Ligation. I didn't want to use Dr. Angel's practice when I knew there were pregnant woman with serious problems who needed him more than me at that point. I prayed a lot about doing this surgery. I knew that in my faith it was not favorable to have your tubes tied or use any kind of contraception for that matter. I was constantly reasoning with God and explaining *my* situation to him.

It went something like this: "Ok God I know I am not supposed to have my tubes tied or take any kind of birth control, HOWEVER you know me and, well, I just can't take these changes God. I am too afraid. I know I am supposed to trust you but, well… ya' see God the doctor also thinks it is best too. I am sure you make some kind of exceptions for situations like mine don't you God? Well it is in your hands now because I am going to get the Tubal Ligation done because now that I have two beautiful children, and I am watching my Chloe have to spend so much time without me due to all of Samantha's care, I just don't think it would be fair to anyone to try for a third. Not to mention what it would do to my mind if I were to have another EB child or, even worse, how about just another child that would get absolutely no attention from me. As it is God, I am feeling a little bit guilty that my little Chloe is having to spend lots of time with everyone but me, so please God just let everything be ok for me and please forgive me for doing what I know I am not supposed to do. I know you Lord, and I know that if you want me to have another child, whether my tubes are tied or not then you will send me one."

That is about the gist of what I would continuously repeat when I talked to God. I had also spoken to a priest about having my tubes tied as well. The guilt that poured over me about closing this chapter in my life and closing it against the very faith in which I practiced and was raised to believe in was overwhelming. The priest that I confided in assured me that God would still love me and that God would not punish me and told me that he as well did not think I should be worrying so much about this subject. He knew my plate was full and that I could barely keep up with what I had, let alone attempt for more children. The kind priest told me what to pray for and to ask for forgiveness just as I had been and to let it go. I don't know why I struggled with the decision so much. I assume many women do struggle with these types of decisions in their lives all the time, maybe some more then others but for some reason I was really struggling with this decision at this time in my life.

The struggle was of course within me. I didn't want to close that chapter in my life because it felt so final. It was like, "Well ok… I am not going to have any more children." Then on the other hand I knew I had to close that chapter because I knew there would be no possible way to take care of all of Samantha's needs while my cup had already runneth over with two children and a business. I had even talked about this with one of my best friends at that time too and I told her, "Well I have to do what I have to do and if God decides that he wants me to have another child, then it will be up to him." She agreed, and supported my decision and was there for me through the whole thing. My husband took me for surgery that day. I know it was sometime in November because it was cold outside that morning. The only time it is cold outside in the mornings in Florida is when it is between the months of October and January. There is another reason I know it was sometime in November and I will get to that in a few minutes.

We had to get to the hospital around 6 am. I had the nicest male nurse. I had never had a male nurse before. He was so funny he had me laughing pretty much the whole time. It was like God hand picked him to take care of me knowing how hard it was for me to make that decision and how sad closing that chapter was going to be so here was this wonderfully funny male nurse to keep me smiling. Jim just kind of sat in the room quiet, never really said too much. He knew I was nervous and really our track record by now in hospitals wasn't something either one of us cared to remember.

One thing I do remember as plain as I remembered that male nurse, was that I asked the nurse just before we went to the OR if they had done a blood pregnancy test on me to make one hundred percent sure I was NOT pregnant. He laughed and answered, "Oh honey you know we did, and as a matter of fact I just checked those results because you know I don't want that hanging over my head". I thought to myself, "Well then ok - I guess I am ready." And I prayed again. I even told the nurse the whole story about why I was doing this and how I prayed about it and how it was all up to God and if he thought I should be having another child, then HE and only HE would have the power to change that.

The surgery went as smooth as any I had ever had, not one complication. The only issue at all was that because of the two prior C-sections there was too much scar tissue around the tubes and my doctor had to spend a little bit longer in me then he had originally planed to get everything in the right place. That is the best way I can describe that to you anyway because that is how I understood things to be. He said it was not a big deal however, because all they did was just give me more anesthesia and I ended up being asleep for an additional hour so that really wasn't too bad for a Tubal Ligation.

The recovery was a bit tougher than I expected - I was so sore. When I went for my checkup and I asked the doctor why he thought I was so sore. He just thought because as he told me he had to move some things around and he had to deal with excess scar tissue so he just told me to stay on the pain pills for a few extra days and try to take it easy.

I was taking it easy, and I also felt like I was mourning the loss of something. Closing that chapter was a bit harder than I thought it was going to be. I was sure if I prayed enough and asked God for forgiveness that somehow he might help me get through the sadness of knowing I would not be having any more children a little bit easier.

My mom stayed with me for a week or so to help me with Samantha and Chloe. My mom was so amazing. She was always with me to help me with whatever I needed whenever I needed it, and she would be there no matter what she was going through in her life. Then I got a sore throat from I guess being intubated and then somehow I ended up with a sinus infection on top of all that, so now I was on antibiotics and pain pills. I was on the couch for a week. My mom was in favor of my decision as she would constantly be worried about me and that I never had time to take care of myself so she was always making me feel good about getting my tubes tied.

Two months later, February 2003 (and this is how I knew it was in November exactly), Jim and I took Samantha and her friend Gina Rae, and little Chloe (who was now three) to Sea World. We made a weekend out of it, stayed in a hotel and decided to see the sites at Sea World. We had been to all the other theme parks more than a few times, but Sea World managed to get knocked out of the vote the past few times so this year we were headed there. We always did theme parks at the coldest time in Florida even if it was in the middle of the school year. We would just pick a weekend, and go and pretty much these were our family vacations because really the summers were just too hot for Samantha so we had to go when it was cold.

As we were walking around the park everyone was noticing that I had to stop to use the restroom facilities like every hour. Jim was making fun of me with the girls and he said, "I feel like I am with my grandmother, you are going to the bathroom so much. What's wrong with you?" I was like, "Ok that's not even funny. I think I have a bladder infection and I don't feel good so be nice to me." Actually I felt awful. I was prone to bladder infections, so I knew what they felt like and I had all of the symptoms; frequent urinating, pain and pressure in my lower abdomen, tired and achy.

That pretty much ruined my whole Sea World weekend. I could not wait to get home to go to my regular Internal Medicine doctor so that I could pee in a cup and get some antibiotics to clear this thing up. Oh, I felt terrible. The girls laughed and thought it was funny that daddy was teasing me about being like his "grandmother" and I guess I thought it was a little bit funny too, but I felt so tired and achy that there wasn't too much that was going to make me laugh.

We got home on Sunday and by Monday a.m. I was at my doctor's office. I got checked in and told the nurse all my symptoms and that

I knew I had a bladder infection so just give me the cup and I will wait for the doctor to come in. So she listened to me and she gave me the cup. I gave her back a urine specimen and then she put me in the room and I waited for the doctor to come in. On that particular Monday my doctors office was unusually busy with colds and flu so I didn't actually get to see my doctor, I had to see a nurse practitioner, but I really didn't care as long as it was someone who could write the script for what I needed to make me feel better. I did not have time to be sick, not with an EB child and a three year-old running around, oh no.

I will never forget that young nurse practitioner's face when she walked through my room. She started to ask me a lot of question about my Tubal Ligation, like when I had it done, where and by whom. In complete denial of any of her thoughts I just said to her, "Hey I have had these before, many times before, so if you could just give me a prescription for an antibiotic I will be fine." Her face was puzzled, and there was a part of me that really didn't want to know why, but I asked anyway, "Why do you have that blank look on your face?"

She said, "Well Mrs. Sheridan, your urine test was normal you do not have a bladder infection, urinary tract infection or any infection of any kind for that matter at all, and your symptoms are a little suspicious. That maybe you could be pregnant."

"What...?"

"What did you just say? Pregnant? No, there is no way. Look here at my stomach - I still have the scar and it is not even healed yet. I had a Tubule Ligation. They did a pregnancy test, and they confirmed by both blood and urine that I was not pregnant so I know for sure that I am not pregnant."

She just paused for a few minutes and stared at me. She was very controlled, and she seemed like she felt pretty certain about her suspicions. Then she said, "Look I know this must be a shock for you."

"No," I replied, "You know what? I want to see my doctor. There has to be some kind of mistake here, I want to see the doctor," and I had a few minutes of panic. Then she very calmly just said, "Ok listen how about we run a pregnancy test on you and I will run it stat. We can take your blood and send it to the lab and I will get the results tonight and I will call you as soon as I get them no matter what time it is, how does that sound Mrs. Sheridan?"

"Ok" I agreed, "but how about you just write me that prescription anyway so that when you find out that you are wrong and I do have a bladder infection I don't have to come back here tomorrow and take another urine test?"

"Well I can't do that," the PA said. "I just can't write a prescription for you for a bladder infection or any kind of UTI when the urine test was negative for that."

"Yes," I agreed, "But isn't it true that sometimes these in office test are not accurate and you have to send them off to a lab to have them tested further and then sometimes you find out by doing further testing that I really did have an infection that you could have been treating all along?"

"Well," she argued back, "You are almost correct but we would had to have seen at least a few whites cells present and your urine looks perfectly clear, but if it will make you feel better I will also send the urine off to the lab and we can see how it comes back. We will most likely get the results from the pregnancy test back first so I will call you with that first ok?"

I just kept asking her to reassure me that she was going to call and that she wouldn't make me wait because, after all, she did not know me and I didn't know her and how did I know if she would really call or not? The real issue too was that I did not feel so great. Now I get to go home with nothing. I guess I will just have to pound down the cranberry juice.

I left the office and got in my car and all of the sudden my mind was doing the Indy 500 again. Ok I knew I couldn't possibly be pregnant so why did this Physician's Assistant think I was? And did I really just leave there without a prescription? I am smarter than that. Oh great - here I go in pain and on my way home without a remedy. As my mind was racing lightning speed I picked up the phone and called my husband. As he answered I didn't greet him with 'hello' or 'hi,' I just went right into, "What would totally blow your mind away right now?" and Jim said, "Uh is this a joke?" He knew with me I was either getting ready to play a huge joke or something really kooky just happened, and probably kooky was more likely. "Well I am just leaving the doctors office, you know since I have a bladder infection and I reminded you of your grandmother. The PA who saw me just now because my regular doctor was too busy, yeah, she told me that SHE thinks I could be pregnant."

"NO WAY, really?" (Almost with a little happy tone in his voice, which just made me not sure if I was mad at him or a little happy myself).

"Yeah really. Yes way."

She even did a blood test that she said she was going to do stat just for me because she thinks I am in shock and she said if she was wrong she would run it stat so she could tell me right away. She was so sure of herself that she wouldn't even give me a prescription for the bladder infection, which she insists I don't have. There were a few moments of silence on the phone from both of us.

"Hey Marybeth just get home and don't worry about this right now, she said she will call so let's just wait for her to call. It is going to be ok. I know you're upset so let's just wait for her to call ok?"

I agreed with him and hung up.

My mind was still doing donuts so I called my girlfriend and when she answered the first thing I said to her was, "What do you think would be the craziest thing to happen to me right now?" She responded in her normal happy tone of voice,

"Oh I don't know. You're pregnant?"

Shocked, stunned, I said, "What? Why would you say that?"

She went on to explain, "Hey girl you prayed about it. You said you didn't want to close that chapter in your life and you put that fate in God's hands, so maybe you are pregnant, maybe this is what He has planned for you Marybeth."

Clearly I was stunned. So many emotions were swirling around inside of me. Believe me I was talking to God... ok, a lot. I decided when I got home that night that I was not going to let this distract me all night and make me crazy. When I walked through the door not another word of it came from my lips. By 10pm Jim was bugging me to call into the doctor's office as if he was a little boy about to get a big surprise. I, on the other hand, was not willing to let my mind agree with anything that PA said to me. I had to tell Jim two or three times to just go to bed, and then finally I was like, "Ok Jim listen - if she doesn't call me tonight I will call the office in the morning. You know if the test was positive she would have called so maybe they are just trying to figure out what is wrong with me and since I am NOT pregnant they have no reason to call"

The next morning when I woke up I pretended like the day before was a dream and it just never happened. Jim was getting ready for work and he was already on me about calling. I told him, "You know what? You are acting crazy. Leave me alone. If they do not call me by eleven am then I will call them. They are probably just busy with sick patients and you know if that test was positive they would have called already, so just go to work and have a good day." I think he was getting a little mad at me by ten am and he was insisting I call in. I was in major denial... major. Soon enough it was 11am and still no phone call from this PA who promised me she was going to call the night before so now I was actually getting a little bit angry. I sat down at the living room table and I called in, "Hello, this is Marybeth Sheridan and I was at your office yesterday...."

The girl who answered the phone interrupted me and said, "Oh yes, Mrs. Sheridan can you hold on one minute please the doctor does want to speak with you?"

Almost nervous I said, "Well hang on a minute, can't you just tell me if the test results are in yet?"

The young receptionist who answered the phone had no interest at all in helping me find out if any test results were in and she almost sounded nervous herself. Here is the funny part – I think everyone was afraid to talk to me because I sat on hold for more than twenty minutes - it was so strange. The longer I held the more nervous I started getting and then finally, "Hello Marybeth, I am sorry I did not call you last night but I wanted to confirm the name of the doctor who did your Tubule Ligation again -."

I stopped her right there, "No we are not doing this. You need to tell me right now, am I pregnant or not?"

Maybe three seconds of quiet then, "Yes, Yes you are definitely pregnant, now if you could give me the name of that –." Again I rudely interrupted her and as tears were rolling down my cheeks instantly, "But I can't be... I just can't be. You see I was in surgery for two hours they had to give me extra drugs to keep me sleeping (I think I started sobbing) there was scar tissue, and then I was on the pain pills, and the antibiotics... and I have a child who has a disease that is terminal and it is genetic and the surgery – the surgery just can not be good for a baby in my womb. Please - I can't be pregnant."

I don't remember anything she said to me. I don't even remember saying goodbye to her. I only remember telling Jim to get home now, and then sitting in that chair and sobbing, and sobbing. Samantha came running to my side the moment she heard me crying. She was so scared and so worried about me, but I couldn't control the tears. I was so scared, too.

The next call was to Dr. Angel, or maybe it was his wife because I don't remember that either. I just remember Jim rushing home and then pulling myself together to talk to Dr. Angel. I gave him dates and answered questions and I am sure I started sounding like a broken record repeating over and over again that it had to be a mistake, I was in surgery for two hours, they had to give me extra anesthesia drugs, and then I was on pain pills, and then antibiotics for two weeks and there is a 25 percent chance of EB and all those things added up together can not be good for a fetus in my womb. Dr. Angel gave me the facts and told me to just stay calm. He assured me and re-assured me that no matter what everything was going to be ok.

Dr. Angel figured I must be about eight weeks pregnant so he wanted me to come in and have an Ultra Sound so we can get a better idea of exactly how the baby was doing. After the tears stopped and I realized that I prayed about this and I even told God that no matter what, this was in His hands, and after all I was the one who said, "Ok God if you want me to have another baby then you will have to be the one to change that. You will be the only one with that kind of power who can make that possible and whatever your will I will be ok with it." After I thought that through for a little bit a very calm and happy emotion just flowed right through me. I wasn't afraid anymore and I realized that I was one lucky girl.

Consequently I ran into Dr. Angel at a football game a couple of days later. I was at the concession stand eating a bag of popcorn just as happy as I could be and he was on his way to the concession stand. He sort of grinned as I was shoving a hand full of popcorn in mouth. I loved to eat while being pregnant. I found it to be one of life's true pleasures; the feeling of life growing inside you and the combination of feeding that life with yummy food was divine pleasure for sure. He was laughing because he knew that too and he also knew I could pack the pounds on through pregnancy as well, so I don't think buttery popcorn is on your list of "foods that are good for you" you know if you want to remain in the normal weight category that is.

It was my MO to gain eighty pounds every baby, and even though I would get right back down to size I don't think any OB doctor wants you to do that.

So as I was eating the popcorn he says, "Hey listen don't get too worried about things because I calculated the dates and there is no way that baby is in your uterus."

Crunching popcorn I said, "What do you mean exactly?"

"Well if the dates of your last period and all the rest of that stuff are correct then there is no way the fetus made it down the tubes before

McNulty (the other doctor) burned them (that just means tied them) so I think the baby maybe stuck in your tubes."

I know Dr. Angel was also worried about all the things I was worried about and he knew why I got my tubes tied to begin with. He knew about my fear of EB, and he also knew that I was an over reactive and highly guarded strictly by the books patient. When I was pregnant with both Samantha and Chloe I wouldn't even take a sip of wine let alone eat a piece of fish... cooked fish that is, because I was always so paranoid that I had to be just be perfect, eat perfect, do everything perfect so my baby would be ok. So really telling me that the now new baby was probably stuck in my tubes was somehow going to make me feel better, when just the opposite happened.

"Oh thanks Jeff (we had become friends by now so calling him by his first name was ok when he wasn't at the office), yeah, that makes me feel so much better. I am pregnant and now I am going to lose this baby because you think it didn't make it in my tubes before the actual tying, or burning (or whatever it is they do) took place. No, that will not make me happy, this baby is where it is supposed to be." He smiled and said, "Well your appointment is in a couple of days and when we get the ultra sound done we will know for sure ok?"

Great - something new to ponder over. Dr. Angel was not someone to be wrong about anything to do with your pregnancy usually so that was not sitting too well with me.

A few days scattered by and I was finally sitting in a chair waiting for One of Dr. Angel's partner's at his practice to come into the room to talk me. Dr. Morales walked in and confirmed that I was pregnant and the baby was exactly where the baby was supposed to be. In my womb. I was elated, we were all so very happy. All I could think was, "I guess either God had different plans for me then what I had for myself or there was a little person who wanted to come into this world in a pretty bad way!"

The entire pregnancy went perfect. Once again I enjoyed every second of having a little human moving around in me. The very best part for me was that this baby was a boy and he did not have EB. Dr. Angel of course ran all of the usual test but after the few couple of tests I knew deep inside of me that somehow this baby was not going to have any problems. The delivery went beautifully and nine months just seemed to breeze by.

Little baby James was born early August 2003 and Chloe and Samantha could not have been happier. They both were part of James's arrival and they both were able to feed him and hold him. In my mind all I could think of was, "Thank you God... and little James you must have some really big work to do here little guy." Something else that was rather funny was that male nurse that I had during the tubal ligation who checked the blood pregnancy test to make sure it was negative – he was the same nurse who took care of me after I delivered James in recovery. He remembered me from the tubal ligation.

Shortly after James was born, post-partum depression sank in. That condition just sort of creeps up on you and really without too much warning. I had recently made a new friend in my neighborhood and she would come and check in on me now and then after James was born. Her name is Anita and although she doesn't really know she pulled me out of that slumper I was in – she did! Nothing made any sense to me. I mean here I had just had a perfectly normal healthy happy baby but I was feeling so blue and down and depressed. I did not go through any of that after Samantha's delivery, nor did I after Chloe was born, so why then would I be going through that now after James? I am not sure anyone really ever knows the reason for these mysteries but one thing for sure is the loaf of bread Anita brought to my door and the day she said, "Here let me hold him and you go in and take a shower and put your self together," was the turning point for me of getting through that period in my life.

Chapter 47.

The Healing Mass

One afternoon a friend called me to tell me that a very special priest was coming to town in our area to a local Catholic church to do a "Healing Mass." I wasn't actually sure what a Healing Mass was since I had never been to one before but I was always open for anything. Through the years after Samantha's birth I had heard many different stories about how some people had visions of our Holy Mother Mary and or visits from her and people from all over would go to where ever those visions or sightings would be happening and wait for the message the Blessed Mother Mary would reveal.

Whenever some one would tell me a story of a Mother Mary sighting I would always listen, try to rationalize the story and make logical sense out of it. I am not sure anything in my life ever really made sense to me or not. I know for the most part that I believed in God because I was always "told that I have to" and then as I got older I would feel these uncanny sort of experiences unfold around me that were completely unexplainable and somehow I just knew that a higher power was definitely in control.

The strangest thing about all of the Mother Mary stories I had heard was that the number 13 always seemed to pop up. Either it was that Mary appeared regularly to a particular person on the 13th of every month, or it was just a one -time appearance that occurred on the 13th of a month, but what was unusual about that was that Samantha was born on the 13th of February so I just found that to be odd.

Being consistent with prayers and learning how to pray more specifically was also a way of learning that God really did exist, however the Mother Mary sightings were partly intriguing and partly hard to believe to be true. One time a girlfriend of mine Erica and I had heard about a specific sighting of the Blessed Mother in Ft. Lauderdale, which was only about three hours from our homes. We both had little girls and they were both the same ages and Erica told me about the sightings because she had heard that a "healing" can sometimes occur at these events. We decided to make a little weekend trip out of it and go see for our selves. Samantha was only a baby at the time this happened.

I will never forget that experience for the rest of my life. We were directed to a tiny little house in a small suburb of Ft. Lauderdale. The home was owned by a little old Spanish woman who had apparently been getting frequent visits or Apparitions from "Mother Mary" (on the 13th of every month), and I guess Mary would tell her things about how we should all start praying and believing in God because Judgment Day was coming. I mean there was a lot more to it than that but that is what I was taking from it. When Erica and I arrived at this house it was packed with literally hundreds of people. It did not look as though we were going to get anywhere near the house, and we were told that our only chance to have any kind of healing for Samantha was to be –In the house – at the time of the apparition.

I do not recall how we got in that house. I think someone noticed that I had a baby who was visibly sick wrapped up in bandages and before I knew it we were being led to the front door of this house squeezing through massive crowds of hundreds of people. Consequently I did get separated from my friend Erica and her baby, but I had Samantha and I had control of us so I was not worried. Oddly I was not afraid of my surrounding at all. Some people were saying that we were going to be able to smell roses when the blessed Mother appeared before this woman, and others said that if we looked outside we would be able to see something strange and unusual happening to the clouds at the time of the apparition.

I have to tell you this story in order for you to understand the course of events that take place a few years later with the same kind of content. Samantha was about six months old at this time, and as we were entering this house she was really fussy. I was worried that they might ask me to leave because as we were entering we were being told that everyone needed to be extremely quiet as this woman who Mary was appearing to was in deep prayer and could not be disturbed. Well that was awkward because here I was with a baby in bandages that was getting everyone's attention and she was crying and fussy. Nothing I was doing was calming Samantha down. I just assumed that the crowd of strangers was the reason she was so upset. Samantha was never fussy, she was always a very happy baby, so for her to be acting like this was weird.

Anyway this old Spanish woman started saying the Rosary out loud and she was sort of walking us through what was happening. She said the Rosary then paused, and then said "Our Blessed Mother is coming down from the Heavens right now." Some people around me were just falling to the floor as if they had passed out or something. I really wasn't sure what was going on, but then I heard someone say that the Blessed Mother was close to being in the room and the people who had passed out were not really passing out but instead it was called "Being Slain in the Spirit," which simply means that the spirit of Mother Mary was so powerful that these people would sort of fall to the ground in an unconscious state, or sleep state, while Mother Mary was entering. I wasn't quite sure what to make of any of it, but I thought well - what the heck - it can't hurt us and anyway being there was interesting to say the least.

The room became very quiet and this all happened very quickly, within 10 to 15 minutes of us entering this house. All of a sudden I had noticed that Samantha was asleep. Strangely enough amongst the chaos and commotion she just went to sleep, which was another very unusual thing for Samantha to do. Then when the apparition was over the old Spanish woman came up to me and she took her hand, poured some kind of oil on it, and she rubbed some of that oil on Samantha's backside area where there were no bandages. Then she turned to me, rubbed that oil on my lower abdomen and told me, "You will bare the fruit in your womb, and your womb will be blessed." And she walked away.

As we left the house and went outside to look for my friend, Samantha woke back up, but she was calm and happy. My friend Erica said she was worried about us because she said she could hear Samantha crying and then all of a sudden she couldn't hear her crying anymore; she said it was so quiet you cold hear a pin drop. We left there kind of feeling like some amazing "thing" did just happen, but we both were not quite sure exactly what that "thing" was.

Consequently that trip to Ft. Lauderdale happened when Samantha was six months old, so a good five years before Chloe was born and eight years before James was born, so I guess the old Spanish woman to some degree knew what she was talking about.

So here we are back in 2004 or somewhere around there and at two o'clock in the afternoon a friend is calling me to tell me about a "Healing Mass" that is taking place at one of our local Catholic Churches at five o'clock that very same night. Since my experience at the old Spanish Woman's house was so intriguing and mysterious I had the urge to want to also go to this Healing Mass. Plus it was also my feeling that, really do we know? I mean do we really know if something is going to be the one thing that could change our lives forever? And the answer is No we do not so if we have nothing to loose then let's go.

I thought my first obstacle was going to be my husband. Jim was a realist and he didn't really believe too much in these sorts of things. Seriously when Erika and I went to Ft. Lauderdale he simply said, "Ok girls have a nice weekend." He thought we were just kooky to be driving three hours away to follow a flock of people who BELIEVE that the Holy Mary Mother of God was actually appearing to some unknown person out in the middle of nowhere. Surprisingly, when I called Jim at work and I asked him if we could all go, which also meant he would have had to come home early on that particular day, much to my surprise he agreed.

I thought, "Well that was just too easy. Hmm…." My dad met us there and saved us some seats right up in the first pews. My girlfriend who called me that day her mom Helen went as well. As we raced to get to the church because we were told that we could not be late something really strange happened. We were about three blocks away and all of the sudden I became very, very sick. Jim had to pull the car over in the worst part of town so I could run into a store to use the bathroom. I was so sick that it was coming out both ends at the same time. I started praying and asking God to help me because I felt like some other kind of strange force was trying to prevent us from getting there. I had never felt anything like that before in my life.

I mean we all hear about Hell and the Devil but I had never actually felt him in my life at all before, but I swear that on that day at that particular time he was doing everything he could from keeping us from getting to that church. As soon as I asked God for help I was mysteriously all better. I got back in the car and Jim was like, "Wow are you ok? You look awful. You are so pale." And I just told him that I had this sick feeling come over me so fast that the second I got into the bathroom I threw up and then had diarrhea instantly and for no apparent reason, but I started to pray and then miraculously and mysteriously I just got all better. Jim looked a little spooked and unsure if what I was saying could possibly be true. He knew I would never ever lie to him about something like that (or anything for that matter) but the whole thing was so strange. There was definitely a force trying to keep us from getting to that church that day.

We literally entered the church with not a second to spare. As soon as we were seated the instructions for the mass began. The priest speaking was Fr. Mary Rookie. He had come from Chicago to do this Mass. I guess this Healing Mass was not public knowledge rather by invitation only and I will tell you there was not an empty seat in that church. Fr. Rookie told us that we would be in prayer for five hours and with no breaks. Jim and I just looked at each other with these "uh-oh" looks as if to say, "Oh no - what did we just get ourselves into?". Then there we were with Samantha maybe she was around eight years old and it was six pm and none of us had eaten since lunchtime. Neither one of us hesitated we just turned our attention back to the priest and we listened to his instructions, and his story. He was telling us how awesome our God is and how as a priest he was privileged to be witness to God's healing powers. There were men and woman in the audience who stood before us and told their stories of how they had been healed or cured from whatever strange illness they had by attending this Healing Mass Fr. Rookie was doing but at an earlier time in life. They went on to explain that since their healing they feel it is part of their thanks to God to come here and share their very powerful life changing stories with all of us.

Fr. Rookie started out by telling all of us how very important it is for us to daily "Thank God." He talked for one solid hour on the importance of Thanking God every day and how vital it is to our very existence to give Thanks to God for every single thing in our life, including our lives every day, maybe even as many times in the day that we can remember to tell God thank you. He said that he thinks one of our most human mistakes here on this earth is that we do not thank God enough.

That was the official day that I started to say Thank You to God everyday!!!!

The strangest thing for me that day was that when we first arrived at the church and after Fr. Rookie had told us that it was going to be a five hour mass, I thought, "Oh man, how are we going to manage this?" We had not eaten and we had never before subjected Samantha to anything this long before.

Probably two hours into the mass Fr. Rookie had called all of the sick to the front of the Alter so that he could pray for them. As we approached I felt this overwhelming need to cry as if I had not cried tears in years. It felt like some kind of release, like emotional pain being lifted from my heart and I could not control the tears. Usually in the past whenever I felt like crying I didn't, and especially if I was around Samantha. This time was different it was as if some other power greater than me had control over my body, but in a good way.

As I stood there sobbing I felt like I was in the presence of The Holy Spirit. Not really knowing what that felt like I guess I felt like something larger than me and bigger than me was holding me up and allowing me to cry a river of tears as sort of a release to my internal pain.

Never before have I done that or have I been able to do that. Then all of the sudden and without any warning people around us were just falling to the ground as if they were passing out. Suddenly the distant memory of being in Ft. Lauderdale with my friend and being in that woman's house where people were just falling to the ground and being in a sleep state rolled back into my mind, and then Fr. Rookie started to speak bringing me to the present moment.

Fr. Rookie had asked all of the sick to take a step forward. We gently put our hands on Samantha as if to push her a little forward and we told her, "It is ok Honey the priest is just going to pray for you, you can step forward"

I could tell she was nervous and probably thinking that now her parents were a bit crazy as well.

There were probably over 50 maybe even more people who stepped forward to get this special blessing of the sick from Fr. Rookie. He very slowly prayed over each person and he seemed to be very intently deep in his words. He had prayed over 10 people before he prayed over Samantha and by this time maybe three hours had passed. The strangest feeling was that time was moving so quickly.

As Fr. Rookie began to pray over Samantha she started to lean towards me to tell me that she could not feel her legs. Jim and I put our hands on her to hold her up and then all of the sudden her legs just gave way and she was falling to the floor, somehow we managed to hold her up. She was so upset that she could not feel her legs and she did not know had happened. The priest continued to pray over her as if nothing unusual was happening. Samantha ended up on the ground and when I looked into the priest eyes he looked as if he had some kind of physical pain.

Somehow I managed to be in this Healing Mass for more than five hours but it never felt like more than 1 hour. Some kind of emotional pain was lifted or some kind of release poured out of me and to this day I am still not exactly sure what happened. A few days after the mass the same friend who alerted us of this mass to begin with had called me to tell me that after we left that night Fr. Rookie was trying to find out who the little girl in the bandages was and if anyone knew her. Apparently he fell to his own knees and then completely out after praying to God specifically for her. My friend did not have anything else to offer me but only that the priest felt some kind of connection to

Samantha.

Chapter 48.

Visionary Communications

With every year that had passed hope for a cure to my daughter's disease seemed to become more distant. I was sure the Healing Mass would offer something, maybe even some improvement but sadly her disease was only getting more complicated and her pain was intensifying. By 2004 Samantha was having more and more reoccurring secondary infections. Every new infection presented new challenges and the wounds just seemed more and more difficult to heal. Our new ID doctor was Dr. Patty Emmanuel. With every new doctor came a new relationship and a learning curve of sorts. We still had our pediatrician Dr.Yee but as Samantha's disease advanced she required more specialized care and as her infections in her wounds became more consistent our ID doctor was becoming our primary contact.

Communicating with Samantha's doctors was extremely important, as details were crucial. Samantha would get an infection and then we would have to strategize with Dr. Emmanuel about a game plan. We would concur one and then a few months would pass and then we would be on to the next issue. We learned so much with Dr. Emmanuel as well. We learned that due to the constant scar tissue and blistering in Samantha's esophagus now it was becoming more difficult for her to eat foods and swallow them and as a result her nutrition was being compromised, thus weakening her body which was already too weak to heal infections and wounds. Also around this time frame we noticed that we were having more and more issues trying to keep her hemoglobin at a normal range, and between the hemoglobin and her nutrition her body was failing.

We added GI doctors to our monthly - sometimes weekly -routine visits along with the pediatrician and ID. Our trusted Dermatologist, Dr. Save Me, became very ill and stopped practicing all together. As soon as she stopped her practice it was if she just vanished in mid air. We couldn't find her or any information out about her.

I lost track of Dr. Save Me as the years passed and every now and then I would hear rumor that she has passed away. Every time I would hear such a rumor I would just happen to be with Sam and she and I would just stop and look into each other's eyes as if we were in shock. Losing Dr. Save Me was not even a reality that either of us could bare. Somehow though our lives started to spin out of control with just keeping track of all of Samantha's needs so we would try to track down Dr. Save Me, but after failed attempts we would get distracted and then more time would pass and still no word or mention of her at all.

We added a psychologist to mix too. As Samantha became more aware about her disease we felt like she needed some professional guidance on a mental level. Sam was in the sixth grade at school, but because of her re-current skin infections she was at home more than she was at school. I began to realize that my sweet girl's life was becoming more and more isolated, as her time at home was always lonely. The kids at school barley even knew Samantha because she was never there, so I understood why no one ever called to invite her to parties or to come and hang out. But still it yanked at my heart like a thorn. She did have one friend who would visit but it wasn't often as Meg had her own studies to do and schoolwork to keep up with. I was hoping the psychologist would offer some help or some recommendations, but sadly after a good long few months of visiting this doctor nothing at all was really gained. I mean what could you offer a young girl in the sixth grade who's life has always been surrounded by doctors and hospital, and daily bandaging and wound care that was filled will pain and horror? This disease EB stumped even the best trained professional when it came to improving a life or adding quality to a child's life who was afflicted with no hope.

By 2006 Samantha had been on dozens of oral antibiotics and had been hospitalized a few times for secondary infection requiring IV antibiotic therapy. I remember Samantha coming home after one hospital stay and the principal from her school came to visit her. She looked so lifeless and sick. The fear of death felt like it was lurking at my door. It rattled anyone who knew her. Some times people would ask me how much longer I thought she had to live, and even though it was a sensible question I never knew the answer but just always knew that I was thankful for that day and any extras days the good Lord would give to us. We lived in fear of losing her all the time.

Some years prior while I was still on the board of directors for the DEBRA organization maybe around 2000 sometime. DEBRA was organizing a world wide Visionary meeting with the top research experts in the world with regards to EB. The idea behind this meeting was to gather all the experts together at one remote location in the USA and assemble a meeting that would allow all the researchers time to collaborate together and share their information and sort of get an idea where they are at in terms of research, finding a cure, and monies needed to accomplish those goals.

I was so excited about this meeting I could hardly stand myself waiting for it to come around. Volunteering my time for DEBRA and helping to raise monies for this not for profit organization was about to put me right where I had always wanted to be… in the know. Strangely enough when the time came for me to make my arrangements to go to this meeting something had happened with Sam and I can't recall exactly what it was but whatever it was I was not going to be able to go to this meeting. I was devastated. By this time I had recruited a friend on the board and her name was Lorraine. Lorraine and I had made friends in Miami at the Appligragh trials that we participated in. Lorraine's baby was the one born that had attracted all the media's attention, which in turn spurred the whole Bio- engineered skin trial to begin with down in Miami in the first place.

I phoned Lorraine and I asked her if she could go to this meeting in my place. I made sure I told her everything I wanted to know and what I was trying to find out. By this time I had been studying all of the cures and methods of treatments that could potentially lead to a cure for EB since about six months after Sam was born.

I was like a little kid on the eve of Christmas morning waiting on the return of my friend from the Visionary meeting. I could not wait to talk to Lorraine, because I just knew that she was sure to tell me that something wonderful was being looked into and that a hope for a better life for my baby girl was really out there. Much, much very much to my surprise it would turn out to be one of the more memorable phone calls I would ever get. When Lorraine called me she had so much enthusiasm and excitement in her voice as she proceeded to tell me that the researchers were not discussing at all a "cure" per-se, but were more intently focusing all of their efforts on a "treatment" not a cure and had discussed that maybe a cure was trying to reach to broadly for something and that maybe it was better to take a step back and try to start looking into a method of treatment.

I was shocked. I was angry instantly, and I know my tone of voice with her must have said it all. My friend did not come back and deliver good news to me, although she thought it was good news. I guess that was easy for her to feel since her daughter had the subtype of EB that gets better with age and than eventually goes away. The anger I felt that day on the phone with her sank in my gut like a bitter poison and in fact I do think something changed in me that day. I told Lorraine that this news that she was so happy to tell me was not news that made me happy at all. I told her that instead she just wrecked my world. "Do you not understand Lorraine that I do not want Sam to live forever like this… I do not want someone to come up with some kind of plan that will just keep her here in these bandages and pain and suffering. I want a cure and nothing else will work, anything less than a cure is just stupid." I don't think my friend ever really truly understood my disappointment but for me it was a huge blow. So as the years passed the whole idea of a cure was becoming more and more distant.

Even as the years followed and I left the DEBRA organization to start my own organization I wasn't trying to raise money for a cure anymore. I started turning my attention to the current needs of the other families who lived with this horrible disease. That is one of the reasons I left DEBRA. I was living in a horrible world full of pain, suffering, sadness and heartache and I would often wonder how others with EB and their families were going to survive. I knew how hard it was for me and I was living comfortably. If you didn't have a lot of money and you had a child with EB it was like adding insult to injury. Not only are you trying to figure out how to pay the rent but at the same time you are fighting to keep your kid alive and juggle a schedule of EB care and daily life that on a good day could take an army of people to just get through.

By this time in our life the idea of a cure for EB seemed so far from reality to me that I started to train my mind on the here and now, and how were we going to make normalcy out of the chaotic crazy life with EB we were living and be happy…

At some point in 2006 my mother became very ill and came to live with me. Both my mother and my father moved into our home. My mother had cancer and had been battling it for about 13 years. Having my mom in my home was the best thing we could have ever done. Mom mom's brought so much cheer and happy to our home. Some times Mom mom's would dress up like a clown and dance around all goofy and just have the kids laughing and giggling. Then when the kids were in bed at night I would go to Mom Mom's room and sip on Franchelica with her and talk about everything.

Before I knew it Samantha was having more and more new EB challenges arise.

Samantha's swallowing problems became so bad in 2006 that her esophagus completely closed up and she couldn't even swallow her own saliva. We had to take the very next flight to California where the best GI EB doctor was and not only have her esophagus dilated (which means opened back up so liquids and foods can pass through) but at the same time we were going to have to have a Gastromitry tube placed in her stomach so that we could now start giving her nutrition from a machine at night that pumps liquid nutrients into her body while she sleeps to insure that we are getting enough calories and proteins in her everyday so that her body can fight off these constant skin infections. Some people call it a "Mickey" button and some people call it a G-tube. All that we knew was that Samantha was so malnourished from not being able to swallow and eat foods that without having the G-tube place she was going to die.

After the G-tube was placed in her stomach we came back home. Having the G-tube was great because it also allowed us to give her all of her medicines through that tube so now she didn't have to drink any more yucky medicines. That was a plus anyway. I don't think that at that time Sam was so crazy about having this little button sticking out from her stomach but after she got some nutrients in her and started to feel better she became more comfortable with the whole idea.

Now we had to find a new GI doctor locally though because the GI doctor that we had been going to ("Dr. W.") wasn't too happy that we went all the way to California to get the G-tube placed. In fact she told me that if I choose to take Samantha there that I could go ahead and find another doctor to take care of her here in Tampa. SO that is exactly what I did. I don't know why some doctors feel the need to be so territorial about things. I mean I even told her that if she were I and she had a child with a rare genetic illness such as EB and her daughter needed to have a huge surgery such as this, than would she herself want to go where they are more familiar with EB and this particular procedure? She said no, but I know different. It is common logical sense. Anyway, I really didn't care what she thought.

Chapter 49.

05/05/05

May 5th 2005 was the official start date for EBAN, Inc. That was the not for profit organization I wanted to create to help families who could not afford EB. There were three of us initially to start EBAN. I birthed the idea in hopes that we could help solve what I thought was the most challenging problem EB families faced... finances. The disease EB can cripple a family financially. Our children lived in bandages from their neck down all day long, every single day of the week. Those bandages can cost anywhere from ten thousand upwards to fifty plus thousand dollars a year. Everything it takes to provide comfort and quality for a child who suffers from EB cost money, and most of these items are not covered under insurance.

First I asked Silvia Corradin and she agreed, and then we asked another woman we knew named Gina. The three of us created EBAN. I was lucky enough to have found a not for profit CPA/Attorney named Cynthia who worked hard for us and at times did not get paid.

I will say it is hard in this time to find a person who is willing to sacrifice their time to benefit a cause that has absolutely no meaning to them. We will always be forever indebted to Cynthia.

Our main goal with EBAN was to provide "Quality of Life" to EB suffers and their families. By doing that we would provide bandages, or any kind of medical supply they needed and did not have the money to pay for. We also provided fun things too, like money to help them go to camp, or maybe just go on vacation, but mostly it was to help pay their medical bills, and help them out if they were going to the hospital, or just to pay for everyday needs such as ointments, bandages, and supplies.

Our secondary goal was to get a Bill on the Hill and passed that would mandate insurance coverage. Most EB families were having a lot of difficulty getting their bandages paid for. If a family's income was 60 thousand dollars a year and their bandages were 30 thousand dollars a year then it doesn't take a rocket scientist to figure out that a middle class family would have to decide whether or not to buy bandages or put food on the table.

I remember very clearly one time being in Washington and meeting with our local Senators and Congressmen. One Congressman in particular seemed very eager to help us. We sat in his office discussing EB and how most families were affected by EB. We explained how extremely important it was to have bandages for an EB child and fresh clean bandages to change every day, not used bandages or reused or washed, dirty bandages. We very clearly educated this one politician on how bandages were their skin and without them EB children would die. Then we explained our dilemma with insurance and how some families were discriminated against because they had a child with a terminal illness who required so much care and so many medical supplies, and some insurance companies just flat out denied bandage coverage. I even shared my own personal story on how my insurance company just terminated my policy back before we had Aetna... done just like that. How I was a self-employed local businesswoman trying to make a living and provide insurance for my employees, but because my insurance company hit me with such drastically high rates none of my employees could afford to have insurance unless I paid for 75% of it or more. I think at some point I was actually paying full price for all of my employees at one time or another just so we could have insurance.

After telling this one Congressman he looked at me in the face and told me, "Ok, well this is like you riding your bike up hill with no peddles." I looked at him said, "Yeah, I know that. That is why we are here to ask for your help because we (EB Families) ride our bikes up hill with no peddles and no handle bars everyday."

Somehow after every visit with a Senator or a Congressman I always walked away feeling like I was still on my way into their office for the first time. Nothing ever got accomplished.

We honestly gave Washington a few visits and often times a Senator or two would bump us from the schedule. Then on one occasion I remember very clearly calling for an appointment with one of my Senators who was actually in my district. I made the appointment three weeks before I arrived there and confirmed the appointment the day before I left. When we arrived in Washington at this one particular Senators' office we sat there and waited for an hour before his staff came in and told us that our appointment had actually been changed to another building that was a couple of blocks away and we had better hurry because this Senator was on a very tight schedule and we only had about three minutes to get there *but* if we walked fast enough we could make it.

Here I was with high heels on and a suit, and so was my partner, and I'm sorry but the building was very far away. It was raining outside and there wasn't a cab in site, so we made the heroic dash to the building, which was like four blocks down a few flight of stairs, down one hall, into another hall, then down another hall only to get to a room that looked like a social gathering of sorts with photographers set up and ready to take pictures. I was out of breath, rained on and now mad. The only issue I was going to be allowed to discus was whether or not I wanted to have this Senator stand on the right side of me or the left.

I cannot tell you how mad that made me considering that we trekked all the way to Washington from Florida, and organizing that time away from work and Samantha was not so easy for me.

Needless to say we rode our bikes hard but we never made up the hill. Our Infamous Bandage Bill never made up the hill either for that matter. So, I started to look around at other ways we could get some attention for EB.

Sometime at the end of 2005, I had met a friend who said they could help us get a big named celebrity to help us with our first big fundraiser. I spent a lot of time on that one trying to organize, write letters and meet with friend of their friends who could get to this particular celebrity. I always had this feeling that this celebrity was never going to pan out and consequently as time went by the celebrity went from wanting to help us to wanting to get paid to help us. I decided to go ahead with this fundraiser anyway and I also decided that maybe paying a celebrity to come was not such a bad idea after all. I mean, geez, I had met a half a dozen of celebrities by this stage in the game and no one I met was interested at all in helping us bring awareness to EB.

The only thing that I could think of was maybe this disease was so horrible that all the celebrities I had met either could not believe such a horrible disease existed, or they thought I was nuts, or both, or worse - maybe they just didn't care. All I knew was that for the past 10 years I had been trying to raise awareness for this little known disease and raise money and every time I tried either of those two things I constantly got, "EB? What is that?" So in my mind, a celebrity speaking out on behalf of EB was the *only* way to go, so if we had to pay him money so be it.

Unfortunately, the closer we got to the actual event the sicker Sam was getting. She was having constant skin infections and her wounds seemed to take longer and longer to heal. Weeks turned into months. Sam was having more and more difficulty eating and swallowing as the strictures in her esophagus were becoming more severe.

We ended up flying to California for a permanent feeding tube placement, or a G-tube, or some people call it a "Mickey" button. Once again we would have to go into the OR and use Propaphal, which is a drug that Samantha does not respond to very well

Dr. Castillo who is her GI doctor in California graciously fit us into his schedule at a moments notice.

We had her feeding tube placed and a dilatation of her esophagus done at the same time. While Sam was in the surgery I got a call from my friend Susan back home regarding the Celebrity Fundraiser we had been working on for EB. Earlier in that year 2006 we had a friend who apparently knew someone who was friends with Cuba Gooding Jr. and was trying to see if we could get him to come to an EB Fundraiser for us. It felt like we had been working on this thing for months and then Sam got sick with her esophagus and we ended up in California. When Sam was in surgery and my friend Susan called me she said that she had spoken to Cuba's agent and his agent wanted to know if we could quarantee a minimum of 300 people to show up to this event. So here I was sitting in the patient surgery waiting area at a hospital in California far, far away from home worried as hell that my daughter might not even make out of the surgery and my friend Susan calls me to ask me this question. Can you guess what my answer was...?

I told her to tell his agent, "Thanks, but no thanks. We don't need him just forget it." I think my friend Susan was a little upset but ya' know what? - I was tired of trying to ask celebrities for their help. Shoot, we were even paying Cuba like twenty thousand dollars to come and flying him in on a private plane that was going to cost someone else ten thousand dollars just to do that, so just forget about it.

I actually never spoke to Cuba myself, so who really knows what happened, or if he was ever even contacted at all anyway. What I did know was that I was at the moment of wondering if this would be the last time I would see Sam so worrying about EBAN's first fundraiser was not on my list of priorities at that moment.

This is how God works: Just after ending that call with Susan regarding not having Cuba as "The Celebrity," Anita, called me to ask me how everything was going with Sam. Anita and I became so close just after I had James. I always joke that she saved my life from the post partum depression that I didn't know I was in. That was back in 2003. Anita's husband was a famous baseball player and now manager of a Major League Baseball team, Lou Piniella. If Anita could have been with Jim and I in California to go through Sam's G-tube surgery, she would have. Anita's schedule was rough as it was but she had always had a special place in heart for Sam.

From the first time I had met Anita sometime in 2001 I could tell she would be someone who *really* cared about Samantha. I could always tell the people that met Sam that had some kind of an instant connection - to the ones who had no connection at all, and that includes family.

So while we were in California, Anita was pretty much on the phone with me round the clock getting updates on how our girl was holding up. Sam never did the OR well anyway because of all the reactions she had all the time to various kinds of drugs, so going in and coming out of the OR was always worrisome for us.

On one of my phone calls with Anita I shared with her the phone call from my friend Susan in which I told Susan basically "thanks but no thanks" for the celebrity and Anita was quick to offer Lou as the celebrity for EBAN's first fundraiser. We accepted and were very excited to have Lou.

Sam ended up recovering from the permanent G-tube placement and first dilatation surgery very well. We came home and Sam started a new life of getting her nutrition at nighttime now that we had a feeding tube placed. At first the whole idea of this rubber tube being inserted into her stomach about three-inches with this sort of button top that rested on the surface of her stomach really creeped me out. That little tube is called a "Mickey" button. The button has this top that you pull out to open sort of like a plug and then there is another tube that hooks into the button on her stomach and that is how you get foods and medicines into her stomach. It is a wonderful idea really because everything bypasses the esophagus all together and goes exactly where it needs to go without causing damage. I know for a fact that Samantha would not have lived another year without this tube being placed because she would have simply died of starvation.

The Mickey button would need to get changed out every three months. Sam learned quickly that she liked to do it herself and that was a good thing because I never fully liked the idea, although it was like putting an earring through an earring hole, and seriously the hole was that tiny and pretty much identical, I just couldn't do it. I did, however, learn how to put the cans of nutrition in this bag that then had to be hooked up to a machine that I had to program which would slowly pump the liquid food directly into her stomach for 10 hours every night as she slept. We were learning that there were many factors to consider with EB and wound healing. As Sam's Nutrican declined with the years so did her health. Right around puberty, or age 10, her body seemed to be less and less able to heal wounds and fight off infection. After we got the feeding tube placed we saw a noticeable improvement in her wound healing. She gained weight and the huge belly she got from always being starved slowly disappeared.

We still battled pseudomonas but so far we were able to keep it under wraps with IV drugs and oral antibiotics. The Nutricin we were now able to give her through her G-tube helped her body to heal the wounds and fight infection and still allowed her to eat food by mouth when she was able. I didn't have to worry anymore about her not eating or not being able to eat once the G-tube was in place. It used to be that when Sam would walk around spitting in a cup I would panic that she wasn't going to eat for a few days because her throat would literally close shut - not even allowing her own saliva to go down.

Those worries were behind us now.

Chapter 50.

The Old Man's Shoes

On one of my trips to the doctors office (For me this time), Chloe and I were walking through the front doors of this office building. Chloe and I were racing through the hallway to get to the elevator because I was always racing the clock to get from point A to Point B.

In our desperate rush to get to the elevator my eyes happen to catch a glimpse of this tall, elderly man in front of us appearing to have difficulty walking. Then I noticed he was using a walker to walk with and he seemed like he was moving at a turtles' pace. People coming in and out of the building were racing past on either side of him. My attention was immediately drawn to his shoelaces flopping all over as he struggled with each step of his walk. I looked around him in hopes of seeing someone assisting him on his travels, but there was no one. What was worse for me was how I quickly noticed that of all these people breezing past this old man with his walker – not one human was aware that this old man's shoelaces were dangling all over as he walked crookedly with his walker. The only thought going through my mind was that this man is going to fall and no one cared. Everyone was in too much of a hurry to stop, bend down and tie the old mans shoes. I was also a part of this careless human society. What was worse was that we were in a medical office building full of doctor's offices. Surely someone else saw this old man right?

The old man walking had such a profound impact on my thoughts at that moment I put my hand up to signal the old man to stop. I quickly knelt down on my knees and hurriedly tied his shoes. Chloe was like, "Mom! What are you doing?" I had one of those "Chloe has no idea that we are supposed to be doing this (for one another) thoughts" which made me realize that we too were part of the blindness in our society today. I was hoping that Chloe had noticed, as I did, that lots of people with their eyes closed had walked past this man who obviously was moving at a snails pace, with both shoe laces untied, desperately grasping his walker with both of his frail arms, which clearly was a huge accident waiting to happen. And because all of these humans were so self absorbed and too involved in their own hurriedness, or maybe too worried about what someone else might think – I am not totally sure - but it sure does leave ones mind to examine every possibility as to why someone had not stopped to help this old man who clearly needed another humans' assistance.

The old man smiled at me and I smiled back. As soon as I was done tying both his shoes I got back up on my feet and he went his way and we ours. I realized that old man's shoelaces being untied, and the fact that our paths crossed, was very symbolic for me and I was thankful. I told Chloe that it was my responsibility to get down and tie that old man's shoes. And really it is all of our responsibilities to get down and tie 'the old mans shoes.' But today, in this world, our lives are becoming so self absorbed and so tuned into what we are doing that most of us humans forget why we are here and what we were put here to do. That all those people walking past him either did not notice that the old man's shoes were not tied and he was walking with a walker, or the other possibility is that they did *see* but *chose* to ignore it because whatever was going on in their lives was more important. Now there is a thought to chew on for a while. Little did I know, but that small moment in my life would be a constant reminder of what defines us as individuals.

As my family and I struggled with the daily challenges of EB and how it was ravaging our lives, I was becoming stronger than I ever thought possible, and at the same time gathering a better understanding that not only was my daughter suffering, but that there was thousands of other children and families out in the world trekking along trying to survive the very same thing we were. In my mind I was wondering if anyone was getting down to tie the shoes of someone close to them who might also need assistance.

The year 2006 brought many changes for us as a family, and more importantly as a family living with EB. I continued to pray for strength and for guidance. There were times I doubted my faith and God altogether. Even with doubt lingering around my faith I still prayed and with all my heart tried to believe God was with me. My mom was very sick now and she had come to live at our house. So both my parents were living in our guest bedroom and nothing could have made us happier. The children loved "mom-moms" always being around. Mom-moms was the "happy" in our house.

We started construction on a guesthouse separate from our main house with the sole purpose of it being my mom's house.

Not only was Sam in the most pain we had ever witnessed another human being in, but emotionally she was responding to the pain with screaming and crying loudly and in a way that left scars on our heart and in our soul. For me as a mother it was like a form a torture and it was happening to my flesh and blood - and prayer was all I had to rely on. Everywhere I went for help, every doctor, every health food store, every homeopathic doctor, and every remedy anyone sent to me – no one and I mean *no one* could help my now 11 year-old daughter, whose life with EB was an insane horror of daily challenges.

Everyday Sam would have issues eating. It was clear that even though we had her first dilatation by the best GI/EB doctor in the country her esophagus was still blistering and making swallowing foods more and more difficult. Not only that but her mouth was always blistering on the inside and had constant EB involvement. Chewing foods was painful and at times impossible. There were plenty of times that we would have to pop blisters inside her mouth before she could eat anything. Not sure if you fully understand what that entails, but we would sit down for a meal. We would pray and than begin to eat. Sam would be the only one not eating and we would notice her doing something with her mouth. Her mouth involvement was so regular that by now we would notice this and ask her, "Do you have a blister in your mouth?" She would respond sadly, "Yes."

I was never very good with anything to do with her mouth so mostly Jim would have to get a flashlight and a super long needle, then ask Sam to open her mouth as wide as she could, while he tried to maneuver his huge hand in her mouth with a needle to find the blister and pop the blister without hurting her or poking her instead of the blister. This was not an easy thing to do. The stress it caused both of us to even think about having to do it was enough to cause a panic attack, and that was nothing compared to the feeling of having to do it or she couldn't eat – feeling we had. Her mouth only opened maybe about one inch, and her tongue was totally adhered to the bottom surface of her palette, her gums adhered to her cheeks, and her teeth were larger then her mouth allowed space for, and over-crowded as well – and all this because of EB. So imagine trying to take your grown adult hand and having to put it in a mouth the size of a nine month-old baby, but with 11-year teeth, while you have an 18 gauge needle trying to find your way to a blister somewhere in the mouth usually in the back to pop… just so your kid can eat. Very Stressful!

Now at 11 years old, because of her EB, her mouth was shrinking by the day from the scar tissue and the webbing occurring on her face which resulted in tightening the skin from all sides of her face. I had noticed years ago this sort of familiar look all EB children would get in their faces starting at or around age 10 and up that was sort of across the board for all EB kids. Their faces would appear to be pulled very tight leaving their noses looking smaller than normal and their mouth and lips smaller than other children their ages. Plus, I noticed the older EB children, as they talked, their faces were expressionless due to their faces becoming so pulled and stretched that even forming a smile was difficult for them.

The bottom line was that if we did not pop the blister she could not eat because it would make the blister get larger and spread, and just make eating food not only difficult but extremely painful. It reduces you to nothing watching your child suffer in constant pain and agony. Nothing in her life was fun. Her largest organ is compromised so eating, walking, wearing clothes, talking, sitting, sleeping, and moving any part of your body causes excruciating painful blisters that have to be popped and popping them hurts. What pleasures does she have in her life? What kind of quality does she have in her life? Why? Why? Why does my daughter have to live this way?

We moved into a new home at the end of 2005. This was truly our dream home that my husband designed, and built with Sam's EB in the back of his mind at every detail. By the time my mom moved in it was late 2006 and she was very sick with cancer.

By January 2007, I put on the first EBAN fundraiser. My partner Silvia lived in California so she couldn't really help me from afar. Silvia and I were and still are extremely close so working together from a distance was just as good, just harder on the one actually hosting the event. Thank God Sam was somewhat stable through that event. I had no idea the work involved in creating and then actually rolling out a golf tournament fundraiser. If my sister Rita had not come down here from Indiana I am telling you that fundraiser would have been a disaster. My sister was good at "saving the moment" if you know what I mean. I sold the event, got the golfers, but I had no idea how to make it work together or organize the golfers or any of that stuff, not to mention I was exhausted. I organized and sold this event in 10 days and I think in 10 days I may have averaged four hours of sleep a night - and I am the type of person who needs a minimum of eight hours a night.

Having Rita come in at the 11th hour and save the day – and the event - was *huge* for me, and for the EB families we raised forty thousand dollars to help!

The day after the EBAN fundraiser I got a call that my other sister Cathy was lying in the hospital with pneumonia, so I rushed to see her an hour away in St. Petersburg only to find her on Life Support fighting for her life. I was at that point in my life familiar with medical jargon but now with my sister some of this stuff was new "medical jargon" I was not familiar with. I knew she had Rheumatoid Arthritis and I knew she had pneumonia and I also knew they had put her on 100 mg Prednisone. She was either on it for three or four weeks. What I didn't know at that time was that when you come off steroids, and especially that kind of high doses of steroids, you have to be weaned off - slowly - and over a long period of time.(I'll explain the consequence in the next few paragraphs down)

Between looking after my sister and still being Nurse to Sam I had no time to think. Before I knew it my sister had let 2 years pass before realizing the consequences of one doctor's mistake. Cathy did try to get some attorney's involved but it was too late. One doctor's mistake with her would become a lifetime of steroid hell combined with lifetime co-pays, prescriptions, etc., and all without being able to work. There was nothing I could do to help her. My sister had been too sick to fight her own battle and I was knee deep in my own battle with EB. By the time I came up for air, 3 years had passed and there wasn't an attorney in town that could help her. The irony of all of this was that I was the girl who used to stand behind the doctors who lobbied for the two-year stipulation for malpractice, so suddenly for me I found myself on the opposite side of that fence. Not a very happy place for me to be as I realized that because of a mistake one doctor made - he pretty much not only ruined my sisters life, but in reality he handed her - her own personal death sentence. I have never been the kind of person who believed in suing anyone for anything. My goodness this country was a "sue happy" place as it was, but in this particular situation I truly believed that because of another human's mistake my sister could not work - nor be able to function normally in life ever again. How could that be fair? And how can we as a society let this sort of thing happen? I am still praying on this specifically.

I went to the hospital everyday to be with her. Fortunately at that time in my life we had just sold a business and neither my husband nor I were working, so Jim looked after the children so I could drive an hour south to be with my sister. As my sister started to recover the doctor had decided to move her from the ICU unit to a regular hospital room on the floor. Somehow someone failed to continue her steroid dosage and after the third day she went into Adrenal Gland Failure. I had no idea what was wrong or why that had happened because, as I said at that time in my life, I had no knowledge of steroids or their use. The consequence of that doctor's mistake was not only life threatening, but a lifetime of hell for my sister. That is when and how I was officially introduced to steroids. Consequently, my sister never fully recovered. Every new day brought a new problem the steroids would offer. The problems were endless and usually with no resolve.

Chapter 51.

Answers Confirmed

I met a lot of new people throughout the years. I am not sure if you have ever had this happen to you or not, but for me it was a sign. Have you ever been told before or complimented on something you do repeatedly? Or maybe the way you show who you are? Well I can't tell you exactly the first time this happened, or the first day I heard it, but what I recall clearly is that with each new day I would start to hear these words over and over again:

"Wow you are the strongest person I know."

Then I remembered what my mom had always taught me:

"With God all things are possible."

Either it was a new person I had met, someone that knew me for a long time or it was a complete stranger, but always after a person had learned about EB that would almost always come out of their mouth. Sometimes it would come from a close friend or a family member, but what really got my attention was the fact that I knew I was *not* strong, ever - which is why I prayed so hard for God to give me strength all the time. So many people had been telling me lately they couldn't believe how strong I was, so just like that - I thanked God, and I knew that my prayer for strength had been answered. They were right. I was strong, incredibly strong, but only because God helped me to be this way. I was handling this life with EB the best that I could and I wasn't running from it either.

Sam had so many battles with secondary infection I lost track of them. I looked forward to the days we didn't have to change a bandage and the nights we got to sleep through. I never thought, dreamed, or imagined that my life would have turned out this way. That I would become this full-time nurse learning how to take care of wounds that looked like third degree burns all over my child's body, and with every year she grew, her disease grew worse, constantly reminding me that at any given day EB was going to claim her life and there would absolutely nothing I could do about it. That is how I knew I was strong because watching her suffer in pain made it hard for me to breathe at times.

I do not know how Samantha made it through school really from 3rd grade on. I know for a fact that she missed more school than she actually went. She was extremely bright and many have thought her IQ to be off-the-charts. I noticed that about EB kids, that they are very smart and extremely bright children. Sam could miss two or three days of school straight and go in and ace a test, no matter what the subject was. As her body grew bigger so did her wounds, and the older she was getting the longer it was taking for her wounds to heal.

By the middle of 2007, which was her seventh grade year, we were on and off IV antibiotics so much it was mind-boggling. The routine was to go to the hospital get the line placed and then come home and I would administer all her medications. I used to think it was funny when others who knew us assumed we had a nurse come in and administer all of her IV medications - no, it was just me. I had a great relationship with her ID doctor at the time, so between Patti Emanuel and I we always had the best plan for Sam.

Chapter 52.

The Whole Year Was a Blur

I knew my mom was sick. I also knew she was going to die too. Subconsciously I blocked the idea of my mom dying from my mind as if it wasn't real. I wanted and expected her to live forever. She was my rock and she was my biggest fan and my largest supporter all of my life. Having her come and live with us for a year was a dream come true. "As little girls you love your mommy, as teenagers you hate your mom, as young woman you are just getting an understanding of what your mom went through and how much you appreciate her. But as a grown woman, you become aware that your mom is the only one true person who really knows you in this life and still loves you." That's my new famous quotation. What is better is that it is true.

My mom tried to warn me. She did her best to prepare me. She told me she was dying and I still put it out of my mind like it was not going to happen. Even up until the end when I was bathing her I still would not come to terms with the notion that she would be leaving me at all. She would try to talk to me and I would tell her, "No mom it's ok your going to be fine don't worry."

It was kind of like I was here with her but I wasn't. If I could make myself busy I did.

When you know someone is going to die but they are here talking and present with you I think it is much more difficult to accept that they are going to leave, or at least that is how it was with me anyway. I was in denial.

We went on a family vacation at the end of June 2007 with my sister Rita and her family to Idaho. I think we all agree it was by far the happiest time in Sam's life, in all of our lives truly. It was by far one of the most meaningful and memorable vacations I have ever had as well. My children and my sister's children are very close and they enjoy being together. Idaho was an amazing place that offered peace and tranquility just from the mountains and untouched earth than we were used to. We were very happy there.

Sam learned how to ice skate while there, as did Chloe and James. I learned to ice skate as a child so I was thrilled for them to learn how to do this. An added bonus was that the famous ice skater Nancy Kerrigan was vacationing with her family at the same resort we were at that very same week. Nancy was one of the nicest most down-to-earth celebrities I have ever met, beside Lou, of course. She even gave Sam some pointers on how best to learn the ice. Now, I bet your thinking, "Hmm… how did Sam do on the ice?" Well, actually, I held her the entire time she was on the ice for fear she would fall - and falling was not an option for me. I didn't ask Nancy for her help with EB either this time, which was very unusual for me. I was starting to look at things a bit differently now with EB. My thoughts were changing about the desperate need to find a celebrity and raise awareness. I think I was just getting to a place in my life where I was starting to accept our EB life.

As soon as we returned from our vacation, my mother's illness seemed to spiral downwards. Her doctors had given her eight months to live and Hospice was ordered in.

I was in the car one night going to the grocery store for one thing or another and I was talking to God as if He were sitting in the seat next to me. Crying, I begged and pleaded with Him not to take my mom away from me. I was sure God needed to know how much I still needed her and how afraid I was going to be if she left me. It was the first time in my heart I felt fear that she was leaving. The next day an angel walked through our door. Her name was Mary. Mary was the nurse from Hospice who came to orient my mom and explain how Hospice was going to work. I was eager to meet Mary, but not so eager to hear the details. I was straggling off into other rooms as they were talking and my mom would call for me to come back in. I know she knew I was not ready for her to go.

Mary was like a ray of sunshine for me and just by meeting her I got the full knowledge of how amazing Hospice really is. I quickly went to the church to get our priest who had now been with our parish for that past two years to come to the house and give my mom a blessing. When I got to the church I learned that a new priest had just started and his name was Fr. Tom Madden. He came to the house in that next day or two. He was by far one of my dearest and most favorite priests ever. I could tell that he was not afraid of death and he seemed to be very comfortable with all that goes with it. He came everyday to the house and would sit and talk with my mom. I was so happy that she was still doing well enough to be able to have these conversations that I know she had wanted to have with a priest, and I was even happier that he was this amazingly nice man Fr. Madden.

By this time I had really great nurses in to help me with Sam, so that allowed me to have some free time. Free time is a luxury for an EB mom and it is not something that comes with ease. I was thankful and grateful for this time with my mom and also time for myself, which was also not something I was used to. I was the youngest of five children for my mom and at that moment in time I felt the youngest too and scared, lonely, and confused. Again, I leaned on God as often as the thought entered my mind. Fr. Madden just randomly popped over every couple of days. My mom went from talking and walking to being confined to her bed and mumbling. My most treasured memory of her before she died was this one:

I was lying on her bed talking to her. I would always tell her about the children and different situations going on with each of them - good and bad. My mom always liked to hear about the children. My dad would sit in his rocking chair reading the paper or playing on his computer and he would just listen. My mom was always giving him orders and telling him things she wanted him to do after she died. As I was in denial I think so was he. I was feeding her a Popsicle and on this day she was unable to speak words. She was in and out of consciousness. I told her, "I love you mom," and she opened her eyes just ever so slightly and she mouthed the words, "I love you too," so sweetly back to me.

It is still so painful for me to write, and this was probably one of the most difficult parts of the book I had to write because I miss her so much. My mom was so lucky to have Fr. Madden at her bedside as she slowly left this earth and went to heaven. We were all there, all of her children and her husband, and all of my children. My sweet Chloe was by far the most affected by her departure. My mom had a very, very, special close bond with all of my children, but especially Chloe. Every day after school Chloe would go into Mom-moms room and color with her or play a game with her. My mom was sure to have candy to share and great stories to tell also.

Chloe cried the loudest and for the longest period of time. I know Sam was equally as disturbed, but she handled her pain in a more controlled way and I knew that Sam was not feeling that great either. My son James was only four years old at the time and although he was crying I knew it was much more painful for the girls. Fr. Madden knew just what to say to each of us and when to say it. He had gotten to know each of us just to know the right words for comfort and he stayed with us through the night and then into the next few days. I know for sure that a part of me died with her that day July 26, 2007. Any girl or woman who has had the misfortune to lose her mom can attest to the fact that something in your soul changes and is forever changed. I am a Catholic and we believe that we will be together again one day, but knowing that *time* will separate us is tremendously difficult. The pain is worse. I think Sam was taking care of me during that time. I know I cried myself to sleep every night. My biggest fan was gone, my largest supporter of my own sufferings with my daughter was gone and I was struggling to get though each day every day.

Shortly after, maybe four or five months after my mom died, I had a dream about her. In my dream my mom was sitting on top of a doctors' table. She was telling me, "Come on Marybeth get up. You have to go to your doctor's appointment today, please get up. I will go with you if you like and I will even drive you, but you have to go. You must stop canceling these appointments."

What was strange about my dream was that I was missing appointments. I was missing everything. I wouldn't leave the house or go anywhere. I was so depressed. I was late getting the kids to school for the longest time. I was having trouble sleeping at night and then at some point during the wee hours of the morning I would fall asleep and then not hear my alarm clock and we would all be late.

I was managing to get to my psychiatrist's office, and he was doing everything he could to help me. The problem was that I refused to take medications. Some years back while trying to cope with EB I tried a number of various drugs or anti-depressant medications and it just seemed liked none of them worked for *me*. I had been seeing the same doctor for years since Sam was about two or three I think and he knew me well. He would always tell me he did not know how I managed to be ok, and if I were his wife I'd be on something.

The drugs just made me feel numb, but I wanted to feel what I was going through. More importantly I wanted God to help me get through it.

I agreed to take a mild sedative occasionally to help me sleep or to help me with my panic attacks, but as far as the medication for depression, I refused.

I kept praying and asking God to help me, and I would talk to my mom as if she were sitting right next to me. Crying to her was more like it. When I was young, about five or six years old, my mom and I shared some tender moments together. One of those moments stands out in my memory very clearly. My mom was a concert pianist and she played the piano much of my life as a child as I was growing up. Mostly she played what I used to refer to as "opera" music but today I call it by its real name: Mozart, Bach and Beethoven or just "classical" music. One thing my mom did have an abundance of was "class." Not often, but occasionally, she would play contemporary music or something off the greatest hits chart. Well, there was this one song called "You Light Up My Life" by Debbie Boone. I have happy memories of her playing that song as I stood there next to her singing it just as loud and proud as I could. I still remember her face beaming with joy, as she loved to hear me sing. That song was popular back in the early 70's and I had not heard it being played on our local radio stations in years, like 30 plus years. Just before my mom died I told her to send me a sign and let me know she was ok wherever it is she was going. We had silent agreements too about her talking face-to-face with God and begging Him to cure Sam from this life of hell with EB as well.

One morning when my alarm clock went off, that song, "You Light Up My Life," started to play from the very beginning. My radio alarm was just set on whatever top hit radio station I happen to be listening to at that time and I can assure you none of them had been playing Debbie Boone anything. I sat straight up in my bed - I felt like someone had just splashed a bucket of cold water on my face. I knew at that very instant that my mom was where she needed to be and that she was letting me know she was ok. That was my sign. Me sitting straight up in my bed was alarm enough for my husband to jump and say, "Are you okay, honey? What's wrong?"

I answered, "Listen… it is the song my mom used to play for me when I was a child and I would sing to her. She is letting me know she is ok and she is helping me wake up. She came to me in a dream and now she is sending me a sign."

Jim was also close to my mom and I know he believed that too. I just smiled and took the comfort in knowing she was there.

One time I was at a doctor's appointment and for some reason I had Sam with me. Now that was unusual because I never brought my children to any of *my* doctor appointments with me. Anyway, this was just a flu shot so I didn't think anything of it. By this time I couldn't remember what I did the day before let alone what I was actually doing.

I also had a hard time staying focused on anything. The sadness that ached in my heart was painful. When the doctor walked into the room she started off her hello with, "Mrs. Sheridan I am sorry to inform you but you have missed two appointments with us. One of them you did not call to let us know, so we are going to have to ask you to find another primary care doctor." Now this wasn't a doctor that I knew very well, and I rarely ever went to the doctors, so I had never really met this particular doctor before. I had changed primary care doctors as my insurance carriers changed. Sam was sitting right next me and I just burst out into tears. I was sobbing. The poor doctor stood up and was visibly shaken by my breakdown. Sam was holding my arm and comforting me. The doctor, confused, said, "Mrs. Sheridan are you ok?" I responded, "My mom just died. I am sorry if I missed the appointments but I am afraid I have missed more than just appointments." Tears were just rushing down my cheeks as I was trying very hard to control myself but to no avail - I was sobbing.

That was the first time I realized that I wasn't functioning.

It took me more than a year but slowly I got up and started to live again. Losing my mom was like nothing I had ever imagined it would be, but honestly I don't think I ever thought too much about losing her. I just always thought she would always be here.

Chapter 53.

Hospice the Second Time Around

About two months after my mom passed on Sam's skin started to take a turn for the worse. Nothing we tried was working to close up her wounds. She had infections constantly which meant she was in her normal pain magnified by 10. Her baths became unbearable. The amount of open raw wounds and blisters on her body was more than 70% of her body. She could barley walk she was in so much pain. I was begging and pleading with all of her doctors to help me. I was even considering not making her get in her bath because the pain was just too much. We had tried almost every pain medicine out there. Sam started to have severe allergy reactions to almost any new drug she was put on. Realizing this, her infectious disease doctor decided it was best for us to use the services at Hospice and see if there wasn't some way to help with the pain control. I remember Dr. Emmanuel calling me up on the phone to discuss the Hospice idea. She was also worried that we would be faced with a life-threatening situation either on a Friday night or in the middle of the night. That is sort of how every situation went with us. Samantha's infections were out of control and antibiotics were just not working. IV or Oral.

Not having any other alternative for the pain, and really no other choices, I agreed. It was a good idea because this way we could try pain medicines in the comfort of our own home and be monitored by professionals who would know what to do in the event we did have a situation.

The surprise for us was that the same nurse that had just been at my home not even two months before for my mom was now walking through my door again for my daughter.

It was a little bit awkward and comforting at the same time. We absolutely adored Mary. She was warm and sweet and everything she ever said just made you feel loved, no matter what was going on.

Everyday someone from Hospice would come out and evaluate Sam. Mostly it was Mary, but sometimes other nurses would come out as well. No matter which nurse it was they all got the same feeling that Sam was in tremendous pain and her prognosis was not good. There were times when Mary or one of the other nurses would come and they were witness to hours of pain and suffering Sam would have to endure. Most often at times they (the nurses) would leave our house crying. I swear it felt like we tried a different pain medicine every three or four days. Nothing was helping or working. At one point the Hospice team had their directors come out to evaluate Sam so that maybe they could come up with some kind of recommendation. They could see her wounds and they could see her pain. They all knew she was very sick and yet nothing they could offer to help relieve the pain was working. The list of drugs Sam was allergic to was growing by the day and now it was starting to include antibiotics.

On bandage change days Jim and I were learning to get Chloe and James out of the house so that when I did the bandages the little children would not hear the screaming and crying. The constant agony was taking a toll on all of us. It was mid-afternoon and only Sam and I were in the house on this particular day. We live in a large house and we have a sophisticated alarm system that allowed us to set it in a way that if the doors open (from outside to inside or vice versa) there would be a little "beep-beep" noise to alert us that someone was either entering or leaving the house.

The phone rang and it was our Hospice nurse Mary. She was calling to tell me that Hospice had tried every medication there was and that she was very sorry but there was nothing she could do. I just stood there holding the phone fighting back the tears and trying to stay strong. Sam was right next to me and I did not want to show her I was scared. I didn't even want her to know really what was being said, although undoubtedly I would have to tell her. At that very moment we heard the door chimes – the 'beep beep' as if someone had opened a door. So I thanked Mary for her help and told her I was in the middle of bandages and that I would get back to her later. As I hung up the phone we heard the door chimes again, but we both knew no one was in the house but her and I. I knew that Jim had taken the kids to the park up the street. Sam and I just looked at each other and then Sam said, "It's Mom-moms." I called Jim and asked him where he was and he confirmed that he was at the park. No one was in the house. I got up and ran around real quick to check to see if by chance anyone was there but there was no one.

We both agreed it had to be Mom-moms as she was the only person who would have known at that very moment the devastation of the news I had just received on the phone. No more medicines for Sam meant no more options to help with the pain. My mom was always the first one to comfort me or be there for me whenever we would get bad news about Sam. For the past twelve years EB had done nothing but offer us bad news over and over again.

So after the door chime incident was over and both Sam and I took comfort in knowing that it was Mom-moms just letting us know she was with us, we sat and talked about the call from Mary. I stayed strong but it was very hard. What was more important was that I stayed positive - which was a very hard thing to do.

I started thinking that praying for a miracle for a cure was pointless. The miracle was feeling more and more out of reach with every passing day that I had to watch her suffer and endure more pain. I was losing hope by the second and my faith in God was weakening. I couldn't grasp why God was letting this happen, and furthermore I really couldn't understand why God would make my beautiful daughter suffer in such an inhumane way. Nothing about Sam's suffering made any sense at all to me. I mean, I had been praying for her to be cured or for a miracle for 12 years now and nothing, *nothing*, was getting any better. Every day, every week, every year was only bringing new challenges, new complications, and more and more pain and suffering. I had decided in my mind that if I was truly selfless and I wanted what was best for my daughter that I would have to start praying differently. I would have to start asking God to please make her suffering stop whatever way He saw fit. If he was not going to cure her then "take her home to be with you Lord and to be in peace, because as her mother I cannot bear to witness one more moment of her suffering, and as her mother I know in my heart that wanting her to be with me like this was wrong." Maybe it is my fault she is not getting better and the miracle has not happened. Maybe it is my fault because maybe I am not praying the right way. I knew for sure I was praying enough because after all these years of "practice praying" I was literally praying to God for a miracle every time I saw her suffer, which was pretty much the entire time she was awake. It was breaking my heart as a mother, and breaking my soul as a person. I knew I would give my life for her so maybe I should give up what I want and start asking God to do what *His will* was to be. From this time on in my life my prayers changed from asking for a miracle to asking for my sweet Sam to just have some peace in her life no matter what that meant: Here on earth, or there with God in heaven. Her peace and freedom of pain was more important to me than anything else in the world.

There were only a few people very close to me that I would ever share this thought with. One was my friend Anita who had just an incredible faith in God. I remember telling her one time that I had changed my prayers. Anita had a strong adverse reaction to my newfound wisdom. She urged me not to pray for this and told me she did not understand. Anita still believed that a miracle was a real possiblilty. I could barley speak the words without tears running down my face, and I was the person who never cried anymore. That's right, I had become so strong that crying never even happened anymore unless I was talking about giving up or giving in. I told my best friends that I have had since middle school what I was feeling and that I just didn't think it was fair to continue on being selfish and praying for her to always be here. Again tears would rush to my cheeks and the pain of speaking this thought was hard to get loose from my lips. I knew they didn't understand, and how could they anyway? You could only understand this if you were living it. I think at times I started to get angry when any of them would say, "Oh she is going to be ok Marybeth, and God is going to cure her. You have to believe in miracles." I would get so angry that I would want to yell at them because they had no clue what they were talking about and how could they, right? Anita had a tiny clue because she witnessed bandage changes a few times. Anita was only one of a very few people who Sam would let into her EB bandage hell.

I mean, they didn't live with EB though, and they really did not have a clue what it was like to live with EB anyway. If I were to have called another EB mom like my friend Denise I could almost always share my new thought with her and she would be able to finish my thought word-for-word. She knew, and she also knew what it was like to have friends all of your life and than to have EB friends.

It was impossible to ask someone to feel something that they just did not know. I knew my sisters both sort of knew because Rita actually did bandages with Sam when she was a baby a whole bunch of times. Cathy had been around us and with us enough to witness the horror Sam endured. Anita had a little understanding because there was a time that Anita would come over and sit with us while I did bandages. Looking at Sam's battered body was difficult for anyone to do and Sam was extremely picky about who she let see her body un-wrapped. If I was doing bandages and having a hard time getting through it because the pain of watching her suffer was unbearable Anita would literally drop what she was doing and race over to sit with me to lend a hand. The look on her face and the tears in her eyes of being witness to the sufferings of this precious, amazing little girl I know forever have scared her soul. How can it not? Watching a child suffer in this way was not normal. It was not right. But that is what EB was.

One of the most valuable lessons in my life that I have ever learned is this: Be very cautious and careful how you treat another person when you do not know what their life is like. Sometimes people are in pain and you don't even know it. Sometimes the pain is so severe it makes the person fragile, and what is worse is that it is a pain that you can't see. The pain a mother feels when her child suffers from getting physically hurt is brutal. Imagine watching your child being tortured day-in and day-out for 12 years and then tell me how that mother should respond in society. It wasn't a wonder that I wasn't asking God to just take me. I didn't do that, but I did start to examine what I was praying for and how, and I also started having compassion for people without even knowing them.

I was also learning how to be less and less selfish about my wants and needs and started to think in terms of what is best for my child - no matter what the expense of my heart.

I do think our prayers get answered, but not always the way in which we ask for them. Most of these chance meetings or situations that have occurred during my journey with Sam I feel were all part of the grand plan to expand and enlighten my understanding of God and all that exist in our life. I think when we are losing our way we are given signs and situations from other people to help steer us back on track. Sometimes it could be that one person that you meet for the first time who just says three words that were meant to be spoken to just you, or maybe it is the "old man" who presented an opportunity for you to see that we are all here to help each other and that life is not always all about getting so self-absorbed, even though you think your problems are much worse than the next person. I think I have lost my way plenty of times, but I was always fortunate enough to have kept my eyes and ears open to the messages God was sending to me.

Chapter 54.

The Story About the Honey

At some point during the year 2007, wounds went from bad to worse and she started running very high temperatures. It had been agreed upon a few years back when the secondary infection first reared its ugly head that I would alert the ID doctor if Sam got any fevers that were over 101. She was starting to run 101, 102 temps and we were all scrambling for what to do. Wound care wasn't working. IV antibiotics were not working. And her wounds were taking longer to heal than ever before. Dr. Emmanuel told me that Sam needed a blood transfusion. Her hemoglobin was hovering around seven and at times lower. Dr. Emmanuel was hesitant to do the blood infusion due to the very strange reactions Sam always has with drugs. She felt that an allergic reaction to a blood transfusion could be deadly.

Regardless, Sam needed another pic line because we needed to be back on IV antibiotics. Maybe now we would do a combination of antibiotic drugs and try for a longer length of time. When we got to the hospital we would than decide if we wanted to do the blood transfusion or not. As we were driving to the hospital Dr. Emmanuel called me to tell me that she may not be able to get to that hospital, but that we would get a direct admit anyway. A direct admit is when the admitting physician phones the hospital prior to your arrival and grants you permission to bypass the Emergency Room and go directly to the room on the unit floor you will be staying in.

When we finally arrived at the hospital I did my usual "clean everything" routine. I am super paranoid about hospitals. I think hospitals have more germs and more ways to get germs than any other place on the planet. I mean, I am crazy about it. I bring my OdoBan in and I clean the door handles, phone, floors, walls, and bed, everything that she comes in contact with. I have read so many stories about normal people without skin conditions like EB walking into the hospital for a routine surgery and leaving with MRSA, which is a worse problem than you can even know. MRSA stands for Methicillin Resistant Staph Aureus

– the resistant means that it is a bacterium that only few drugs will kill -
and *few* meaning one or two. For an EB child, MRSA can be deadly and
much more worrisome than pseudomonas. So it was always my goal
when going to a hospital with Sam for any reason to get in and get out,
and if we have to be in for any length of time - even if it is for an hour or
two - then I bring my own cleaning supplies.

So while I was being a clean-a-phobic Dr. Emmanuel phoned me
again to tell me that she really didn't want to inform me of what she was
about to say over the phone, but she really had no other choice.
I thought she was going to tell me something was wrong with her. I had
no idea what was getting ready to come out of her mouth. Then she
explained, "You see I have been working on this other project for the
University and I really am not practicing Infectious Disease anymore, but
I didn't want to lose you guys as patients. I thought I could keep you but
now here you are in the hospital and I can't get to you. So what I am
trying to say to you is that right now right outside your door there is
a new ID doctor who will be taking care of you from now on."

'Wow' – that is all I could think.

I can't even remember what I said back to her I was in such shock.
I know she felt bad, but, man alive, here I was with Sam in this hospital
where the only doctor that I knew who worked out of there had just
dumped me over the phone. Sam was sick and she needed a pic line.
What other choice did I have? I figured I might as well go outside the
room and meet our new doctor, but I wasn't happy. I know I wasn't nice
about it either.

So I opened up the door and walked outside the room. He was
sitting there in this chair, very calm looking and quiet. The only thing
I could think of was, " Oh My God, I have a brand new ID doctor that
knows *nothing* about EB and we are in the middle of a dog fight with
EB." I went rambling on about what we wanted and what Sam needed
and he just listened. I told him, "Look we just need a pic line placed or
a central line so it stays in the vein for longer than 10 days. A regular pic
line will only be good for seven to ten days at the most, and we need
a line in place for at least two weeks so we can give her a good long dose
of IV antibiotics." Here I was acting like the doctor and telling him what
to do. It can be very unsettling when you lose a doctor you trust on the
spot while your child is extremely ill and in need of medical attention.
God had other plans for us though. His name was Dr. Juan Dumois. He
was nice - he listened - he agreed we needed IV drugs and he agreed we

needed a line to be in for longer than 10 days. I am not so sure he was crazy about giving us a line and sending us home for me to administer IV drugs, but he didn't know me yet.

We got the line in. That was a whole ordeal all by itself because Sam does not tolerate the OR too well. She always opts for having the IV teams come to the room, numbing the area and placing the line while she is awake. Most kids go to the Operating Room and go completely under sedation to have their lines placed. There we were in a room. I was standing to one side of her bed rubbing her head and my husband was next to me down by her legs. On the other side of the bed was the IV team attempting to insert this little rubber plastic tube line in a vein in her arm that would go up her arm across her chest and to her heart. Between Sam's fear and anxiety, and the stress of not hurting her skin, I could feel the stress and tension in the room building. There were two ladies from the IV team in the room. As my focus shifted from Samantha's face to the area where the two ladies were working, I noticed dark red blood everywhere instantly. Next thing I know my husband is face down on the bed. I think he passed out from the sight of the blood. The ladies on the IV team asked me, "Is he ok?" To which I answered, "We don't have time to worry about him, he will be fine let's just get that line in." They both giggled, I think Sam may have even thought that was funny too.

The line went in. The blood transfusion was discussed but decided against due to all of the drug allergies. What was decided on was a shot that we would give her in her stomach that would stimulate red cell production. We went home and a few days had passed. I had been giving Sam her IV medications faithfully around the clock and I didn't miss even one dose. Still nothing seemed to be working. Sam was still running high fevers and her wounds were looking worse than ever. The Hospice nurses were still coming out and offering support, but really they were at a loss as to what to do too. So Dr. Dumois had us come into his office so he could take a look at Sam's wounds. After he looked at all of her wounds he sat down in his chair and he told me that since the IV drugs did not seem to be helping that he thought we should pull the line out. I remember having this awful feeling of "oh no he is giving up on her." He told me that he wanted to try something new, new to me maybe, but not necessarily new to him. He told me that he wanted me to go and get some honey. I said, "What did you just say? Did I hear you right? You said honey, as in 'the honey we eat' honey?" And he said "yes" and then went on to explain that in past experiences he has had plenty of success with the use of honey on a skin infection that was troublesome to heal. He said that he tried to find some actual case studies on wound healing and honey for EB and was not successful, but he wanted to try it anyway as bacteria cannot live in honey. Ok… so I thought this man was nuts. Either that or he was trying to get rid of us. But honey? No way.

The entire ride home in the car I was ranting and raving about how 'the really great doctor' (or so I thought) was a wacko. I mean, is this man crazy or what? I never heard of anyone using honey to put on their wounds. Actually, I really did hear about honey a few years ago from another EB mom named Nancy. Nancy is one the most amazing women I know and she served her time well in the EB community. Sadly Nancy lost two beautiful daughters to EB. I have a ton of respect for her as well but when she told me about the honey and how well it was helping her daughters I thought to myself, "Well it sounds ok I guess, but I am just not ready to try that yet." And honestly the honey was just one of those things that I put on the back burner of my mind for another day. Having a child with special needs presents opportunity for lots of people to come into your life and offer lots of different kinds of products and ideas. As a matter of fact in the past 12 years of Sam's life I have had so many products and things suggested to us to try for Samantha that at some point everything was going to 'the back' burner.

Sam is the level headed one and I am the emotional train wreck. She was like, "Mom can you just stop at the store and get the honey?" So we did! Then we went home, did bandages, and tried the honey. At first it was tricky to use and challenging to figure out. We had to learn how to put it on the wounds, and by learning that we learned that it couldn't go directly on the wounds - it had to first be applied to the actual bandage we were going to use. Finding the right bandage and the correct way to apply the honey took trial and error to get it right. We learned that when honey is on your body your body temperature will melt it and it will leak off of you like water, so we had to find ways to prevent sticky from getting all over everything. Did you know bees love honey? Well Sam was a walking bee magnet. We learned, and we were thankful and grateful for what we learned.

After about two weeks of using the honey Sam's wounds healed up and completely closed. Her fevers stopped and almost magically she felt better. I just could not believe it. I mean who would have ever thought that something as simple as honey could save my daughter's life? And yes, I say 'save' because one of the leading causes of death for an EB child is secondary infection and/or complications that arise due to secondary infection. So if you can manage an EB child's infections then that is half the battle. The other part is if you can slow the blistering down or reduce the amount of wounds on an EB's child's body at any given time then their quality of life becomes so much better, too.

You can imagine what out next office visit to our new ID doctor was like. My tail was between my legs. He was our new hero. Our local NBC news station got wind of our success with honey and contacted us for an interview. I believe you can still go to their website ("Myfoxtampabay.com"). Click on the Health button and search for the story called "The Golden Elixir" to see the story. The reporter's name is Dr. Joette Giovinco. The coverage that our local news gave the honey was amazing. Not only did people get to learn how great honey can be to heal any kind of wound or infection, but they also got to learn a little bit about EB as well. That was great all by itself because by this time in Sam's life I had scaled way back on all of my volunteering for EB and all of my fundraising for EB due to the plain and simple fact that there were just not enough hours in the day to do any of that. Sam's bandages by now were taking four to eight hours every other day and three to four hours on the opposite days due to the amount of wounds and blistering that was occurring. The beauty about the honey was that it allowed her skin to heal allowing us more free time to live instead of being held hostage to the almighty wound care we had become so used to. Also, the honey allowed Sam to have a much-needed break from the use of all the antibiotics she had to be on for the past couple of years.

The way certain people came into our lives at just the right time was only something I know divine intervention could have been responsible for, when I prayed for things. For example, I prayed for strength all the time and before I knew it I was strong. Then I prayed for a miracle to heal Sam, and really that had been a favorite prayer for years and years, well, since she was born really, but instead of the miracle I was getting people that would come into our lives and represent this value that could have only come from God and His answers to the prayers that I was clinging onto as a lifeline. The miracle was in the rescuing of our sanity, and in the comfort of our souls.

When I say people, I mean friends, doctors, strangers like the old man who needed his shoes tied, all of these people played meaningful, but very different roles in our life, and ultimately came to us because I asked for them to come. Sort of like a lifeline in the course of this life.

I was becoming more aware of these gifts that God was sending with every new day. Dr. Dumois was an answer to prayer and literally with something as simple as honey we now had quality in our lives. My friend Mary from Hospice was tearful but happy the day she had to come to our home and disorient Samantha from Hospice care. Mary told me that it was the first time that she ever disoriented a patient from Hospice's care. I am sure you all are aware of what Hospice is and that all of their patients are, for the most part, terminally ill. Well Sam was terminally ill, too, but because the honey had sort of put her in this 'remission' (if you will – because I really don't what else to call it), Hospice had no real reason to continue their care or visits.

Sam was getting better and stronger by the day and by the beginning of her eighth grade year she was seeing light in her day.

Chapter 55.

Miley

Samantha always had a love for music. I am sure it is no coincidence that her love for music had something to with my mother's passion for music. My mom used to tell all of us that music was the way to the soul, and incorporating classical music in a child's life at a young age not only made them brilliant, but taught so many valuable life lessons and skills. From the time Sam was very young she was attracted to the female guitarist and vocalist. When she was in kindergarten her "Make a Wish" was to meet Brittney Spears and she did. Then when Sam was about 10 or 11, the Hannah Montana show first started to air with Miley Cyrus and her dad Billy Ray Cyrus. Sam became a Miley fan instantly. I remember in 2006 Chloe and Sam both wanted to go see "The Cheetah Girls." One of my best friend's Kristy and her daughter Kassidy went with us as well. At that time I didn't even know who Miley Cyrus was but I knew she was opening for The Cheetah Girls, and I also knew Sam was very enamored with her. We did not have front row seats, but I think our seat we pretty good and I just remember when Miley opened for The Cheetah Girls Sam stood up and really zoned in on her performance. The crowd did seem to go crazy for Miley back then and that was long before the rest of the world knew who she was, but Sam was in awe of her at the very beginning. Sam always was a good judge of character.

About a year or so after The Cheetah Girls concert Miley Cyrus and The Hannah Montana Show had really taken off and Miley was the biggest name on TV and on the radio station at the same time. The second she heard that Miley was coming into town for the concert she didn't ask if she could go, she just asked what time are we gonna' get there?

Jim got us tickets. He got four for us and four for my friend Anita. I took Sam, Chloe and Sam's BFF Meghan, and Anita took her two grandchildren along with a close friend and neighbor's daughter as well. It was Allison's (our neighbor's daughter) first concert. Maybe about a year before the concert, or as soon as it became available, Sam became a member of the Miley Fan Club. When you do that you pay a fee and they send you a Miley Fan Club Card that had Sam's name on it and a picture of Miley. It kind of looks like a drivers license, very cool idea actually.

Anita and I decided that we would meet at our house. Sam was going to need her wheelchair but instead of her power chair she wanted me to bring the manual pushchair so that we could sit in a regular chair at the concert and fold her pushchair up and get it out of the way. Anita and her crew came to the house and we were getting ready to get in the car when I noticed Sam pulling papers off the printer.

"Sam what are you doing?" I asked as she was counting the papers in her hand.

She said, "I'm printing out photos of Miley, mom." And then I saw her looking for permanent markers in my drawer.

"Oh. Why are you doing that honey?"

Sam sort of paused and said nothing. That is her way of telling me that she doesn't want the entire room to hear her. Then she said quietly, "So when we meet Miley she can sign these photographs for all of us."

Anita and I looked at each other as if to say, "Oh my, hmm... yeah, I don't think we are going to meet Miley at the concert," but we didn't say that we just thought it. Sam gave each of the girls an 8x10 photo of Miley very nicely printed out on photo quality paper and a pen to go with the photo. We all piled in the car and started on our way. Anita was secretly and quietly telling me as I was driving, "Hey, you better let these kids know that they are not going to meet the celebrity at this concert," and I was secretly and quietly responding back to her, "Yeah I know. Believe me I am thinking about how to do that right now." Just then we passed the back of the Ice Palace in Tampa where the concert was going to take place. As we were driving past, the Miley tour bus was parked and loads of people looked to be unloading the bus. We couldn't really make out who was around the bus but the girls got very excited in the car and started screaming and yelling with excitement that they couldn't wait to get to the concert and that they couldn't wait to meet Miley. That was my queue: "Girls, I am sorry to have to tell you this but I don't think we are going to get to meet the celebrity tonight. I mean I have been to loads of concerts myself and not one time did I ever meet the person singing or performing. It just doesn't work like that. First of all, thousands of people are going to be there and we are not even close to sitting around where the front of the stage is, or where she will be performing, so I just don't think that is going to happen."

But I followed up my bad news with, "Well, maybe, I guess. You just never know about these kinds of things and, well, Sam seems to think she is going to meet her so let's just get in there and enjoy the show."

Sam wanted us to get to the concert early because since she was a member of the Miley Fan Club she got invited to the Miley pre-party prior to the concert. The concert started at 6 pm and we got there around 4:30 pm, so we were there in plenty of time for the pre-party. We found a parking spot and walked up to the open area where the pre-party was gathering, which was right out side of the building of where the actual concert was going to take place. Parked right out front was a huge, pink, RV-looking bus with a gigantic picture of Miley Cyrus's face on both sides. There was a very long line of people standing out front of the bus. We couldn't make out what everyone was waiting on though, and then there was just hundreds of people sort of scattered everywhere. There was a small boxed shaped booth situated right in the center of the whole pre-party and it sat in-between the building the concert was in and the bus, then, in a diamond-shaped sort of way, they had a make shift stage set up. From the sound of things we guessed that the person on the stage talking must be the person running the whole Miley Fan Club.

Frankly I was overwhelmed and stressed out just thinking about getting into any of those lines. I think the stress was coming from the idea that Sam was a target for pain, the only thing running through my mind was, How am I going to protect her from this raging crowd of people who are not even going to notice that she is (number one) – in bandages and, (number two) - in a wheelchair?"

So we sort of stood around grasping the whole situation and really confused as to what to do or where to go. It really didn't feel like a pre-party, but then again I wasn't sure what a pre-party for the most popular actress/teen sensation pop star would be like. You can believe that Sam knew what to do though. She wanted to go stand in line at this booth because they were giving out raffle tickets. We did not know at that time what the raffle tickets were for. All we knew was that we were standing in line to get one – all eight of us. As we approached the person before the counter of the booth we noticed that she handed the person in front of us green tickets, but the girl in front of that one she gave pink tickets too. So Sam asked her why she was giving out different colored tickets, and happily she answered, "Oh, well if you are a Miley Fan Club member you get the green tickets, and if you are not a member you get the pink tickets." Sam told the girl that we were all members and she pulled out her Miley Fan Club card from her wallet and handed it to her, and sure enough she gave all of us two each of the green raffle tickets. All the girls were happy and thanked Sam and I know no one even knew why we were happy, but just that we felt lucky that we were getting special tickets now. I can laugh thinking about it because we still at that point had no idea what the tickets were even for. Then, as we walked away from the booth the man on the stage was talking so loudly that our attention was drawn to him immediately.

We heard "raffle ticket drawing ten minutes for back stage passes, bus tour passes, and front row seats", and other Miley novelty items as well. We were racing to get to where we could see that person on the stage better and where we could hear him better. I swear there were fifteen thousand people crowded around this stage by now and we could barley move we were squeezed in there so tightly. Seriously, my elbows were hitting the persons on either side of me and it was all I could do to protect Sam from getting bumped or tripped over or worse. The announcer explained to all of us that he was only giving out two backstage passes and two front row seat tickets, but that he had lots of other goodies to give out as well. He told the massive crowd of people that if he called their raffle ticket numbers and they did not respond to him in a matter of minutes that he would pick another raffle ticket out of the hat and call a different number. He also stated that if you get the winning number and he acknowledges you that you had better get to the front of the stage pronto or else he would be forced to give your prize to someone else because they were going to be in a serious time crunch as the concert was going to start on time whether you were where you were supposed to be or not.

I very clearly remember looking at our raffle tickets and looking up to the sky as if my mom were right up there looking down on us, and in my mind blocking everything else out except for this, "Please let 456817 (or whatever the number was because that was not it I am just using that as an example) win. Please let Sam's wish come true." The announcer started to call out the numbers. Anita and I looked so frantic or at least it was how I was feeling at that moment. I was also thinking, "Gosh - how the heck are we going to make it to the stage if we are called?" We were about one hundred feet from the stage, and then about five hundred feet from the building, and there were thousands of people between those to destinations and us.

The next thing I heard was "456818." My heart stopped. I knew we had to have had that number because it was so close to the one I just saw. I looked at Anita and she at me and then suddenly Meghan (Sam's BFF) started jumping up and down screaming, "I won, I won, I have the winning ticket." Meghan's raffle ticket had won and it was for one of the backstage passes. We were all crazy screaming and yelling, hugging and crying, and trying to move to get the announcer to get the ticket but people were so crammed together I couldn't move the wheelchair. There was so much noise and utter chaos and as I am trying to move I looked up at Anita who was jumping up and down and yelling at the announcer, "We won, we have the other ticket!" I get chills down my back writing about it because the irony of all of that was unreal. Anita's granddaughter Sophie had won the second backstage pass!!!! What were the odds of that? It was destiny: it was Sam's wish and it was coming true. We were like crazy caged up animals getting to that stage to only then discover that the announcer said that only the ticket holder and one other person could go back to meet Miley. Awww man! Right on top of the instant, massive high was a massive blow to the ground. "What? You are kidding right? There are 8 of us, are you telling me we have to choose which child gets to meet her?" Can you imagine the emotion we were feeling and on top of the emotion was this pressure that time was slipping away as the announcer said firmly, "Yes only two get to go back and the rest have to wait outside, and if you don't get to the building in three minutes you will miss your chance to meet her at all."

We had no time to argue... We RAN!

I still don't remember how we got to the building or how we managed to squeeze past all those people but we did. As we flew through the door a security person was there to greet us. She looked at our tickets. She was holding this clip board and as she was flipping the pages looking for what floor and area we needed to be, she was explaining that all of us could not go back and that, in fact, we probably already missed the chance to meet her because Miley was already done with the "meet and greet." We were experiencing major ups and major downs in a matter of minutes apart from each other, and the intensity was unreal. I looked dead into that woman's eyes and said, "We are not late and we are going to meet her. Now look - I just had to get her and her wheelchair through hundreds of people and she won. Now you are not going to tell her she can't meet Miley after all we had to do to get here to this spot? And what do you think I am going to do with my other children? Leave them here to get kidnapped? No they are at least going up to the floor with me to where we need to go and they can wait outside the door!" She looked at me, looked at Sam and signaled us to go back. As we were getting on the elevator Anita was giving me that frantic friend look and saying, "How? How are we going to do this Marybeth? That woman said we have to go through three more security checkpoints? How are we going to choose between the eight of us?"

I just looked at Anita and said, "Don't worry, don't say anything, stay behind me and follow me - no matter what I do, ok?"

Out of the corner of my eye was this elderly man with a suit on signaling me to come to him. He overheard me telling the girls not to worry to follow my instruction and stay close. With a wink of his eye he whispered in my ear, "Follow me. I am security and I will get you past the next two checkpoints. What you do beyond that is up to you". He got the biggest smile of relief from Sam and I. Little angels were all around us helping to make this moment magical for sweet Sam. We did exactly what he told us and we followed him past the next security checkpoints, at which time the girl with the winning ticket and one of us had to go one way and the others had to go another way. In a matter of split seconds Anita and I had to not only choose, but have a plan and pray. That is exactly what we did too, because I don't remember discussing a plan. I went with Sam. Kassidy went with her younger niece Sophie, or at least I think that is how we split up, all I know is that I told Meghan to stay with Chloe and meet us on the next floor up where we were headed and if anyone gave them a hard time to run.

Sam and I got to the "meet and greet" station they had set up. There she was: Miley sitting at a six-foot long banquet table as each girl in line walked up to her and got their pictures taken and *if they brought a photo*, they got to get their photo's (or whatever it is they brought) signed by Miley too. I was so frantic and worried about Anita and Chloe and Meghan, Sophie and Allison that I could barely stay focused on any one thing.

First of all, I could not believe that we were actually standing in a line about to meet the celebrity of this huge concert that I was certain before we even came that we were not going to meet. Second I was in utter amazement of how my Samantha knew from the moment she knew we had tickets to go to this concert that she was going to meet this person that she idolized. Miley represented all of the things that Sam wanted to be – healthy, pretty, popular, singer, songwriter and guitar player and able to do what ever she wanted in life. Free from pain, and free from bandages.

Suddenly my little angel Chloe came running down the hall towards me. Oh, what a relief it was to see her face among all of the girls! Anita came up behind them and we hugged and cried and gave thanks to God for this incredibly special moment that was about to happen. Sam went in front of me, but she insisted I fold up her wheelchair and hide it out of the way so Miley would not see her in it. Sam had her bandages covered up with a long sleeve shirt she was wearing. Sam almost always wore long sleeve shirts to cover up her bandages. I understood why, but we live in Florida where the temperature is always 100 degrees and I would worry that she was going to get too hot or cause more blisters by creating heat. Heat and sweat were not her friends and at times I would notice that those two earth elements together would only cause more damage to her skin. I admired Sam - though mostly for her bravery. As her mom I watched her walk up to that table to meet this person that in my heart I knew my sweet Sam wanted to be just like, and in my heart I also knew that Miley would not know what bravery it would take for Sam to meet her.

My intense awe of that moment was abruptly disrupted when, all of a sudden, a man trying to hurry the line of people meeting Miley gave Sam a little shove as if to say, "Ok, hurry up now and move on." I know Sam did not even have enough time to get words out. Scrambling for what to do just like that it was too late. The man had pretty much put his hand on Sam's back and gently pushed her away from the table. As she walked away my heart sank to the ground. I was mortified. My tiger instincts were flying out and ready to attack, but I was next up so in another moment of making a split-second choice I decided to make the best of it and tell Miley who Sam was while I was there. That is exactly what I did, as I leaned across the table for the photo op I said to Miley, "That precious little girl that was just in front of me was my daughter Sam and I am not sure if you noticed but she has a problem with her skin." Miley made eye contact with me and replied, "Oh really?" So I quickly wrote down my EBAN & DEBRA website and handed her the piece of paper and said, "Yeah and I know how busy you must be, but if you have a chance can you check out these two websites because actually we desperately need a celebrity to help our campaign for awareness."

Of course the man that shoed Sam away way shooing me as I was talking and as quick as it all happened it was over. We all met at the elevators and we were escorted back to the concert area and our seats. The girls were on the magical high - beaming with over-zealous excitement.

The whole experience of meeting Miley made the concert one of those concerts that you go to that you will never forget. Every song she sang was amazing and every day from that day reminded us of just how lucky we are.

About six months after we had the chance meeting of Miley, our neighbor gave us tickets to the Billy Rae Cyrus concert, which was being held at the Strawberry Festival. They also arranged for Samantha to meet Billy Ray backstage before the concert. It was really a weird set of circumstances. I mean who would have ever thought Sam would get to meet Miley and then six months later get to meet her dad? We took a family picture with Billy Ray (who, by the way, was very nice). You can tell when you meet him he is genuinely nice. I went prepared to that backstage meeting. I had written a three-page letter asking him for his help or if he knew any celebrity who could help get the awareness out about EB. Sam wrote Miley a letter and we put my letter, Sam's letter, and the photo of Miley and Sam in a large envelope. I personally handed it to Billy Ray and told him that there was a letter in there from Sam to his daughter, and another letter from me to he and his wife to ask for their support of our non-profit organization DEBRA or EBAN. He handed the envelope to a man who looked like his brother. Billy Ray asked the man to make sure he took special care of that envelope so he could read it when the concert was over.

We never heard from him. I have to tell you that we were disappointed, but at the same time we understand that these celebrities must get asked to support everything on the planet. They probably get so much mail and so many letters like the one I wrote that it is humanly impossible to read all of them. Still it was a let down.

Chapter 56.

New Discoveries

By 2008 Sam was feeling good. Her wounds and her skin were almost all better because of our new friend "The Honey." The blistering had slowed from 50-plus a day down to 10 or 20 a day. Sam was entering the 8th grade which also meant she was ending her middle school year and ending a nine-year stretch at her favorite school ever, Most Holy Redeemer. By eighth grade, every single faculty member and student pretty much in the entire school knew who Samantha Sheridan was. Sam was a person many would admire and be inspired by. By this point most of the students and teachers knew what Sam had to go through just to get to school, and how extremely difficult and painful her life was.

With every grade she entered I would always work with Mr. Coffaro (the Principal) and her teachers to create this student support plan due to the rigid schedule of bath and bandages. Most of the times Sam would be late to school or not go at all depending on what was going on at that point. I can't recall every single person by name, but many people would always tell me that by having met Sam she changed their lives one way or another. Mostly people would say that by seeing her human suffering they felt a need to get closer to God or to make their relationship with God stronger. Some people would tell me that by watching me function through life, knowing what I go through as her mother, that it was another reason people felt the need to enrich their faith in God. I guess in their eyes it was sort of like: Well if that mom can get her kids to school and function, or if that mom can volunteer for this or whatever the case may be, then it gave them hope that they, too, could deal with whatever problems or challenges were happening in their lives as well. Sometimes it is human nature to feel hope for your own set of circumstances just by witnessing another human's circumstances that just might be a whole lot worse then yours.

I knew our life was incredibly hard and anyone who was ever remotely close to our family unit also knew this. There were times that I had friends who would be in our house and hear the cries of pain, or witness the wounds. Sam was always extremely private about her body and her wounds and she never let me share too much with people. I think by the 7th grade I did start sharing photographs with some of the staff and teachers at her school because sometimes I got the feeling that some of them did not fully understand what Sam had to go through just to be there. The day I shared the photos changed everything for us. Don't get me wrong - the school, Most Holy Redeemer, was more than generous with their love and support, but sometimes I would get an occasional question from someone, or I would hear another student say how they think it is not fair that Sam got to turn her work in late. Or that it wasn't fair that Sam always got to be late to school and at times not come at all. Those things would drive me absolutely crazy because I knew better than anyone that Sam wanted nothing more than to be just like them. She wanted to go to school and she wanted to be given the same assignments as everyone else. It was time to share the pictures of her pain, it was time for people to understand. You couldn't see her wounds because they were always bandaged up. After a while I realized this and that is when I decided maybe these folks needed to know. Also by sharing her pain I was showing her courage and bravery and to me that was extremely vital.

Sam was her own worst enemy though. She would go to school with raging wounds and fever. She would fight me at every turn. I knew why, I got it. School was her 'Happy Place,' and home was a place of constant medical treatments and pain. I was the full time nurse struggling to be the mom so when it was time to stand up for her I was always ready.

The honey in many respects changed our lives forever. I felt like we had a new lease on life and for the first time in her life, or all of the years while she was at school, I knew that the eighth grade was going to be the best year of her life. Sam was able to attend school almost every day, which was something she had not done in years. A funny thing about that year of school: For the first time ever I had an awakening. You see, it used to bother me that Sam was not really ever a part of any of the girls at school. She rarely got invited to parties. The girls in her class were not calling her after school, nor were they asking her to meet them at the mall either. I knew girls her age were doing stuff together so sometimes that part would really bother me. Sam had her best friend Meghan all of the years there, and for that I was grateful. She really had two, but her first close friend Gina Rae left MHR by the second grade and when she did that their friendship slowly diminished and really never recovered. Gina Rae's mom (Regina) and I always stayed close and remained very close friends through the years even though Sam and Gina Rae seemed to grow apart.

The awakening I had was this: I suddenly realized that because Sam had never really gone to school. I mean she missed out on so many things: field trips, after school activities, pretty much all the fun stuff at school like PE and recess. She had to miss those two favorite subjects because the heat was bad for her to be in - not to mention that she is wrapped in bandages from her neck down all the time and then has clothes on, so those two things together can make a 98 degree day feel like a 108 degree day. It was almost like a little light bulb went off in my head and I realized the reason the girls at school never really involved Sam in any of their lives - it was because they really never got the chance to really know Sam. EB was scary enough to those who know nothing about it, but being absent from school more than you actually attend school can have its consequences as well. The school MHR went above and beyond to make Sam feel as comfortable and part of everything as they could, but if your not there – you just not there.

Meghan and Sam had an instant connection from the moment they met. I believe in my heart that, upon meeting Sam, Meghan never once saw a bandage or a boo-boo. She only saw a friend. As the years went on, Meghan and Sam grew a friendship that is not to be reckoned with and one that is very near and dear to my heart. Their friendship taught me many things about sticking it out and staying together. There were times they would have little arguments but when the cards were down for Sam, Meg was always there.

For example, one of the first moments that I realized how much the kids barely knew Sam was in her seventh grade year at this school dance. It was at a time when she wasn't feeling that good. I volunteered to be one of the chaperones because I would have to have been there anyway. Anytime Sam went anywhere I always had to tag along in some way just to be able to get her wheelchair there and also to be close by in the event anything happened, like if she were to get hurt or something. Her boo-boos would need to get tended to almost immediately.

This dance was at our local church St. Mary's, which is the church we attend and love dearly. The dance was held in the parish center of the church. By the time we got there it was a little bit after the dance had already started. It was nighttime and dark outside, and even though it was

October it felt like it was May with the temperatures hovering in the 90's (and feels like of 100 degrees). We were starting to wonder if living in Florida was a very good idea at all for our Sam. All the kids were standing around the dance floor and every now and then the DJ would play a song that the entire group of kids seemed to know the dance skit to. All of the kids except for Sam. I was sitting in one of those fold-up chairs against the wall a few chairs away from the other mom that was there to chaperone as well. So my biggest nightmare was developing right in front of my eyes. I watched as Sam got up from her wheelchair, which she looked as if she was going to park in the corner. I knew what she was about to do. She was about to get out on that dance floor and have some fun with those kids. I wanted her to have fun, but what I knew that no one else knew was that Sam had big painful wounds on her legs and on her feet and on her arms, and as she hobbled over to the congregation of teens dancing on the dance floor my heart was sinking down to my feet. I think my physical body was actually slumping down in the chair as if I wanted to hide.

My mind was racing with all of these crazy thoughts like: I wonder how much pain she is in? I wonder if the kids will watch out for her and not bump into her or step on her feet?

I was more nervous for her than she was for herself. I don't think she was nervous at all. So one of those dances where all the kids were doing these dance steps in unison started and I watched in horror as Sam tried to keep up. All the kids were smiling and dancing and laughing and then there was Sam hobbling along trying to watch her feet as if to try and learn the dance for the first time, while the other kids must have done this dance many times before. Oh God - that was it. I was already thinking of how I was going to talk her into coming home and preparing for her to say 'no,' but I just wanted to protect her.

I didn't want Sam to figure out that the kids were really not even paying attention to her at all anyway. I thought, "Wow can they not see that she doesn't even know the dance routine and why aren't any of the girls offering to show her?"

Oh that was torture for me to have to watch; so many emotions rolling around in my mind, sitting there watching this little person that I gave life too trying to fit in, trying to have fun and be like everyone else, but because of this awful disease EB she can barely even walk let alone dance. Then to see her stick out in that crowd like the only one who has no clue how to do that dance, and to top it off to see her hobble along because I know the reason she hobbling is because her feet are bloody and raw with open wounds and the pain is excruciating. Why God? Why does my baby have to endure this? Why do I have to witness it happening? Why God?

By the time the eighth grade dance had arrived Sam had gotten a chance to know the girls a little bit better and I was able to witness a happier time for Sam at that dance.

When eighth grade came it brought on a sense of "wow we made here," because honestly I was not sure she would see the eighth grade. Since I had become so involved in the EB community for the past 12 years I knew anyone and everyone who had anything to do with EB. I studied every single treatment being worked on and paid very close attention to any new possible cures and treatments being funded by research. I had met hundreds of EB families and suffered through many deaths. As hard as the deaths were for me I kept a running inventory in my mind of how these EB kids died, how old they were, and what was the main complication leading to the death. Plus I educated myself medically so that I could grasp a better understanding of how EB works and stops working. There are so many different subtypes of EB it really is hard to gain an understanding of just one particular subtype just because in that one particular subtype the variations are tremendous. For the past 12 years of all the EB kids I had met my Sam was by far one of the most severely affected. That was hard to tell just by looking at her because I was meticulous about keeping her bandages clean and diligent with her wound care. Sam was one of the very few EB kids who was allergic to all oral sedation medications, most pain medications, and now some antibiotics making the treatment of her disease almost impossible. Also, she lost the use of her hands at a young age. For me as her mom it was very difficult to balance out keeping things as normal and routine as possible with a disease that was extremely unpredictable and ruthless.

I had a few very close friends who were EB mom's and I found that when EB was getting the best of me my EB friends understood my pain so much more than my non-EB friends, and simply because they too were living the same torturous life of hell. My friend Denise and I would go weeks - sometimes even months - without talking, but when she was calling, or when I called her, we both knew what the others' life was like since our children were very similar in age. Her son Hunter was nowhere near as severe as my Sam, but EB has a way of creating such a suffering hell in your life that really it doesn't matter because at the end of the day pain is pain.

I thought I was a pretty good medical student when it came to EB or wound care, but my friend Denise was definitely the PHD in the EB mom family. Whenever a rumor was spreading about a new treatment or medicine (or whatever it was) she and I would always keep each other in the loop. Sometimes I would have to call Denise just so she could put things into layman's terms for me. Denise is not a doctor, but a highly self-educated EB mom who could run circles around the best doctors in the world. This woman can break down molecules with you, if you know what I mean. I really don't want to know the molecules breakdown - all I really want to know is if they work. And how can I get them?

Sometime in 2007 Silvia (my EBAN partner and one of my best friends) went to Washington for another one of our attempts to get some support for the EB Bandage Bill. We were also invited by the American Academy of Dermatology to visit the NIH (National Institute of Health) for a meeting for non-profits collaborating efforts to get grants and research monies for various different diseases. Just as Silvia and I were getting to Washington there was breaking news about a possible CURE on the horizon for EB. While in Washington there was mumbling about this new cure, but no one was talking. At the time it appeared as though there was a tight lid of security on any information about this boy who apparently had just undergone a Bone Marrow Stem Cell transplant in Minnesota and survived. Since no one was talking, nor would anyone answer any questions, I decided to take matters into my own hands.

I managed to find out where the transplant had been done, and then I managed to find out who the family was. So I Googled the mom's name and just-like-that I got the mom's email address. I wrote what I thought was a very nice, friendly, desperate email to this woman asking her about this new "cure" that I had heard about. I guess the woman didn't want to communicate with anyone because she wrote a very nasty email back - but not me, she wrote it to my partner Silvia. I thought that was really flipping weird. The woman must have Googled me to find out that I had this non-profit organization with Silvia and for some unknown reason and answered my partner not me. In my email to this woman I gave her all of my contact information, so why she felt like she needed to rant and rave to my partner was just plain weird. It just pissed me off to tell ya' the truth. Here I was trying to find out any information about a possible cure for a disease that was killing my daughter by the day and this woman has a child with the same disease who is apparently undergoing a treatment that could be a possible cure and she doesn't want to communicate with me? Why? I think the first thought that came to my mind was 'WHY?' Then I answered back her nasty email to my partner. I very gracefully apologized for making her mad but explained that I was only making a desperate attempt to reach out to her to see if she would tell me anything about how her boys were doing and if she could tell me anything. By that time I had heard that she had two boys going through the same procedure, which left me thinking, "Well geez - if she put one boy through and now a second, then something really good must be happening and I wanted to know what it was."

That was it. My apology and response back to her turned her into a crazy woman. Again, I did not understand why. I mean, shit, if you are going to pioneer something that could save thousands of lives, why not share? This woman was definitely not getting down to 'tie the old man's shoes' i.e.: the 'old man' being me. Didn't she know that death for my daughter was not an option? And *I need* to know was. All of us EB mom's who want to know need to know.

Well part of me felt bad for my friend Silvia because, after all, she was getting her butt reamed by this crazy woman because of me, so I figured I should just let this one go and not respond to her anymore. I decided that I would just try to find out who the doctor was and contact him directly.

A few months later I was in my kitchen chatting with a dear friend, Jeff Angel, who happened to be the OB doctor who delivered Chloe and James, and was the doctor who did my CVS on both babies. He and his wife are good friends of ours. Jeff also cared very much for Sam and on many occasions would be there for us to help with anything or any problem - no matter what time of night it was. We happen to live in the same neighborhood. Every crazy insane moment with EB usually happened to us on a Friday night or weekend leaving us with few options to reach for help. 911 was really not an option due to the plain fact that since not too many folks in the medical community knew about EB. A 911 call could potentially make things worse for the EB child, so we always tried to manage those 911 calls ourselves and with help from our friends. As Sam grew older her list of allergies to medication grew longer. Sam's allergies were rashes, and then difficulty breathing followed by blood pressure issues. On several occasions Jeff would come over to help us with those and we were always so thankful for that. His wife was always so gracious letting us invade on their family time. He saved Sam from many tragedies that could have been (if you know what I am saying).

Back to the kitchen scene: Jim and I were telling Jeff the story about the EB mom I tried to contact and how she refused to talk to me, and then we told him about what we had heard about the transplant, which really wasn't much. There were other friends that lived in neighborhood who also had heard about the Bone Marrow Transplant in Minnesota as well. There was a story that was released in the USA Today Newspaper, which was how most people were hearing about it. Then, to complicate things further, now we had heard that there were two places doing this Bone Marrow Transplantation. One was in New York and with well-respected physicians I had known for years, and another in Minnesota with a handful of doctors whom I knew nothing about. After discussing it with Jeff for a little bit he wanted me to call the doctor while he was there because he wanted me to ask this doctor a few doctor questions.

Standing around the kitchen I picked up the telephone and I called the office of the doctor doing these transplants: Dr. John Wagner. He was not available to speak with me but there was a man who was specifically assigned to the EB transplant prospects to discuss the details. I started out my conversation by telling him who I was and why I was calling. The man, Tim Krepsky, seemed to talk very fast as if he had too much to do and had no time to talk to anyone. Jeff could hear me ask questions and then I would repeat the answer so Jeff could hear. Jeff told me specifically to ask this question: "What is your protocol?" I asked. Mr. Krepski answered, "We don't give that out! That is our own special protocol and we do not share the details of that with anyone!" I would repeat what Tim was saying on the phone so Jeff could hear the answer and as soon as I said that Jeff was like, "Hang up the phone! If they won't tell you the protocol then they are either hiding something they do not want you to know or they are not doing things properly."

Jeff was a trusted friend and well respected physician in town so no doubt about it I was going to hang up the phone and just forget about Minnesota all together. Of course I thanked Mr. Krepski but told him that we were not interested at this time anyway. Plus Mr. Krepski told me that in order for us to qualify as a candidate we would have to have a 'sibling donor match.' I didn't really understand what that meant, nor did I understand what the word "protocol" meant either at this point. Jeff further explained that the protocol was the formula of drugs used in the transplant that Sam would be exposed to. He went on to tell us that these drugs they use for transplantation are often chemotherapy drugs and cannot only cause death, but long lasting harmful side effects. Ok -

that was enough for me to shy away from the whole idea of transplant. Plus at this point we could not find out anything about the two boys from this family who had been transplanted, and we knew for sure that the first child was well over a 100 days out. The rumor on the second child was that he had died, but no one would confirm or deny anything - not even the EB contact person in Minnesota, Mr. Krepski.

Before I hung up the phone I asked Mr. Krepski if this Dr. Wagner could return my call and Mr. Krepski told me that Dr. Wagner was getting so inundated with phone calls from the EB community and that unless I was considering a consult that he would more than likely not be able to call me back. Knowing in my mind at that time that New York was also now doing this transplant, and at safer level than Dr. Wagner, I really didn't care if he called me back because from what I had heard by now I was already anxious to call New York. One of my friends had told me at some point that she didn't understand why we were not just getting on a plane and camping out at the University of Minnesota until they would just let us in. I had to explain to her that it just doesn't work like that and I was sure that they were going to need certain test and test results from our doctors here before we could ever just go there. Now that Jeff was with us while we made that first initial call and the response was not favorable I was even more convinced that our next phone call would be to New York.

In the meantime, my friend Denise started to have more frequent calls to me regarding the transplant and she would try to explain the technicalities to me, but it all just seemed so overwhelming and foreign. What we knew at this point was that Minnesota had transplanted two children with EB, both of them were brothers and apparently one of them had died. The mother of the two boys refused to speak to anyone and the doctor who did the transplant was not reachable either. We had heard that the protocol was something called "full ablative," which Denise at that time had tried to explain to me a hundred times and I still was not getting it. All I could hear was 'death.' We also had heard that New York was choosing to do the same transplant but with a more reduced drug regiment, and by doing that it was less life threatening and worked just as well.

Denise had finally decided that she and her family were going to travel to New York for a consult with the doctor there whose name was Dr. Mitch Cairo. His counterpart for this stem cell transplant was a very well respected EB Researcher/doctor/PHd. named Angela Christiano.

Dr. Christiano was also one of the doctors on board at Jefferson University in Philadelphia who discovered what the missing gene which causes EB is: Collagen #7. She is also the same scientist who discovered the gene that causes alopecia as well. She has been recognized for many accomplishments and is highly respected by her fellow physicians as well as researchers around the world.

Chapter 57.

Denise's Trip to New York

My not-for-profit organization EBAN had pretty much stood still since our very first fundraiser in January 2007 with Lou Piniella. That was largely in part to EB consuming every moment of my time and no real volunteers able to work for free. We raised forty thousand dollars at that one event so we were able to help a whole lot of families with a variety of needs. One of our dear friends and long time supports wanted to make a charitable contribution to EBAN, but they only wanted it to be used for local EB families here in the Tampa area. That was going to be a little challenging because since I had been out of the family sector loop for a few years I really didn't know any EB families in the area except for one – my friends Denise & John and their little boy Hunter.

The rumblings of the Bone Marrow Stem Cell Transplant were starting to get louder and louder. By this time little flurries of information were being scattered around very sparsely and getting solid information seemed to be extremely difficult. I tried to contact the only one family that I, at this point, had heard of that had gone through and I tried to contact the doctor as well. I took the fact that I could not get any information as a sign for us that it was just not meant to be at this point. Denise, on the other hand, decided she would contact New York and look into what was going on there. She was talking to me about her findings and discussing the notion that she and her family may travel up there for a consult. I had told Denise at this point about this generous family who had made the contribution to EBAN to help Hunter with anything he may need and, if Denise would like, EBAN could pay for the airfare to get to New York. I automatically knew without question that if you were an EB family no matter how much money you think you had it was never enough. The out-of-pocket expense would eventually drown you.

So Denise, John and Hunter traveled to New York and met with Dr. Cairo. She came back home elated with hope. Still I felt the hope for us was drifting away and becoming a distant part of our past. I felt like

I was giving in to the acceptance that maybe the doctor that we had met in the very beginning days of Samantha's life was right - maybe there would not be a cure for EB in his lifetime, or ours either for that matter. Denise kept urging me to at least go and get a consult. I kept refusing, and more importantly I purposely did not absorb any information she was sharing. Anyway, the one and only article that came out about this transplant was on a family who would not communicate. Not only with just me, but any EB family. Nor would the doctor. So I was convinced that there wasn't anything really concrete to get too excited about. Instead, I stayed focused on the day in which we were living and not too much into the future.

I missed my mom horribly, and even though a good full year had passed I was still crying myself to sleep at night and wishing she would be by me to help me with the pain that was burrowing in my heart. It was because of my mom that I started to write this book in the first place and now I had more stories to share and now more than ever I needed her to tell me that no matter what, 'everything was still going to be ok.'

Denise had nagged me enough to go for consult that probably about one month into the nagging process I decided I would try and give New York a call. Since I had been on the DEBRA Board for so many years and I was still friends with a few people on the Board, so I reached out to them as well to ask for their opinions about what was transpiring in New York. I learned that Dr. Christiano was involved with Dr. Wagner from the beginning. Although it was not quite clear whose idea it was for transplant, or who had discovered what. All that I had heard was that one boy lived and was showing signs of improvement and one boy died. I also heard that Dr. Christiano left Minnesota's team because she wanted to form her own team and try this newfound treatment a less severe way - a better way that was less risk-of-death to the EB child. I also heard something about some mice that Dr. Christiano had taken and something foggy about how out of 13 mice tested 10 died and three were cured from EB. When I say 'foggy' that is because I did not get that information straight from Dr. Christiano herself. I was getting it second-hand and I knew the data was not exactly accurate, but it was enough data for me to hear the words: 'cure.'

For the first time since Sam was born I felt these tiny little butterflies fluttering around in the pit of my stomach and somehow the idea that Sam might have a chance was starting to surface in my mind. So I got the phone numbers from Denise to call New York, she even gave me a contact person to speak with too. How awesome was that? Because trying to call Minnesota was such a trial of daunting experiences it just sounded too good to be true that calling New York was going to be so easy. I actually had the person's contact name and number for New York for a good week before I tried to call. The good news was that I was finally starting to accept the possibility that something good for EB could be brewing and it was just a matter of making a simple phone call to find out.

We had just celebrated Sam's 14th birthday. It was February something - I can't remember the exact date (although it could have been the actual date of her birthday) - but I had finally made the call to New York about a week prior. Denise told me that the contact person there was very friendly and full of all the answers I had questions to. She also warned me that I might have to leave a message, but not to get discouraged because she knew for sure that I would get a return call. February was probably one the only coldest months in Florida, and when I say that I mean 60 degrees was cold for us Floridians. I was always thankful Sam's birthday was in that month because it made planning activities better because of the weather. On the night that we celebrated Sam's birthday, it was late in the evening and we were about to eat dinner. The phone rang:

"Hello," I answered.

"Hello may I speak to Mrs. Sheridan?" is what I heard on the other end.

I answered, "This is Marybeth Sheridan."

She replied, "Hi, this is Alana Smilo from Columbia Presbyterian in New York returning your call regarding the Bone Marrow Stem Cell Transplantation for EB."

I was so excited I could hardly stand myself.

"Thank you," I said. "Thank you for taking the time to return my call. I have some questions for you." Of course the first question was: "What is your protocol?"

To my surprise she was happy to share that information, although the words coming from her mouth sounded like some foreign language that I had never heard before so I couldn't even begin to imagine how they were spelled. That really wasn't important at the moment because since she was happy to share and I figured that our friend Jeff could call her himself if he wanted those drug names translated to him. I began to ask her all kinds of questions like: What is the criterion? Have you all tried your procedure on a patient before? Is it covered by insurance? How long does it take? How do know if Sam is a candidate?

Mrs. Smilo answered all of my questions in a friendly, cheerful way. It was the extreme opposite of what we had experienced from Minnesota, so already I was feeling a certain warmth and acceptance from her voice. She explained the whole mouse story to me about how Dr. Christiano had tried her theory on 13 mice and how a couple of those mice had been cured and that they (New York) felt that this was a possible cure for EB. Her words took my breath away as I felt this wave of emotion come over me that made me gasp for my next breath - so much so I paused for a moment and then Mrs. Smilo said, "Mrs. Sheridan are you there?" I could barley talk due to the lump that formed in my throat. I started to cry in a way that I could not speak words, and if I did speak words you could clearly tell that I was crying intensely. The kind of crying that you have these deep breaths of air in-between tears rushing, which is followed by a wavering, whimper in your voice. Mrs. Smilo compassionately responded to my tears with, "Oh Mrs. Sheridan are you ok? Why are you crying?" Trying to gather myself and get words out after a few seconds I told her, "Because you see I had resolved to the notion that my baby girl was going to be taken by this disease." Following that was a few more deep breaths and tears and on with, "You just gave me some hope back that I thought was completely diminished."

It was tears of joy. Opposite of pain, but pure elation of the feeling that something really good is still on the horizon for a situation that was looking so doom and gloom for so many years. Elation, happiness, a sense of relief in a few short moments with Mrs. Smilo overpowered everything in my being.

Mrs. Smilo went on to explain the age requirements it was: nine months to 14 years of age. Sam was right at the cut-off limit. Sam would have to have RDEB, which is a particular subtype of EB (which she had), and more important than anything else, Mrs. Smilo (who liked to be called by her first name, Alana) very meticulously made sure that I understood that Sam would not be a candidate if we did not have a sibling match for the transplant.

"Sibling match?" I said, confused.

"Yes," she answered, "You have to have a sister or a brother to Samantha that has the same HLA typing as Samantha."

Suddenly fear crept back into my spine. Once again as Alana was talking to me about the details of how to go about getting the blood work done for this kind of testing, my mind was scrambling for the "what ifs" of all of this: Wow what if Chloe and James are not a match? And just as that thought entered my mind, Alano's voice came back into the forefront of everything I was hearing as she said, "And Mrs. Sheridan I have to tell you that we have already had plenty of families come through who had two or three siblings and none of them turned out to be matches, so that eliminated that particular family from this trial altogether. Dr. Ciaro is not taking non-sibling donor matches at this time." She went on to tell me that I would need to get a doctor to give me a prescription for the blood work that needed to be done. That particular test is called HLA typing.

Uh-oh. Oh my - and I only have two children to choose from. As quickly as my mind was racing for the 'what if' scenario again, that little voice inside my head that talks to me all the time was telling me to pray about it. My little voice was saying, "Stop thinking negative thoughts, Marybeth. You know better than this. You know that if it is God's will and this is what He wants you to do then all you have to do is ask Him to guide you. The prayer for you now is simple, just ask God that if this transplant is meant to be then the choice will be up to God and He will answer that choice by giving Sam the perfect match."

I bravely calmed my self down and focused in on what Alana was still explaining to me. I wrote on paper what my "to do" list was going to be.

- Call Dr. Yee and ask him if he will write the orders for the HLA typing.

- Pray for guidance.

- Find a way to explain to all three of my children why they were going to be stuck with a needle

- Start planning on a trip to New York to meet Dr. Cairo and discuss all of the pros and cons to this possible cure for EB

One more item that needed to be discussed was insurance. Alana told me frankly that this procedure was a minimum one million dollars, and that if our insurance company did not approve us we would not be able to come unless we paid cash. I was like, "Really... cash? Wow! That is a lot of money. Are you requiring the whole amount up front?"

She responded, "Eighty percent."

Well, if insurance did not approve us we were done because we did not have eight hundred thousand dollars lying around. I didn't want to spin too much energy on the "what ifs" again, though. Thinking about that for a few minutes I suddenly became the tiger again, and in my mind I said to myself, "Well, it doesn't matter. We can sell our house and everything we own if this is a cure for Sam." I had always said I would give everything I owned, including my home and the shirt off my back, if Sam could be cured and saved from this really horrible, nasty disease called EB. Little flashbacks of conversations I would have with Denise were rolling in and out of my mind of this very same conversation, because Denise always said the very same thing: "You can have everything just give me my child without EB!"

By the time Alana and I hung up the phone together a good hour had past and it was closer to 8pm now. That meant that I wasn't going to be calling Dr. Yee until the following day. I can understand now why doctors do not give out their cell phone numbers. I wanted so desperately to get everything on my to do list done right at that very moment.

The next day rolled in and Dr. Yee was more than happy to give me the prescription for the HLA typing. He further explained that this type of test would take a few weeks (six to eight to be exact) to get back and that I was about to enter an area of medicine that was not in his general knowledge. He had been one of our biggest fans since the day we met. He had supported us through every infection, every up, every down, and even through every single nightmare that came with EB. I knew without him ever saying that he was just as excited at this new prospect to help Sam as we were.

On the way to the Quest lab where we were going to get the blood drawn I told all three of the children that we needed to go get some blood work done because we had to find out if their blood matched Sam's blood. Chloe and James really didn't ask me too many questions why - just "Is it going to hurt, mommy?"

"Well, maybe just a tiny pinch, but we have to get it done so we are going to be brave and just do it ok?"

I have to say my kids are the best. I guess all moms around the globe will attest to the fact that their children are, for the most part, all around good. We as parents are their biggest fans, right?

We got the blood taken. We waited. I prayed.

Chapter 58.

The Buddhist Priest

We were heading to Camp Wonder again for the second year now. Just Sam and I were traveling because this was a camp for children with skin conditions. Only the children with the condition were allowed to be at the campgrounds and mainly because these kinds of camps only run off of donated funds. That being said, Chloe and James didn't want to go on this trip because there wasn't anything fun for them to do. At times this could be tremendously hard for Jim and I as parents because what was good for Sam at times was not always good for the kids and vice-versa, so often times it would be just me going somewhere with Sam and Jim doing something different with the other two.

When Sam is traveling and flying we always have to make sure her medicines that are hard to replace are in our carryon luggage and that a certain amount of bandaging supplies are in the carryon bags as well. Usually when we travel together we have bags on both arms (well, I do anyway) and bags hanging off her wheelchair. When we board the plane we usually get to board first, even though we are not sitting in first class but because she is in a wheelchair and that is just what the airlines do. I like that about the airlines. They always take into consideration people, children, and their families traveling with a special needs child or person, and they allow you extra time to board the plane and almost always allow you to board first.

When Sam and I boarded this flight to California we were walking to our seat only to find that a rather large over-sized man wearing some sort of smock/robe type of garment. It looked like it was a robe with some kind of smock throw over the robe. This man had already occupied the seat next to the window (Sam's favorite seat). Usually I get Sam in her seat first then I put whatever bags away on top that we won't need during the flight and then I sit and get comfy. I knew already without even asking that Sam did not want to sit by this man, so I had her sit on the seat closest to the isle and I sat in the middle. I was already (in my mind) trying to figure out who this man was and what type of religion he was because immediately I knew he was wearing these kinds of garments due to his religion. We got comfortable in our seats and Sam and I were happily chatting together. We both like to fly. The idea of getting on a plane and just "getting way" is almost an instant happy pick-me-up that we are always just happy on the plane.

The man we were sitting next to was very quiet and his body language didn't really yell out to me that he wanted to converse either. He appeared almost tense and stern looking. I, on the other hand, was really curious as to why he was wearing those strange clothes that look like something a religious clergy-type of person from a hundred years ago would wear. His gown was orange and his cloak that draped over to one side of his robe was red (or vice-versa with the colors). Sam and I were pulling out our snacks and eating them. I offered the man some but he declined. Then I just asked him, "So are you heading home or away from home?" and he responded, "No actually I am heading to visit a friend for a month and I just left a friend that I visited for a month." I joked around with him that he must have a lot of friends and how fun is it that he can travel to different states to visit all of his friends. He was an older man and his demeanor was calm and serine. He seemed so gentle but he was an enormous man. I asked him where he was from and he told he lives in Hawaii but his native land is Tibet, so I said to him, "Oh - so you are a priest from Tibet?"

"Yes," he said, "I am a Buddhist Monk from Tibet"

I smiled at him as if to say to him – 'well that's ok with me I like all religions.' I told him that I just got done reading a book about Karma and Buddhism and that I was Catholic, but I like his religion very much. I went on to tell him that I believe in Karma, too. He smiled and looked relieved that I was knowledgeable about his faith. He leaned forward in his seat and then over me and he looked at Sam. He paused for a few minutes as he was looking at her. He never had any expression on his face - just this blank sort of stare. That was unusual for me as most people that look at Sam always have some kind of emotion on their faces. After 13 years of EB I could always tell when a stranger was going to make a comment to me about Sam, but with this Man I honestly could not tell you what was going through his mind. He studied her for a very long time. After about one minute he very slowly started to lean back into his seat and as he did his eyes connected with mine. He said to me in a very adamant sort of way, "You must take very good care of her."

I quickly responded with, "I do take good care of her."

I was a tiny bit insulted and had to catch myself from going into full blown insult as I realized I was sitting next to a Buddhist Priest, and I was fully aware that if he was a monk then he himself did not mean me any ill will or ill thought. He was simply telling me a fact. His expression never changed as he told me that. He repeated that again to me, "No, but I mean YOU MUST take very good care for her and SHE must receive your care as well. This is your Karma."

I gently leaned back into my chair. I decided I would stop telling him that I DO take really good of her because I assumed he knew that. There was this tiny thought rolling through my mind that maybe there was something about to happen that might give "taking care of her" a whole new meaning. Sam asked me what he said so I told her and the three of us just sort of sat quietly for a little while. After about an hour I started making small talk with the man again which gave me a doorway for all sorts of thoughts I was having and questions popping into my thoughts.

We were starting to converse a little bit about past lives and the idea of all of that. My religion didn't believe in past lives, but I knew that the Buddhist people did believe in that. He explained how we are all here to learn something and if we do not learn here in this life that we will come back again in a different life to learn whatever it is that we are here to learn. He was just so serious. I was still on the fence about the whole past life philosophy, but part of me was eager to keep asking him questions. Plus if he was right about the whole thing I had better find out as much as I could because according to him I must have done some really bad stuff not only in my past life but Sam's, too. OK, well, hmm… I wasn't quite sure about all of his beliefs but I enjoyed inquiring and religion had always been a favorite subject. I thought for a few more minutes quietly by myself and after three or four minutes I had this question for him, "Well, can you tell me what I have to do in this life so that I do not have to come back here to learn anymore?" I ended the question with a familiar giggle. He, on the other hand, did not smile back but informed me that in fact there was something I could do and if he could find someone to interpret the book that was written in Tibet he would send it to me. I gave him my address and made sure he knew that I would be eager to read that book. I also told him that I wasn't at all happy about my mom leaving. He offered his beliefs about what happens with our loved ones after they die. According to him we are all connected, but when we die we do not see our loved ones again. Instead we all come back as a different people.... Ugh! I liked that version less and I told him, "Well, I like my belief on that subject. We Catholics believe that we will be reunited with our loved ones in heaven. That is if we all make it to heaven right?" Giggling.

Chapter 59.

And She Played The Guitar

Most Holy Redeemer School had so many wonderful things to offer children who attended their school. One activity that was offered every two years was called "The MHR Variety Show." This program was run strictly on volunteers mostly made up of staff and parents of children who attend. The Variety show was a talent show of sorts in which the students were given the chance to get up on stage and perform any talent they had in front of the entire school and all of the family members who wished to attend. I remember this show would pack the house always. Sometimes getting a good seat was challenging.

Sam was always drawn to this event and always wanted to participate. I remember one year I think she was in third or fourth grade she sang a song by Hillary Duff. Most of the children would either, sing, dance, play a musical instrument, or act out a skit. By far this program being offered at MHR was on everybody's favorites list.

At that time we had this baby sitter coming to help me with the kids mostly on the days I had to do bandages. Her name was Katie Lozado. Oh how my children loved Katie. She was pretty, fun and had tons of talents herself. We were so lucky to have Katie in our life, but then again nothing in our life was by accident. The more time passed the more I would come to realize that each person we met was a true gift from God.

Katie immediately bonded with Sam. She bonded with all of my children but especially with Sam. Katie would only work part time as she was attending the local college here. Her goal was to one day become a dentist. One day Katie played her guitar for the kids. Sparklers flew out of Sam's eye the moment Katie played a tune and then sang. Her voice was incredible and we often told her that SHE should be trying out for "American Idol" as she could win it. Katie was well grounded and her goal in life was education first and everything else that happened was secondary. I liked that about her, but I also thought that her voice was an amazing gift and if someone heard her sing she would be discovered to be the next mega super star.

Katie could see the sparkle in Sam's eyes when it came to the guitar. Next thing I knew Katie would spend a little bit of time here and there teaching Sam how to play the guitar. Sam was in awe of Katie's talent. Sam was always so excited to learn this musical instrument that she had always been attracted to. Now you have to keep in mind that Sam does not have fingers, so learning how to play the guitar was going to be tricky. Katie thought of ideas and different ways for Sam to get the basics down and still manage even without fingers. Before long Sam was playing tunes and experimenting with her voice.

Sam announced that she was going to be in the Talent show that year. I think it was her seventh grade year. She practiced any chance she could. She chose the song "I'd Lie" by Taylor Swift. I had not heard that song on the radio before. I asked Sam how she heard of that song since I knew it had not been played on the radio. Sam said that since she loved Taylor Swift she wanted to pick out one of her songs. When I would go in Sam's room to hear her play the guitar and sing I would get all these mixed up emotions scurrying around in my mind. First of all it was a hard song. Second, she was going to be sitting in a chair on the stage in front of hundreds of people playing a song with a guitar and singing the tunes without any background music... at all. I was amazed at her determination and courage. Nothing was going to stop Sam from mastering the guitar. Still my heart fluttered and sank all at the same moment thinking of her sitting up there on stage.

The big night finally arrived. We got to the program especially early that night to ensure the best seats. We got front row seats and I did that on purpose so in case Sam got nervous she could focus in on me. The anticipation of how that night was going to roll out was building with a splurge of excitement. I was worried about all of the obvious things: What if she messes up? Will she be ok? Will she cry? Will the kids laugh at her? I knew the kids at *that* school would not laugh at Sam. I had better sense than that. For goodness sakes these kids had known her all of her school life. The kids at MHR were never mean to Sam, but just the opposite everyone there had always, *always*, been so warm and loving to her. Sending her to MHR was one of the best decisions we ever made for Sam. The nervous "worry-wart mother syndrome" was emerging like a volcano inside of me. Jim and I were sitting in the seats waiting for her to come out. There were approximately twenty students who came on the stage just before her. Those children did all kinds of various talent show acts. When it was Sam's turn I had to jump up and help her to the stage. I helped her up the stairs and then handed her the guitar. When she went to sit in the chair the woman organizing the event (Sue Ellen) was trying to maneuver the microphone closer to Sam. I asked Sue Ellen if she could make sure the microphone was as close to Sam's mouth as possible, she assured me she would. I quickly went back to sit down in my seat. As Sam sat in her spot and got comfy I saw that the microphone was not where it was supposed to be and the problem now was that Sam did not have the hands to move it. I know Sue Ellen tried to put it where I asked so I am not sure exactly what happened there. What I did know is that everyone was nervous that night for all of the same reasons we were. Most of the crowd was friends and family of the students performing that night, including Sue Ellen as she also had children doing skits.

Jim and I, crunched up in our seats, were so nervous we could barely stand ourselves - it was awful. My lips were quivering. I felt like I was going to throw up. At that same exact moment Jim told me he was going to throw up, with a grin. When I noticed the microphone issue it was too late as it was time for her to start. I was praying for God to have mercy on her and please don't let this night be a total embarrassment for Sam. Sam was her own worst critic. When she set out to do something – anything - she always propelled towards perfection. Anything less than perfection was just not acceptable for my Sam.

She began to play. I felt my heart stop, skip a few beats and my face turned hot red. I was frozen with fear of the "what ifs." I held my breath with every movement she made. Jim was in the exact same state of affairs as I was. I know both of us felt like stopping the show and just talking her off that stage that night. Here she was sitting in a chair beginning to play a guitar with no hands, bandages from her neck down, and about to sing a song with absolutely no background anything – in front of 350 people!!! Oh God!

She started playing and we could tell the microphone was not properly placed. You could barely hear her voice. All of the sudden, as if Sam's thoughts were somehow intertwined with my thoughts, I knew exactly what was going to happen next. She stopped! She realized the microphone was not picking up her voice. Only for a split second she stopped and our eyes made contact. I mouthed the words "keep going" to her in hopes that she would know what to do. I have tears rushing from my eyes as I write this because I still feel so emotional about that night. No one had any idea what kind of courage it takes to do what she did that night. But I knew. I was having such guilt about being so damn nervous that I should have just gotten up there myself and put the microphone where it needed to go. I knew that Sam was timid and shy and that belting out a song while playing the guitar was HUGE for her. Just as that thought left me she continued on her performance. You could hear her loud and clear and she sang and played her song beautifully, not missing one cord or one beat to any word. Her voice was magical. I was crying, Jim was crying and as I looked around everyone sitting anywhere around me was – crying. People were putting their hands on my shoulder as if to say, "We support you. We love you, and we love Sam."

She rocked! Sam brought 350 people to their knees. It was the first time in my life I saw so many grown men in tears. I was moved by their expressions and reactions to our sweet Sam. Her performance was monumental in many ways. She sang with HOPE and showed no fear. Her own ability to inspire and create love was astounding. So many people came up to me that night with complete and utter astonishment that our amazing, extremely talented daughter, with no hands and a very visible disability, got up on that stage and did something that I am sure has never been done.

I still wanted to pick her up and run out the door. That was the "Tiger Protect My Cub" mode surfacing, really for no reason. Her performance was a huge success. The faculty and families have talked about that night for weeks after. It is without a doubt one of my most prized stories to tell about Sam. Her gift of inspiration and admiration were shining through her like huge rays of light. I was so proud to be her mommy!

Chapter 60.

The Bridge

Some people would say that EB instills a certain kind of patience in an EB parent. I never agreed with that method of rationalization. I never had patience, and I believed with my whole heart that a person is either born with it or not at all. I did not ever believe that patience was a learned behavior and I was living proof of that. I downright did not like waiting for anything. I don't care what it was - let alone a friggen' test that was going to determine the outcome of my oldest daughter's life. Oh, and I was praying, praying, praying and more praying. I even called my closest friends and asked all of them to pray for the same thing.

By this time I had told everyone what was going on and how we were back on the edge of our chairs again. EB has a way of constantly putting you on the edge of your seat a lot. The prayer that I asked everyone to help me with was this:

Please, God, heal Samantha. If this transplantation is to be hope for our sweet Sam then let the doors to our journey fly wide open with bold, clear signs that say: "This way please! Move in a forwardly direction." AND, God, if you should *not* want my Sam to follow through with this, then put a lightning bolt down in front of my car and stop me from going - so clearly - there will be no mistake about what it is that you want for us to do. I could only hope dear Lord that if it is *'your will'* for us to proceed, that you will give Sam a perfect donor match from either Chloe or James.

I had this feeling somewhere inside of me that we were going to find out we had a match. Somehow I felt like the match was going to be my James. That would make sense since James came into this world AFTER I got my tubes tied, right? Honestly whenever I tell that story (how James after my tubes were tied) to someone I always joke around about James coming here for a reason, for a purpose, and it must be a really important one. What could be more important than saving his sister's life? I mean, think about it for a minute: I made the decision to get my tubes tied after Jeff saved my life from hemorrhaging to death with Chloe and urged me not to have any more children for the safety of my own life. So I get my tubes tied with much sadness and despair because I really wanted to have more children, but again I put it in God's hands and I prayed about it. Really, just gave it to him and said, "Ok God it is all up to you now. I have to close this chapter in my life, but if it is *your will* and YOU want me to have more children, then I know that only you, the All-mighty and all powerful God, can make that happen. But for now please give me the strength to endure this sadness. And then I found out after I had the Tubal Ligation that I was pregnant, and it was a perfectly healthy unaffected-by-EB-or-anything little boy – what could more amazing than that? Right. Everything about James was amazing. Then at his baptism when Fr. Bob Morris held him up and introduced the newly baptized James Sheridan Jr., my little baby flew his arms wide open to the audience (which was all of our family and close friends) as if to say, "Here I am and peace be with all of you." There is not one person who attended James's Baptism that does not have full memory of that very moment when he flew his arms open. All you could hear from the crowd was this huge "gasp" and in the perfect moment of timing all together so it almost sounded like music. Fr. Bob even smiled loudly and commented on how God was shining through this glorious child.

So ok, it had to be James and pretty much for the next six weeks that's all I could leave in my mind.

The excitement growing around us was illuminating. The anticipation of this phone call to identify whether or not we had a match or not was growing by the week – no, by the second.

Still even with the idea that we could have a match there were also the unknown worries. Like: Are we ready for this chapter in our life? Are we ready to do such a 'life threatening' procedure on Sam? And more importantly, were we all ready for the outcome: good or bad? We were sitting on nails - not pins and needles - and we were forced to exercise patience. Extreme patience.

Six weeks later on just an ordinary day I drove over to Clearwater to see Carrie who not only was one of my best friends since middle school but she also did my hair. Carrie owns her own salon in Seminole, Florida, which is about an hour from where I live in Tampa. I really enjoyed the drive over and the drive back. I never got to have time alone for just me, so when the opportunity arose I would always volunteer to drive to her to get my hair colored. I guess you can probably figure, by now, that due to the constant state of stress I lived in with EB, my hair was about 2 inches grey all the way around, so I had to color my hair faithfully every four weeks. Going to hang out with my best friend while doing that was a huge break in the action for me and one I looked forward to every month.

On the way there and on the way back I would always roll the sunroof down and put my I-tunes on really loud. I do love music and the fresh air outside. Now although Florida happened to be the hottest place on earth, there was something magical about driving with the windows down, wind blowing in my face, and my I-tunes blasting my favorite tunes in my ears. I guess it was like my own personal vacation. Any parent who has a child with EB will tell you that you learn to accept and enjoy these little breaks when they present themselves because EB works hard to consume you.

I will remember this moment for the rest of my life as if it happened yesterday. I was on my way back home and it was later in the day. The traffic was a bit backed up, but I didn't care if it had come to a complete halt. My favorite music was playing, the windows were down, fresh Florida sunshine was beating on my face, and the mixture of cool air from my ac in the car (along with the warm air from the windows outside) was the remedy for any kind of stress. I usually ignored any calls on my little "me time" drives - unless of course I were to have gotten a call from my husband, or Sam, or any of my children for that matter. I always had to have my cell phone with me wherever I went all of the time. You just never know when EB is going to create havoc in your life and Sam might need me.

The phone rang just as I was passing over the Howard Franklin Bridge, which gets you to and from Tampa to Clearwater, or in this case I was coming from Clearwater to Tampa.

"Hello," I said, as I knew whom the call was from instantly. Number one, no one ever called me from that area code in New York, and number two, I knew it was Columbia with the call.

"Hi Marybeth this is Alana from Columbia."

I could hear the excitement in her voice just from her 'hello.'

"I have the best news for you Marybeth. We are all so happy over here and we could hardly wait to call you. We got the HLA typing results back and you have a match."

And she paused

I paused too, waiting for her to speak.

"Ok so who is it? No, let me guess, it is James right?"

I am telling you I could feel this woman's smile over the phone. What a cool feeling to have someone as happy as me and as excited for our family as we were – that she got to deliver such awesome news.

"No," she said. "It's Chloe!"

She went on to tell me that she had to have the test read again by two doctors because Chloe's HLA was such a perfect match that no one at Columbia could believe it. She said that, so far, they had not gotten this kind of perfect match from any other EB child and their sibling.

"It is a perfect match Marybeth, and we all are so very excited over here."

Instantly my mind drifted to: "Thank you God – Thank you God – Thank you so much. You have answered my prayers, God."

The first door was opened for us to walk through. Now the next hurdle was going to be insurance. Alana told me that if our insurance company approved the consult, then more than likely they would approve the transplant.

Alana was spilling with joy, which filled me up. I was so excited I could barely stand myself.

Oh my God we have a MATCH!

Having a match meant having Hope. Could it be that Sam might actually be cured? Is it true – is this really a cure? The next phase of our life was about to begin. Would we ever truly know what was really going on in Minnesota with Dr. John Wagner? What we did know was that now we have a match and we will be going to New York for our first consult that will open the door to the next chapter in our life.

We have a match! Will we have a cure? What is coming next?

References for EB

DEBRA of America
www.debra.org

Debra of America was founded in 1980 by, Arlene Pessar, whose son was born with Epidermolysis Bullosa (EB). Frustrated with the lack of available medical information on the disease, Arlene wrote countless letters to nursing journals seeking information about EB. The young organization sought to fill the large gaps in knowledge about the cause, diagnosis, treatment and a cure for the disease. After writing the first informational materials on EB, the organization identified regional representatives to promote awareness and disseminate this information. Initial television, radio and newspaper publicity drew attention to the rare disease. In the inaugural year, the first Debra newsletter was published and mailed to 100 EB families. Today, Debra Currents is mailed to approximately 13,000 families, health professionals, corporations, and public officials.

Throughout its 30 years, Debra has remained committed to funding research toward a cure, while responding to the increased need to provide direct services to patients and their families.

Debra of America, Inc.
16 East 41st Street
3rd Floor
New York, NY 10017

Tel: (212) 868-1573
Email: staff@debra.org

EB Info-World

A great website for information about EB
www.ebinfoworl.com

EBAN, Inc.

www.EBANUSA.com

National Rehab

Founded 18 years ago, National Rehab has grown from its root as a local supplier of off the shelf bracing in Sewickley, Pennsylvania to a nationally recognized leader in the provision of healthcare products.

National Rehab now operates its business in Moon Township, Pennsylvania (suburban Pittsburgh. The 25,000 square foot corporate headquarters houses all customer service, billing and warehousing activities, utilizing the latest in computer and operational technology.

Today, National Rehab is a regional provider of orthotics and prosthetics, and a national leader in the provision of specialty wound care dressings, urological and ostomy supplies. However large the company is or will be, Customer Service is the top priority. The staff is expertly trained and personally dedicated.

Doctors, nurses and healthcare professionals exhibit confidence in National rehab each time they refer a patient to our care. National rehab works with these dedicated professionals to achieve successful healthcare outcomes and improve the quality of patients' lives.

The commitment that national rehab exhibits toward its client base is extended to the community in which it operates. Many charities are the recipient of the company's commitment to community health and dedicated spirit of giving back.

Customer Service:
Phone: 1-800-451-6510, or 1-800-813-6080
Fax: 1-800-749-0711

National Rehab Equipment, Inc.
Airside Business Park
540 Lindbergh drive
Moon Township, PA 15108
Phone: 412-507-0077, or 412-472-0680
Fax: 412-472-0311
For medical equipment emergencies, please call 1-412-507-0077
The answering service is staffed 24 hours/7 days a week.
If you would like to receive company literature, have a salesperson contact you, or just give your comments and suggestions, you can e-mail us at:
feedback@nationalrehab.com

Be sure to leave us your name, address, and telephone number at which you can be reached.

Direct Medical

www.directmedical.com

A note about insurance:

Direct medical, Inc. can bill Medicare, Medicaid, and/or private insurance for you medical supplies. Your cost may be reduced to almost nothing. If you believe you may be eligible, please call our insurance department at 1-800-900-7054 to discuss these options. We will be pleased to assist you in any way we can.

Direct Medical, Inc. has been working with EB families for over ten years. In 2002 we were awarded the Corporate Award from DEBRA for our work in helping spread EB awareness and education.

If you wish to contact us; our customer service representatives are available Monday through Friday from 8 am to 5 pm CST. Or if you prefer you can email me at:
Aaron.deutmeyer@directmedicalince.com.
Our toll free number is: 1-800-659-8037
Or locally at: 713-869-5585

> **Direct Medical, Inc.**
> **(800) 659-8037**
> **5422 Kiam Street**
> **Houston, Texas 77007**
> **Phone: 713-869-5585**
> **Fax: 713-869-5568**

EBMRF
Epidermolysis Bullosa Medical Research Foundation

The EB Medical Research Foundation was established in 1991 b Gary and Lynn Fescher Anderson at the request of Dr. Eugene Bauer, then Professor and Chairman of the Department of dermatology at the Stanford University School of Medicine. His research team was exciting progress of their study of EB but needed additional funding to realize their goals.

The Andersons lost two children, Chuck and Christine, to Epidermolysis Bullosa. Both children suffered deformities of the hands and feet, chronic anemia, malnutrition and growth retardation. Neither child ever weighed more than 84 pounds. The worst part of the disease was their constant pain.

Near the end of their lives, they suffered as much as 75% of their bodies in open wounds. Relief came only when they were sedated to the point of sleep.

Chuck died at age 27 of skin cancer, another side effect of the disease and Christine died of heart failure at age 14.

In 2005, the EBMRF expanded its efforts by adding the Joseph Family, whose son, Brandon, was born with RDEB in 2003, to its Board of Directors and opening Administration offices in Los Angeles. Both Paul and Andrea Joseph, and their immediate family, are committed to raising funds for ongoing research, as well as awareness through the media and various fundraising programs.

To date, the EBMRF has raised over 5 million dollars for research.

The EBMRF is unique in that the Foundation pays no salaries. All work, including executive, development and administrative, is done on a volunteer basis. It is the goal of the Foundation to keep operating costs at less than one percent of incoming donations so that a full 90% of contributions can go directly to our research programs.

EBMRF

8909 W. Olympic Blvd. #222
Beverly Hills, CA 90211
President/Founder: Lynn Anderson
Executive Vice President: Andrea Pett-Joseph
Phone: 310-854-0957
EB Clinic Coordinator at Stanford University:
Lorraine Spaulding
Phone: 650-804-4820

similar pain. And instead of being honest about that pain, we dress it up, put some makeup over it, throw a smile and some swag on it, and keep it moving. I did that for so long because I thought my career depended on it. What was slowly happening is that my real life was in some trouble. The more I hid it, the deeper the trouble. Abuse began for me very early and showed up over and over again. There have been nights where I was ready to go. Go where? To heaven. Home. Away from this planet. I'm thankful to have friends who knew when I had these troubles and showed up! They are God's reminders to me that I am deeply loved, and that I have work to do. I grateful to God for helping me realize the truth: Moving through and healing from my pain is essential; my work is now helping others heal from theirs.

I stopped showing everyone this perfect image on the mic and in front of the camera. I stopped pretending that it was all good all the time.

After watching little girls in my neighborhood, women in my life and women in culture get abused and still have to move through life with that pain, I turned my work into a place for learning healing. My foundation, *JJ's I'm Me Foundation* encourages middle school, high school and college-aged young ladies like me, who didn't have healthy women to model wholeness to them. My first book, *Without Bruises*, is my manual for ending an emotionally abusive relationship for good. I'm in the middle of launching "Respect My Crown," a community and support system that encourages women to deepen their spirituality, grow in sisterhood, connect through accountability and expand in service. My work with my therapist, my service in the world, and my choice to create a "chosen family" of friends who love and respect me is helping me heal. Being a part of other women's healing is turning my dark places into light that guides other women out of their pain.

Bianca's story is so important to me. The way she is bringing these stories into the light and being vulnerable takes courage. I am grateful for her decision to uncover some of the things that may cause people to judge and criticize. She knows that it's more important that people feel understood and read how she got through it. How many of us have been bullied? How many of us have been ready to end it all? Her work is literally saving lives. I encourage you to read her words. Find yourself in her story. Then, make your own plan to understand your own pain, and seek healing. Your life is valuable, Queen! We need you to be here, your story will unlock so much for so many others.

Love,
Jillian "JJ" Simmons

Introduction:

Have you ever thought that life would be better if you were no longer here? Is mental health something you have or are struggling with or are you one who is unable to see the light under all your darkness? Welcome to the club! For a long time I was challenged; I kept hiding one of the biggest skeletons in my closet, while wearing a smile that led everyone to believe that I had it all together. I had made peace with living this life until I was forced to speak out without warning. I tried to hide it for way too long and I could no longer live with the guilt, shame or silence. After losing my cousin to suicide in 2010, the episodic moments began to run a common theme; TRAGEDY. How often have you found yourself feeling like there is absolutely no hope? That everywhere you turn life hit you like a ton of bricks. That was me. If you asked the people who know me, you would never think I struggled with major depression and tried to take my own life twice.

I grew up in a traditional Christian home. A place of love. My dad working in corporate America and minister, my mother a domestic engineer and 3 amazing siblings. Life was good! At least I told myself that. Let me be clear, this had nothing to do with my upbringing, I lacked what I needed in myself. Graduating with my Bachelors in Psychology, landing a gig right out of college you would think this is life right? No! There was so much I hid behind in order to appear polished so it didn't place light on me or create an environment where people felt the need to ask me what was wrong or ask how they can help? It all came to head more and more; and one day the tape I placed over my mouth had to be removed after a series of events I never wanted to share. Who knew it would land me here doing the VERY thing I never wanted to do. TELL THE STORY and more importantly become whole so I could be a catalyst for those who are tied to my purpose.

For the past two years I have fought hard to be a blessing to someone who feels their voice was removed from them by pain and strife. During my suicide attempts each time I heard a voice say "NOT YET" and I never interpreted the finality of what that truly meant for my life. I SURVIVED and NOT YET, planted the seed for me to be the "VOICE FOR THE VOICELESS". I feel so blessed to be walking in my purpose. I am able to look back at my snapshot of a young girl longing for love from people instead of unveiling it from within and now standing here to speak, teach and educate with multiple credentials, platforms and a nonprofit that is now helping the very audience I once crumbled in. None of this is my doing, as I give all credit to my Lord and Savior! I cannot even begin to take credit for what I know I am walking in and the shift that is about to take place. I have experienced such a whirlwind to get here, touched hands of other survivors and created a community of safety for those seeking to HEAL. I am learning even to this day that people need each other and if we are so brave to dig deeper than the surface we actually become someone's hero with no cape. I am so ecstatic that you are now the proud owner of this book. Can You Hear Me Now was only an idea in my sleep and became a reality at 3:40 am. This is a major step towards you finding light in the darkest of times. How, you ask? This book is designed with you in mind, it is one tool that will help you visualize in a better headspace. Sometimes we heal by connecting with like individuals and this is exactly my intention. It will assist you in times where you feel like giving up, but remember to grab the book, read a personal story of overcoming and refuel! Go to the journal and affirm yourself to keep fighting. I guess you are wondering how this book will truly help you. I stand to tell you that there are several tools needed to become the CEO of your life but this book is a great start. The journal in the back allows you to write down those emotions you may not want to speak out about. It gives you specific positive statements to say to yourself daily. Waking up saying one positive thing to yourself; you are already training your mind to start on a great note.

This book also has self-acknowledgement tools from a licensed therapist that will help you evaluate where you are and triggers. This was something I could do alone but instead I wanted to give my contributors an opportunity to speak out to help you break out. I truly believe that you CAN and will adapt a new appreciation for where you are and ready to push yourself to new heights! I believe in your healing, I believe in your voice! The WORLD needs you!

Dear Self……..

Dear Bianca,

Ha, I never thought I would be writing a letter like this to myself. Growing up people always thought that I had it all together, but boy were they wrong. As I sit here typing, I feel confused and tired while I listen to HillSong, "Music Is Therapy." I keep getting up, trying to talk myself out of reality, but it keeps guiding me right on back to saying these words: "I am so sorry!" I asked myself, "Why am I apologizing?" But then I thought about how I tried to give up on my life, not once, but TWICE. But I constantly told myself that this would never be me. Yet here I am, suffering in silence.

Do you remember when you were younger, you had the love of your parents but you knew that the love you wanted from your grandmothers was lacking? Why wasn't my grandmothers as loving as the grandmothers you saw on TV? As a child, you never felt that from "you know who (Dad's mom)" and her lack of love made you feel unlovable, misunderstood and confused. You couldn't understand why someone would want to deny their own blood. It seemed so absurd. You felt crazy for longing for the love of someone who never showed you she even deserved it. But then it came down to all the family crap you saw. The absence of love always made you question whether your existence really mattered, which was just another reason why you wanted to wave the white flag.

Growing up your parents did all they could to protect you and your siblings from hurting. They tried to keep you all from basically being the black sheep of the family. You did all you could to hold in the pain, but your beautiful smile is what in the most hurt.

As a child, you didn't know what troubles meant. You came home to loving parents who greeted you with a hug and a kiss, you had a loving home, food, clothes, and care. Oh, and let's not forget your parents introduced you to

Jesus. So how could you be unhappy? You often wondered why your grandma would mistreat you. You knew something wasn't right but you longed for her love. Maybe that was asking too much. You wondered why she treated you differently than the other grandkids. But when you got home, daddy and mommy would join you in love. You knew you were safe.

During middle school, you began to notice that something was not right. You began telling mom and dad that you didn't want to go to Momo's (Mom's mom) house. Even though she never told you she loved you, at least she tried. She showed you through your late nights of making the traditional Easter Bunny cake before Easter Sunday. You always wanted to ask her why she hid things and asked you not to tell the other grandkids… so you held that pain, too.

So high school comes along and after going to all the "white schools" you begged your parents to send you to the "black school." You wanted to follow your best friend because y'all were stuck together at the hip! You had a decent high school experience, but everything was still hidden in pain. There were times even back then when you questioned your sanity. You had no clue about life. It was weird in high school because all the emotions were heightened, and you never understood it. You remember going to church and "You know who" wouldn't even walk over to you and your family like she didn't have our blood running through her, but daddy and mommy kept you! You were so glad you had your sister at the same high school to protect you from the demons of family that walked the same halls as you. Do you remember how embarrassed you were when your own family would torment you in front of people? It hurt so badly because you weren't a fighter. You just wanted to go to school and get the hell out so you could run... run far away!

Do you remember when the body image issues started? In 10th grade, you kept telling yourself you were fat. Even though you cheered, ran track and were super fit in 10th grade. For some reason, you made yourself throw up one day and then again and again. You hid it as much as you could. But you knew you couldn't hide it for too long. Remember telling mom your stomach hurt really bad? She inquired and you had to tell her you were making yourself sick.

Years later, on graduation day despite graduating with honors, you felt proud and sad all at the same time. Sad because you were left wondering where is my family, how come everyone's family is attending and mine was limited? Did you think just because you accomplished something that this would change things with your family, Ha proved you wrong? You hated going to church, and school became an afterthought so you told your parents after graduation you were leaving and not coming back.

Well when you made it to college, you really lived life! You were partying like there was no tomorrow, running track, getting on academic probation and making amazing friendships. Until that one party your junior year, where a drunken guy told you he would blow your head off because you tried to protect your friend from being hurt. Remember running to your best friend's house and locking the door, crying hysterically? You couldn't call your parents because you wanted to be brave and you knew what would happen if you called. So you dealt! Life was okay… I mean you made it the best ride you could.

Oh, but remember graduation day! You thought it was an amazing day until "you know who" showed up. This time that child-like longing for her love was gone. Your grandmother had done nothing for you. You always wanted to make your parents proud, and you would stop at nothing to do so. They had gone through enough hell, why would the child who loved them beyond life disappoint them? You wondered why your grandmother showed up, but here is the kicker, you NEVER even saw her on graduation day, your dad told you that she was there. She left a card with money in it like we were cool or something. You harbored so much resentment and pain for her that you threw the card in the trash. You never understood how your amazing parents had to deal with all of that. You often questioned God as to how he let us have this person in our lives. You often thought about an award she deserved, you know how we give that #1 GRANDMA pendant, I would say more like, we don't really know you but we have the same last name PLAQUE, because God knew at this point the sound of her name made your skin crawl and made you cry all at once. You packed your house up and headed to start your new life with your psychology degree! You began to find your way, find a job (not a career) but it worked. You partied even more still just dealing the best way you can.

One year later, your cousin took her life. Do you remember the conversation you and her had that day? Remember how much you both loved tattoos. You planned to go pick her up after work but who knew that would be the last thing you talked about. Do you remember the text? Do you remember blacking out? Do you remember the funeral? Do you remember life never making sense after that? That is when everything changed girl, all the bottled up things you held in had you ready to explode. So much happened leading up to that next moment, things that you've held in until now. Remember getting in that awful car accident, receiving eviction notices, and losing your job? Do you remember that day you found yourself researching the best and easiest way to take your life? Do you remember the day you said you were done? You grabbed the pills and you thought that was it? But you failed.

You ran again but this time further away. You lived a life of sin, shacking up and miserable. You moved to Atlanta thinking everything would work out. It was like an overnight tornado that turned into a rainbow. Until it was no longer that sweet fantasy, you know the notebook stuff you sought out from somebody. Nope, instead you found yourself lonelier than before working a job making amazing money, more than you ever should have trusted yourself with. You purchased your happiness at the mall. You bought gifts for everyone, especially your baby brother because remember that promise you made to yourself? The promise that you would never let them hurt or corrupt him! And you made sure he knew he was loved. You often thought "F--- family!" But not my parents and siblings but everyone else who gave us hell. Yes, it was true, you rebelled in your head. This time it was scarier than ever to thrive because you moved thousands of miles away only for it not to work. But then you said to yourself - No! You were not going back home, you were destined to for something greater, so you decided you would stay in Georgia and make it work. But do you remember all the things going through your head? You didn't know anyone but your coworkers, you were only familiar with your church, malls (spending thousands on a weekly basis to convince yourself that you were happy)) and how to get to work with a few things in between. So how would you make it? Until that day... the day you felt haunted by your emotions when Momo got sick and all hell broke loose. You know how family gets when someone is ill...They wasn't worried about her health, they wanted the money. Do you remember the days of fighting for your mom as she fought hard to protect Momo from those demons? It was scary at times, taxing on your health but yet you watched your mom be a warrior! Although Momo wasn't the best, she tried and we fought for her to have the best of her last days. You were so lonely and you were ready to check out. Only this time you were determined to do it and be successful, but NOPE! God said no to you! He denied you ending your life again! This time you were so shattered, you had made peace. You held in more pain than ever. And life had no more value. I mean how could you forgive people, let along forgive yourself for doing the unthinkable AGAIN.

Fast forward to failed relationships again, from friends to lovers and many others. You decided to take your life back! You had to make yourself a project of healing. But first, you had to right your wrongs with God. It became personal this time around no one could tell you that God was not for you girl. He REDEEMED you, He saved you, He longed for you to come back and you did just that. Kicking and screaming but you went. You still had pain because you were still in chains, you never shared it because you didn't want those closest to you to know you were done with life. But one day it came out and damage control was in order. You had to free yourself, no longer fearing judgment, no longer trying to please anyone, no longer wanting to explode in pain but more in hope. The healing has not been easy but it is happening. Thank you God for saving me from destruction, thank you for my understanding family. God gave me life's true purpose when he gave me my parents, my siblings, some blood relatives and old and new friends that are more like family. This is my story, and I am not ashamed. I went back to further my education, who knew it would become a part of my healing and on the path to take it to that last step. Here I am standing in my 30's when in my late 20's I was done with life. I am not afraid to say yes I tried, failed, survived and so many people say it could be worse, but back then that was the WORSE. Well here is some hope. This may be your story too – embrace it. Allow yourself to feel. Know that you should not try to rush your healing. My pain led to my power. I felt empowered to take my life back for a greater purpose. I used everything I endured and overcame to help others and that is the ultimate goal of living purposefully. When you learn that you are here for a reason, your life will have an even greater meaning. I promise you that your life will change. Today, I am the CEO/Founder of Crying Voice Project, an Atlanta- based nonprofit that deals with suicide rehabilitation and anti-bullying. I have been afforded the opportunity to work with individuals from all walks of life. I am blessed to speak in many different facets of my story, just being a small piece of hope. I am also a Life Coach and Speaker. I can't tell you this will be easy but it is worth the fight. I overcame so others can overcome! Will you join me?

Love Always, Bianca

Dear Ajanae,

Tis' the season to be jolly! You have survived yet another nerve-wracking holiday season. I am so proud you hung in there. As the snowflakes gather on my bedroom window, I can vividly remember the time I survived the coldest winter of my life. In 2010, my holiday season was kick-started with a birthday card inside an eviction notice from my adopted mother. I was totally unprepared. I had no savings, no plan, and no family to stay with. I remember having to drop out of college because I could no longer afford it. I mustered the courage to leave behind my then two-year-old daughter because I didn't have the guts to drag my baby into the streets with me.

Some nights I stayed with friends, but most nights I found the parking lot of the nearest church or a park to sleep because that's where I felt safe. A few months later, I returned to my childhood home to see if the "holiday spirit" had visited my mother. I had hopes that she'd be kind enough to allow me to use her restroom to wash up. It was no secret, the relationship between my mother and I had been severed for years. According to her, there were plenty of things about me that left a bitter taste in her mouth. Much of which was biologically out of my control. I always had hope for us, but there was nothing in my spirit that justified why she would continuously turn me away. Despite what I had already known to be true, I constantly tested the waters, hoping one day she'll want to have a relationship with me. After all, I didn't ask for much. I was homeless, hungry, and dirty and above all, I was still her child. I just needed to take a bath. As I walked towards the door of my childhood home, I was able to catch a glance of my younger siblings and their friends setting the dinner table. What a rare sight! They seemed to be enjoying themselves. I could feel my heart racing, and the knots in my stomach as I watched my family, being a family, without me.

I managed to find the courage to knock anyway. After what seemed like forever, the front door finally opened, just enough to realize I was definitely un-welcomed. "Happy Holidays," I said. "I was wondering if I could use the bathroom for a few minutes, I won't be long." My mother laughed in my face and replied, "No Nikki, I do not want you in my house." I tried really hard to compose myself. I really just wanted to tell her how bad I had been living ever since my birthday, but the harsh reality was that she did not care. With tears rolling down my face, I begged and pleaded for a few more minutes, but my cries fell on deaf ears. The optimistic orphan in me wanted to try one more time. "Well can I have a plate to go?" I asked. She laughed once more before closing the door in my face. "Nikki, I would feed my dogs before I feed you anything." She meant that. I'll never forget how cold I felt at that moment, I was almost numb. My mother had left me out in the cold again.

The thought of being abandoned gave me chills unmatched by any winter storm I've ever witnessed. "Nobody cares," I thought to myself. At the time, there was no one around to make me feel any different. This had become my "norm" and I was sick of it. I was tired of living every single day constantly reminded of the fact that my loved ones didn't love me. I thought the best thing to do for myself was to end the misery and eliminate my pain. I decided very quickly that I would end my life by overdosing on prescription medication.

There wasn't enough time for me to consider how it would affect my beautiful baby girl or my baby sister, who was always rooting for me in the shadows. I did not think about how devastated my friends would have been. All I kept thinking was how unfair this game called "life" had been for me, and I did not want to play anymore. So, I chose to forfeit.

But then God called for a change of narrative. A friend of mine was miraculously at the right place, at the right time to rush me to the local hospital. In the midst of the lifesaving procedures I had to undergo, the first thing I remember thinking was "what a terrible ending." A story like mine deserved to be told, after all, I've been through. I deserved to live and be the one to tell it. I felt a mixture of emotions then but eventually was overcome by a familiar warmth of passion. It was the same passion I used to have whenever I fought for somewhere or someone to belong to. I had a passion for everything but myself. It was a horrible feeling. I was punishing myself with all of the many reasons why I should've been dead. I let my own compassion for myself die. The truth is, I deserve to be here! With the help of an amazing group of mental health professionals, I was able to turn a lot of that negative energy into the fuel I needed for a life-changing comeback. Once I made the decision to LIVE again, I had to immediately accept that my road to recovery would not be a stroll in the park. No matter what I was going through, I had to be honest with myself and my support team so when the "worst days" came around, my tribe and I were well prepared to deal with it. "You can't stop the rain from coming, but you can always carry an umbrella." Keeping a "crisis-prevention-kit" available at all times is very important. I make sure to include various items that can be used for coping skills, positive affirmations and a list of emergency contacts.

I have learned to make my mental health my priority. The boundaries around my peace and happiness are non-negotiable. Journaling daily helps me keep track of my overall mood, goals, and areas of improvement. Aside from creating various forms of art and music, I also share my stories with others. Being able to speak out has been the most rewarding. I am often gifted with empathy, constantly reminded that I am not in this fight alone. There is no doubt in my mind, God has a greater purpose for my pain. May this letter always be a reminder that the most beautiful days are seen after the darkest hours. Don't ever give up!

Love Always,
Ajanae Nicole

Dear Dana,

Oh precious, powerful Dana. Why did you ever see yourself as not enough? Why did you ever question your existence? Why did you let someone come in and validate you? Where did you lose yourself? Have you no purpose? Well, in my mind I didn't.

These are some of the questions I asked myself when I looked back on the things I endured in my lifetime. I tried to take my life. Not once, but twice. Funny thing is both attempts were tied to the "love" for a man. Actually looking back, two men, two different times, with the same name. Oh, Dana! You yearned for love so much. I remember the first time. He was my high school sweetheart, I knew we were going to get married, have kids, a house, a dog; the whole nine. But when the time came for us to go to college, we both went down south, but we chose different schools. Since our schools were only a few hours away, we stayed in a relationship. We were determined to make it work. I was in a brand new city and state all by myself. No family, no familiar friends really; I was literally starting over. It hurt so badly! I felt so alone. But I knew I could talk to my mom or family on the phone and talk to my long-time boyfriend at any time. It was a short bus ride to get to him if I needed to, so I knew I could get through this. But I wasn't prepared for what would come next. Over the first couple of months, we were acclimating ourselves to new areas, new people, and really just new everything. It was rough! I traveled down to his college after a month of being in school and we were making it work. But about five months into college, things started to get shaky. The calls became less frequent, the conversations were getting shorter, and the "passion" was dying. I started to feel the disconnect. Well, my feelings were right! He started cheating with someone from school; actually a few people he met there. I was all he knew when we were back home and he said: "he wanted to live now." Here I was, with all this hope that we were going to make it through college and get married, have kids, the house, and the dog; not realizing I was dating the dog. We broke up over the phone. There I was heartbroken, in my little jail cell-like single dorm room. I cried so much that night. I didn't go to class the next day or the day after. I think I missed the whole week actually. I literally only came out of my room to go eat and use the bathroom. I started smoking cigarettes more, drinking more, getting high, partying more and studying less. I was just so broken. I felt so lonely. Not just in a physical sense, but I was so dead on the inside. I would stay in my dorm and just get high and drunk and go to sleep. It was a repeat cycle. I don't think people knew what I was going through because I always masked it so well. I was good at acting like it was all good. I remember about a week or so after we broke up, I started looking through pictures, old pictures of us and I became full of so many emotions. I was running around my room high as ever and so upset. I was crying so much that my heart was racing so fast, my eyes were so red, and I was shaking and completely outside myself. I just couldn't fathom life anymore, I had so much built up anger from my teenage life and then moving here to Atlanta to feel alone, abandoned, not good enough, fat, ugly, unwanted and so much more; some of which was verbalized by him. It was all just too much. That night, I tried so hard to leave this earth. I drank a gallon of vodka and cognac, took some pills, and smoked as much weed as I could get my hands on. I was really trying to overdose on so much that I would never wake up. I screamed and I cried. I begged God to take me that night! I started to think of other ways to make it happen when it didn't feel like I was dying. Then, out of nowhere, I felt my body going numb. I felt like I was leaving my body. I started to sweat extremely badly. My hands were shaking. My eyes were rolling back and I could barely see anything. I said, thank you, God it's time, and then I passed out. The next morning came and that was the problem, THE NEXT MORNING CAME. I said, "God why? Why am I still here? Why didn't I die?" and I heard a voice say, "Save yourself" and I couldn't understand what that meant or why I was still here. This showed me that no matter what plan you try to put in place, God has your steps ordered. I should have been dead! I wanted to die! He wouldn't let me go. He saw more in me than I saw for myself. I tied my happiness to a man, to "love" and God showed me, He is love. He is the man that will give me love unconditionally. In my times of loneliness, I had to remind myself that God told me to "save myself." In my time of doubt, God told me to "save myself." In my time of feeling less than, God told me to "save myself." God saw me worthy! From then on, I knew I was not only worthy, but I knew that whatever life throws at me, I WOULD HAVE

TO SAVE ME! When you are drowning in life's sea of problems, experiencing hurt, pain, lack of self-love, brokenness, health problems, deceit, infidelity, loneliness or any other life issues – just know you are going to have to be the one to save yourself. God will give you the map, the directions, the address to type into your GPS to get to your destination, but it is up to you to DRIVE there. I have learned the importance of making sure my "vehicle" is up to par for the drive that I'm going to have to take. But, I remember that time when my "vehicle" almost had a total loss, again.

You would think after learning that valuable lesson Dana, you would know better now. Oh powerful, Dana. How did we end up here again? I remember it like it was yesterday. I met this guy. He wasn't really my type. He was short, not really as groomed as I like, and he didn't really have any of the things I required in a man, but I was single for a little while and I was in need of some love and companionship.

So I fell into the trap of getting wined and dined by this man. It started out pretty good. He took me on dates to nice places. He cooked. He cleaned my house. He got along with some of my friends. We laughed together and had a lot of "sexual chemistry," but only sexual chemistry. I confused it with real chemistry. Things were moving so fast. He was always at my house and started moving some of his things over to my house slowly. Fast forward, about five months into our relationship, I moved out of my house and we got a place together. He started to act different. He talked down to me. Took my car and just did whatever he wanted. He has disrespected me, my beliefs, my family, and even my friends. We started to argue more, and it would get so heated he would call me out of my name, smack me, choke me, and force me to do things. I no longer knew this person. I no longer knew me. It was all about what he wanted. I remember the day he told me that he cheated on me with 20 different women. What possessed me to still want to stay? Did I want or need love that bad? Or was it because he told me that no one would want me but him? Either way, I stayed longer than I was supposed to. I know I did because when I went to get my annual women's exam, my doctor called a few days later to tell me that I had contracted an STD. As I hung up the phone in complete shock, I threw my head back on the headboard and screamed, then I picked up the phone to call him. I remember telling him with so much anger and asking him why he did this to me. And his response was nothing but mind control. He tried to make me feel like I did this. Like I'm the one who cheated and gave him an STD. I knew I was faithful. I knew I didn't step out, but I knew he did. After a long argument, he finally musters up the words "I used a condom every time I cheated on you." My heart dropped at that moment. He said it with no remorse! As a matter of fact, he had already gotten an antibiotic for himself because he knew he had it and told me nothing. He didn't care about me or my life! On this day, I was stuck in the house, he was out of town and I was technically disabled and unable to drive my car. I sat in the room crying my eyes out. I had nothing but pain pills in the house and alcohol. I sat down in a corner of the house completely blank. Dead on the inside. I took about 10 pills and drank about 20 shots of vodka. With tears in my eyes, hurt in my heart, complete brokenness and lack of love for myself, I grabbed a knife. I tried to research ways to kill myself quickly with the tools I had on hand. As I attempted to take my life, I heard the doorbell ring. It frightened me. I don't think I was expecting anyone, and I knew he was out of town. I went downstairs and it was a friend of mine randomly bringing me something that she promised. That friend has since passed away, but I'll always remember this moment because I truly believe God sent her to me.

She saved me. That doorbell was right on time. God wanted me here for a reason. He kept telling me throughout this process that I was worth it. I thought back to the time when he told me to "save myself." I never knew I would have to save myself time and time again. I didn't realize until years later what it meant to truly save myself. Was it true? Am I worthy of more? Do I possess a power within? Do I have a purpose? I found my greatness, my power, my purpose and myself in the brokenness of my circumstances. Through all the trials I had been through, it was up to me to finally learn the lesson. God sent interferences to distract me from ending my life. Ultimately, it came down to me, saving me. I had to want more for myself. I had to want to be free. I had to choose me and take back my power. I had to learn to re-love me and learn that love was not a man, it was God and it was in me.

Suicide is so real. We don't talk about it because we don't want to be judged. We're too afraid people will see us as being crazy. I know so many would say, well why didn't you just leave? Are you stupid to allow a man to make you feel the way you did – to the point of suicide? But I ask you not to judge because it could be you. You, too, could be so far outside yourself and in need of love that you do unthinkable things and find yourself in my shoes. There are so many things that can lead to these feelings, this pain, and the need to leave this earth. My story begins and ends with love. It started with an extreme love for men and ended with an extreme love for myself. I had to build my own lifeboat to save myself from drowning because no one can help a drowning person when they don't even know the person is drowning. I encourage you to seek help. Talk about it. Find yourself. Live free. Choose you. Dream big. Be who you're meant to be. Don't let anyone steal your joy. Learn true love for what it is and not what people make it look like. Don't suffer alone.

Don't be scared of what people say. How you feel and what you go through is valid. But always remember your story. The story has to be told. But always remember, just like me you are still here. And even for those that are no longer here, you have to LIVE FOR THEM! Just know that what you went through was temporary, but it was necessary. Now go live, truly inspired!

Sincerely,

Dana "Truly Inspired Martin"

Dear Jameka,

I want to say you are a unique individual and don't ever allow anyone to tell you differently. You know God has placed a special calling on your life, but that was almost taken too soon. Let's travel back to your junior year of high school when you felt there was no purpose in being here. No one will ever truly understand the emotions and mental state you were in – they didn't walk a mile in your shoes. It was a few hours after being home, isolated in your room and you just felt hopeless. You were dealing with personal insecurities and family issues that no one knew you were battling with. You sat in the dark for hours and finally sent three text messages out to your closest friends. This is what others called the "cry for help." Just shortly after sending the first message, you heard a knock on your bedroom door. As your friend walked in, you knew this wasn't what God had planned for your life. God has a special assignment on your life and he doesn't want you to end it all! If it wasn't for that person coming as soon as they did, we don't know where you would be right now. You were called crazy for wanting to take your own life. We know that's not true. We know you weren't crazy. Later that week, the same friend said, "I didn't feel your spirit was here anymore. Walking into your room, I felt as though you weren't there." After speaking with a spiritual leader about the incident you felt a little more at ease. You didn't have any more incidents like that one the remainder of your high school career. You graduated high school and went on to college. There was a catch… you thought that you would never return to that dark place again. In 2015, you fell into a dark place again without understanding why. You were living the average college student life, but battling with your own demons. You became involved with men you shouldn't have. Engaged in sexual acts when you knew you shouldn't have. You lost your faith and didn't know if God was hearing your prayers. You would get drunk almost every night and weekend just to find a high and escape from everything. You placed yourself in toxic relationships which led to a domestic violence incident. You were embarrassed. You were ashamed of what you allowed to happen to yourself. You lost your sense of identity. You lost your purpose. You became insecure with yourself. You weren't YOU! The enemy continued to put suicide into your mind. The enemy said, "Just do it. End it now! You won't have to worry about this anymore." As the months passed by, you were slowly recovering from everything. No one knew the battles you were fighting mentally and emotionally because you were too embarrassed to speak on them. People placed you on a high pedal-stool. You couldn't bear to confess this to anyone - to have them look down on you. You have younger cousins who look up to you. You continued to push through and found a new focus. April 2016, you launched your non-profit organization, F.R.E.E. Foundation, Inc. The acronym is *Freedom Restores Everlasting Empowerment*. The mission is to help empower youth and young adults through leadership and community service. August 2016, you became a mentor to youth in the Atlanta area. You wanted an intimate relationship with God. You had not been to church in a year. October 2016, you attended Fusion, a young adults' Bible study at Victory World Church. That night opened your eyes! You shared a special moment with God that night. From that night forward, your life began to change in ways you didn't imagine. December 2016, you vowed to God that you would reclaim your purity and remain pure for your husband. You chose to be celibate in a sex-driven generation, where temptation is lurking in every corner. April 2017, a stranger stopped you as you were walking to your car and spoke blessings on your life and told you "God wants to bless you in ways you CANNOT

IMAGINE. He wants you to step out of your box, allow him to come in. He hears your cries and prayers." As the year 2017 passed by and God continued to work in your life, you chose to make another commitment. You publicly confessed yourself to the young adult ministry at Fusion and was baptized. You felt like everything that once almost broke you, the dark times, the insecurities, etc. had been washed away. November 2017, you and your best friend were obedient to what God told y'all to do for a family. That night can't even be put into words! It's a feeling that you praise God for every day. As you were driving home that night, the Holy Spirit continued to use you. You spoke life over three people and informed them about the talk you had with God and wanted to share with them. You had no idea what they were dealing with, you didn't know what was really happening. You were obedient. That same night you went into complete worship until 4 am. You didn't just stop with the family.

You allowed the Holy Spirit to continue to use you. Today, I want to personally tell you – don't ever stop listening to what the Holy Spirit gives you. Continue to place God at the center of your life. You have shared your suicidal and domestic violence incident with the generation under you. Not to "brag" about these things happening to you, but to inform them. That IF YOU CAN make it out of this dark place when you felt you couldn't, they can as well! You learned through this process that younger and older people have dealt with these same issues that you once had to deal with. You're helping to raise a new generation to learn to express themselves. Don't be ashamed. We all have a story that needs to be told. You never know who may be dealing with the same issues but don't know how to handle it. Please allow my story and my testimony to help you. God isn't done writing my story. I know he has assignments over my life that I'm going to conquer in different seasons of my life. Now, this doesn't mean you won't come to a bump in the road of life or a dead end. You now have a different approach to what life throws at you. Male, female, young or old it doesn't matter – you can overcome anything.

Tell yourself you are a strong, inspiring, ambitious, God-fearing, phenomenal individual! I am proud of your growth and your continuous growth.

"Peace I leave with you; my peace I give you. I do not give to you as the world gives. Do not let your hearts be troubled and do not be afraid."

-John 14:27

Love,

Jameka

Dear Jason,

It has been almost six years since… that night. The night I started taking pills and didn't want to stop. The night I had not an ounce of hope for the future and could see no way forward. The night I could not reach God, as if He were not at home to receive my call or maybe I had the wrong number all along. You know the circumstances leading up to that night, how the ground was shaken beneath you and you stood as reactively firm as possible… until that moment.

I was fortunate to wake up the next morning. From that point, I made a promise to myself to live in my truth even if it meant ignoring the impositions and expectations of others. I embraced cognitive therapy and mindfulness. I found a new personal meaning in my faith. I walked… I walk through every day in spite of uncertainty and doubt. I do what I need to take care of myself, to recharge and renew. I value myself in a way I never did before, so if that good can come out of such an ugly moment, I am grateful.

It has been almost six years since… since I was born anew.

With love,

Jason

Dear KJ,

I grew up in a small town in central Maine. I lived the good life being raised on a dairy farm with two older sisters and two younger brothers. Life was amazing… or so I thought. On June 14, 2009, at approximately 9 p.m. I was sitting in my bedroom which was in the attic of our old farmhouse. My sister and I heard a loud BANG. She grabbed her wooden sword from karate and we both bolted downstairs. Instantly in tears, as we scurried to find out what had happened. Our first thought was that our dad was beating our mother. She was screaming, screams that you can never forget. When my sister and I reached the office in the house, what we discovered was years to come of pain. A new life that was going to change us forever. A journey that we thought was not possible.

Our father had shot himself. He put a gun to his chin and pulled the trigger. The bullet had hit the top of his mouth and ricochet to the back of his head but it never exited. He was vomiting blood, and my mother was screaming on the phone for 911 to hurry up. I asked him if he was okay, but he just kept shaking his head no. The look on his face, knowing that he had fucked up is one I will never forget. My sister was pissed. She was angry. I pulled her in close to my chest and told her everything was going to be okay, but in reality, I knew that the good life we were so used to was now over. My father was brain dead but still alive for three days. On June 17, 2009, we received the phone call from the hospital that he had passed. It was very sobering.

In December of 2009, I expressed to some friends in my middle school class that I was going to hang myself on December 23. I did not want to be here for Christmas. I just wanted to be with my father. Ending my life seemed like the best thing that was going to happen to me. Thankfully, those friends told the principal. When I got home from school that day my mother gave me two choices. I could go to the ER with her or I would be escorted by the police. At that time, I had no idea that she knew what I had told my friends earlier that day at school. I didn't want to hurt my family any more than my father had already done, but I wanted the pain that I was feeling to end. I chose to go to the ER with my mother. It was the longest hour ever. When we reached the ER we waited for what seemed like forever. I was asked so many times why I wanted to hurt myself, and if I was planning on hurting anyone else.

It was close to midnight when I was told that I had to be admitted to a mental health institution for my own safety. I was so pissed. I spent one week in confinement. I couldn't shower alone, I didn't sleep, the food was shit, and I was away from my farm animals, which helped me the most. Luckily, I got released a few days before Christmas. I was watched very closely considering I had made plans to take my life before Christmas. The dreadful holiday came and passed. I continued to get mental help but I took myself off the depression medicine. It made me feel so drowsy. I was not myself for quite some time. It was the best decision I ever made. I ended up graduating high school a year early because I hated it. I was miserable being around people that didn't understand what I had been through. I had one good friend who I still talk to. She has been there for me a lot. Jenna is her name.

In September of 2013, I made the decision to join the United States Air Force. I was sworn in and just had to wait for a date to ship out to basic training. In March, I received the call that I would ship out on March 24. I picked my bags and left my family thinking I would never see them again.

It was a long eight weeks of adapting to a lifestyle I never even thought of. I knew nothing about the military. It gave my mind structure. It gave me a reason to live. It gave me balance.

In May of 2014, I graduated from basic training. My mother, little sister and little brother, Harvey came to Texas to see me graduate. When I left for training, my mother and I were not on good terms. I despised the decisions she had made with her life. When I left she honestly thought I would never talk to her or see her again. It warmed my heart to see them after a long eight weeks of finding out who I truly was.

In July of 2014, I received orders to go to Germany. I was so excited because I had never traveled outside of the country or the state of Maine. I left the country August 16 for an adventure I will never regret. I learned my job, kicked ass and worked hard.

Fast Forward to July of 2016, a summer I will never forget. My soul twin (brother) Henry flew to Germany to travel with me for two weeks. It was a dream come true. Henry and I have always been two peas in a pod. We are only two years apart, so growing up we were always close. We traveled to England, Paris, and a small town in Germany for the day. Spending time with Henry was an amazing feeling. Seeing him grow into a handsome young man was bittersweet. The day he left was the last time I gave him a hug. We were at the Frankfort airport in front of customs, and I hugged him and immediately the tears started flowing. I said to be safe and told him I loved him. Text me when you get back on the ground. For some reason, at that very moment, I knew it would be the last time I saw Henry. I watched him walk away as I slowly walked back to my car. I cried the entire way home. I wished our time hadn't gone by so fast. I was hoping it wouldn't be long before I saw him again.

On February 7, 2017, I awoke abruptly and saw a text message on my phone from my supervisor. It read "I am at your door." I quickly jumped out of bed and ran downstairs. I thought he needed something. I opened the door and two of my supervisors were standing

there with a look of utter disbelief. I was
informed that my brother had passed away in
the night. I was breathless. I have two younger
brothers but I knew it was my other half, Henry.
I felt empty. I ran upstairs to call my mother. I
was worried about her. I asked who was it, and
she said it was Henry. Then I asked what
happened… She said he committed suicide.
My heart sank. My best friend was gone
forever and the worst part was he did it to
himself.

The next few days, I got a flight home and
attended Henry's memorial. I was in shock,
disbelief, but relieved that we got to spend
those two weeks together the summer before.
Since losing both my father and brother to
suicide, I continue to climb mountains of
depression, anxiety, and PTSD daily. Every
day I wake up and I make the decision to live. I
am constantly telling myself that I need to live
for my brother. I have to finish what he started.
Henry was such a kind soul. He would give the

shirt off his back, and the cash in his wallet to anyone in need. At 22 years old, I have been hit with a very true reality that life is very short. I now live life from a very different perspective than I did ten years ago. To whoever is reading this, thank you for staying. Please make the choice to continue to stay. Your time on earth is not over yet.

I chose life for you,
KJ

Dear Tasha,

I'm proud of the woman you are today. Today is the day I celebrate your life and the happiness it brings to so many. You came a long way and with every breath you inhale and exhale, it brings on new opportunities to reinvent yourself.

You suffered from depression since childhood and no one in the family had a clue. It was painful. Growing up in a home where you saw men come and go beating on your mother was not easy to experience. You found yourself getting caught in between helping mom and the survival of yourself and your siblings. Being touched in places you didn't know existed, feeling feelings for the first time and being exposed to naked bodies had your mind in a whirlwind at such a young age. I'm elated you are even in your right mind. To experience being homeless three times does something to your mental state. To have your parent pick you up from school not knowing that the car you were in would be your home for the next few weeks.

As we fast forward into your young adult years, it took a broken heart to erupt years of silent pain, leaving you lifeless yet living.

You fell in love with someone who was willing to cover your insecurities. He was willing to hide you from outside hurt and pain. He made you believe that you were everything he wanted and you believed him. You made some bad choices because as long as he was happy, everybody else would just have to adjust. He was everything your father was not, yet that still didn't save you from the damage that came out of this union.

The day you found out he cheated broke your heart. The day he told you, you knew who he was, that was his way of saying you got what you deserved, and that didn't help at all. It felt like a slap in the face. It pulled you back into that closet you use to hide in as a child because you were afraid to save your mother once again from the beatings of a man you had to later speak to when you prepare the family breakfast.

Finally, you lost all hope in the marriage and there was nothing else to do but take the pain away by carving lines that represented a way out.

Trying to hold it together for the sake of titles; preacher, wife, and mom. Dealing with it head on and in public.

Remembering the breaking point... laying on the bathroom floor with the razor in your hand, crying out for help ever so silently. Not wanting anyone in the house to know what was happening because no one would understand and besides it's hard being the stronger one in the family.

So I write this to thank you for not surviving but for being a warrior. Although you wanted to die and each day was so hard to face, you did it. You pushed yourself to seek outside counsel. You found people that you could trust with your deep thoughts, people that loved on you when you were too ashamed to go to your family members. You felt every hurt of abuse growing up and you mourned your marriage. Look at you now – you're career driven, goal oriented and making life happen the way you want it to go.

Through all the ups and downs, you put God first! You prayed daily. You even read self-help books, listened to positive music, watched positive shows, and more importantly, you gave social media a break.

You made it out of darkness not only for yourself but to show others there is always a light and I'm here to show you how to find it!

Thank you for choosing life,

Tasha.

Dear Rae-Lonnie,

I remember all the times I have tried to take my life. The first time I was just so tired of not being heard or feeling loved and feeling like I was a mistake. I was in my room, I grabbed some pills and I took them. I remember getting sleepy. I went to sleep and woke up hours later with a headache. I didn't understand why I didn't die. I always felt like no one understood me. The last time I tried to kill myself, I had a gun.

I'll never forget I was 17, I was tired of going unheard. I felt my life crashing down. I was depressed and had no one to really explain what was going through my mind. I got kicked out of school and went to another one and problems kept coming. It seemed like God had forgotten about me.

I dropped out of school for a while. I wasn't going to go back. When I got home I was crying, I was hurting and I was done. You could see the anger and hurt all in my eyes. I went to my pawpaw's room & I grappled his gun, but before I did that I wrote a post on Instagram saying I was about to kill myself.

I was tired, fed up, I felt nobody loved me. I felt worthless. I went in the restroom crying and looked at myself in the mirror. My phone kept going off but I didn't care. The last time it went off I was pulling the trigger and the bullet hit the wall and not me. I dropped to my knees crying, so scared because I realized what I could have done. I picked up my phone and it was a lady I never met or even knew followed me. She was telling me not to do it and that it will be okay. She told me that God didn't leave me. I kept crying and I was talking to her, letting her know that she saved my life.

At that moment, I had to start fighting for my life. The past two years, I have been baptized and I graduated which I never thought I would be able to do. I literally have to stay prayed up every night. When I'm going to sleep I make sure my worship music is on, because it feeds my spirit. I have to pray non-stop.

I ask for help when I need and I can honestly say it has helped. The main thing I have been doing to live free and stay free is communicating with God. I always rebuke evil spirits and negative thoughts. I ask God to show me where to go and what to do. I keep a positive attitude and I have a better mindset now. Reading God's word and knowing that God loves me more than anyone else does is so reassuring. Now I know that everything happens for a reason and that things get better with prayer and faithfulness. I am now 19-years-old and will be going to college for nursing.

Things happen in life and sometimes we feel like we will not make it, but God always has our back even if we don't have our own. He will.

Love,

Rae-Lonnie

Dear Richard,

How could we have ever guessed that being bullied and feeling like an outcast could lead to so many negative feelings, self-hatred and destruction so early on in one's life? Before we dive into this, I must let you know that none of the initial things that happened were your fault. Just because you speak, look and act differently than those considered "popular" or "normal" doesn't mean that you deserved any of the negative treatment. You might have been embarrassed, talked about and mistreated, but it doesn't mean that your life is any less important. I'll never take away from your experiences because they all are meaningful.

However, what I will say is that none of those experiences are worth you taking your own life. You matter so much and all the things that you've had to face are temporary. I know that it doesn't feel like it at the moment, but you can overcome every bit of adversity in your life &

stay alive in the process. Your life matters so much, and you deserve to live. This concept might not make sense and I get that. I spent so much time wanting to die and be left alone that I never actually took the time to know what it is to live. Not just living to survive, but to truly thrive in life.

I remember being bullied for my weight and going home one day after school thinking that I could cut some of the fat off my body in an attempt to be loved and accepted by my peers. I was so young and had no clue what I was doing as I tried to take that butter knife across my stomach. It's crazy that our young imaginations can really lead us to places that can be detrimental later. I don't know why I was so intrigued by the blade as I cut myself, but I felt this rush of adrenaline take over. Even with that rush, I was scared because of the mess I was starting to make. I remember saying that my parents would be home soon, and I had to hide all of what had been done. As

I tried to move hastily, I slipped the knife under my bed, opening a doorway of access for more harm to come.

Over the next few years, I started dealing with my mental and emotional pain by trying to balance it out with physical pain. Knives and other sharp objects became a huge part of me. With so much chaos in my young life from seeking validation and wanting to be accepted, it seemed like the only time I found peace was when I gave into that depressing feeling and the voice that encouraged cutting. Something shifted however because it wasn't just a thing of wanting to cut anymore. It grew deeper and stronger. The urges to cut became an urge to leave it all behind.

I started functioning with a mindset to die and thinking that everyone would be better off if I wasn't around to cause such a mess. During my teen years, this feeling seemed to grow stronger as I always felt stuck or like I was never enough. By this time, the knife wasn't enough. My attempts became more along the lines of painkillers and homemade nooses accompanied by a goodbye letter. It's crazy to think that every attempt failed, but I'm glad that they did, after a period. My young adult life was the hardest, however. Seeing such a change from friends towards the end of high school to losing out on the opportunity to pursue football because of a health condition.

Depression seeped in something heavy as I entered college. I was fully consumed by the feelings of neglect and rejection and the thoughts seemed to skip past being a single action, but rather a full-blown lifestyle. I lived like I had no regard for my life. Not going to class and failing with a 1.4 GPA, gaining 170lbs in 18 months, getting into an abusive relationship and accepting the abuse and blaming myself for it. I was a complete mess. My relationship with my parents was all but gone and I tried to do so much to cover it up in front of people I encountered. I used my position in organizations and leadership opportunities to feel important. Arrogance became the fuel to hide so many insecurities. The only issue is that I couldn't hide for much longer. By January of 2008, I was running out of energy and didn't care to try anymore. With everything seeming to spiral out of control and my intimate relationship on its last line – I finally had enough. On Dr. King's birthday, I took a big cutting knife and tried to end it all. Five huge gashes down my left wrist and I found myself in the back of an ambulance headed to the ER.

I blacked out from losing so much blood. I remember waking up to the doctor pouring some type of liquid on the open wounds to help stop the bleeding. He told me how lucky I was to be alive and just how much damage I had done. He then said to me that I had a purpose in life and I need to figure out what it is. I had a lot of time to reflect in that hospital and even more during that semester as I found all my secrets being put on blast around the campus. Having to go back and face so much ridicule and judgment and trying to figure out if I should try suicide again and succeed this time or do I face what's in front of me and crawl my way to freedom eventually.

I chose the latter for one major reason and that was the genuine love and help I received from a handful of people who saw me for who I was and still decided to take a chance on me. They didn't judge me but rather loved me through and out of all the hell that I had been in for the ten years leading up to that point. It was through the investment of these people and me paying attention to it and learning to appreciate it that really changed a lot for me mentally. So often we focus on everything that's going wrong and we don't give a thought to the highlights in our life.

Even if there aren't that many highlights, the truth is that they exist, and we must start focusing on them. The more I gave into what wasn't happening, the more I allowed my mind to go to empty spaces where I didn't see a purpose in my own existence. The road to recovery was tough at times. There was a lot of mental, emotional, spiritual & physical work that went into this process. While the work seemed tough at times, the results have been well worth it. Depression, the thoughts of suicide and the actions that follow don't own me anymore.

They don't control you and they don't own you either!

Love,

Richard

Dear Sholante,

Life is way tougher and complicated than I ever imagined. It seems like a downward spiral... a never-ending struggle. We all have fight in us but there comes a time when we get tired of fighting, lose hope and start to give up. I'm exhausted because I am tired of being tired. The feeling of life is slowly being drained from my body. There's a consuming pain that is such a burden that you're willing to do ANYTHING to make it go away.

I had felt this way for months, but for no particular reason. I would sleep for 17 hours a day and cry myself to sleep every night. I would cry in the shower every chance I had. I barely had enough energy to wake up and go to work. I would get off work and smoke weed and drink until I couldn't feel anything anymore... but that didn't really work either. My family didn't even notice the change in my behavior. I always told them I was tired and they never thought much of it.

Depressed? No, not me! How could that even be possible? I know I don't have the worst life. Others have gone through way worse than I have. I am clearly overreacting, or am I?

It was March 1, 2017, the day I thought about ending my life. I thought about it every single day. I wanted it to be as quick as possible with as little suffering as possible. On March 6, many ideas ran through my head, but only one stuck with me. I wanted to try heroin for the first time and overdose on it. I figured, why not go out with a bang and feel good at the same time? I was desperate and willing to do anything. I sat in my dark room by myself and thought hard. Why do I feel like I'm dying to live? Why won't it go away? Why me? I was pretty settled on ending my life that night, and all I had to do was make a few phone calls and get the merchandise I needed. Then the 0.001% of fight left in me said, "Sholante, beg for help one last time, and if it doesn't come your way then you know you tried your best. If you try to get help one last time, then you won't die with any regrets." With the last bit of fight and energy I had, I begged my older brother (J) to please help me. I told him that I was desperate and even though he didn't see it, I was in a deep dark place and needed to be checked into a hospital immediately or something bad might happen. J was my last resort. I tried to explain the situation to my mother plenty of times, but she failed to realize or believe anything. The following morning March 7, J checked me into a psychiatric facility where I began treatment for 5150 and severe depression. I was in a hospital for nine days and was put on antidepressants and anti-anxiety meds. My first few days were the hardest. I had no clue what to expect.

To my surprise, all the patients had all gone through a traumatic event in their life that made life seem impossible at the moment. We all had a story we needed to tell.

Every individual has a story of their own and

here is mine. I am a child of three born to a teenage mother and a father who was in my life only when it was convenient for him. I feel like I lived a pretty normal childhood until the age of four. I was molested repeatedly and raped by my uncle. I somehow buried this away in my subconscious but lived with all the scaring effects of this traumatic event. At the age of four, my innocence was lost. I no longer trusted anyone. I was confused about love. I started to become self-conscious about my body. I felt different than most kids my age and that's because I was different. I didn't have many friends and couldn't talk or relate to anyone about my situation at such a young age. I started having unexplainable sexual desires at the age of nine. I didn't know where they were stemming from and I didn't have anyone to talk to about it. Throughout high school and college, my sexual behavior became extreme. I sought love through sex and attention. At the end of each hookup or verbally abusive relationship, it seemed to hurt me more and more. I started to feel objectified and knew that men only wanted me for my body. While going to school, I started working at the age of 14 to support myself – which was a huge stressor on top of becoming a teenager. By the time I was in college, I was working, going to school and drinking almost every night to help me deal with my emotions. In 2015, my junior year at university I almost flunked out. I was so overwhelmed with life, that I was forgetting everything, losing important things and I was always so tired. The ironic part of this is I majored in psychology. For two semesters as I walked to my classes, I passed by a mental health office and was scared shitless to go in and see if the services offered could help me. When I started failing my classes that's when I decided to put on my big girl panties and take a visit to the mental health office. That was probably one of the healthiest decisions I made. The health office offered me free one-on-one counseling as well as anti- depressants to get me out of my rut. Six months into my treatment I felt the need to tell my mother that I suffered from depression and was receiving medical attention for it. My mother didn't take the news so well. She told me that I didn't have depression, I had no reason to even be sad, and that I was just ungrateful. She wanted me to go off my meds because they were changing my behavior. I stopped taking the meds and less than a year later I relapsed extremely tough in 2017. Growing up my father wasn't always around, except when it seemed convenient for him. As a child, I only really remember when he was around to give me and my siblings excessive spankings. He was never really a father figure but was always around when it came to our harsh punishments growing up. I grew up in a backward dictatorship type family. It was "do as I say, not as I do." I remember my dad would lock the garage door with my brother in and blast the stereo for what seemed like 25 minutes while he was beating my little brother. Since K was 14 he has been either in camp or jail majority of the time. It is very hard for me at times.

Throughout all of my struggles, I have been free from suicidal thoughts for almost a year. I have learned that it is okay to ask for help. I am a very independent woman and I never ask for help, because it's almost like a sign of weakness in my eyes. Boy was I wrong! Asking for help makes you a stronger person. Everybody has their opinion on anti-depressants, but I needed them and they helped save my life.

Never compare yourself to other people, Sholante!!! I've learned to focus on the now, not the future and not the past. I cannot rewrite my own history. I have also learned that if I need to get something off my chest then do it. I finally had a talk with my mother and wanted her to acknowledge my mental health. I forgive my father for being a crummy dad. Now it's time to live my life without any regrets or any extra baggage holding me down. DO WHAT MAKES YOU HAPPY WITHOUT ANYONE'S APPROVAL. I've learned that it's my life's so my happiness comes first, whereas I used to put others happiness before mine. There are good days and I definitely have my bad days... some days are harder than others. I enjoy going to the beach and listening to the waves, it calms my anxiety after a long stressful day. Some days my anxiety gets the best of me and I can't help but think about a relapse. I have learned to talk about what triggers my anxiety. I have learned to be a lot more open with my depression. More individuals are depressed than you think. I didn't know until I wound up in a hospital. My message to myself and anyone reading this: SPEAK UP ABOUT DEPRESSION, TALK ABOUT IT. I know if I heard more individuals talking about depression I would have sought help a lot earlier and not been so ashamed. Sholante, you have come a long way in your young life. At the age of 26, you have accomplished and beat many odds. Sometimes you need a reminder that you are kicking ass so here is a letter to yourself to show you how far you have come.

Love,
Sholante

P.S you are stronger than you think so keep fighting, your fight isn't over yet!

Dear Rhonda,

As I sit here in the living room watching the kids run around in the neighborhood, I reflect on what happened to me. I remember the many times I didn't want to play because crying was easier. The abuse you received from mom and dad left you exceptionally vulnerable to toxic relationships. The first time you tried to kill yourself was when you were 13-years-old and had your first miscarriage. After you healed from that, you found out that your boyfriend was cheating on you and boy did that scar you for an extremely long time. I can still remember when mom was sleep you went in her medicine cabinet and grabbed her sleeping pills and you counted them; I'm not sure why you did that but you came up with 23 sleeping pills and you took them all. Shortly thereafter you laid in your bed and fell asleep.

For whatever reason, your boyfriend came over unannounced and came into your bedroom and noticed something odd about your body language. He told the ambulance that you were non-responsive and hallucinating at the same time. I can even recall him slapping you a few times calling your name "Rhonda". You appeared to those around you that you were drunk, you then pointed to the empty pill bottle on the floor. I was so scared for you as they rushed you into the emergency room to pump your stomach, you were just out of it! Your eyes were rolling around because the pills were starting to take effect. Thank God your boyfriend got there in time, otherwise, you would have succeeded. After they pumped your stomach I remember you asking if he could stay with you and he told you they would say no. You asked anyway and low and behold the answer was no. Your boyfriend later told you he knew the answer was going to be no because the hospital turned you over to the youth psych-ward. You stayed for four days and quickly learned how to play the role to get released. Your family thought you were crazy but never took the time to get you help. They didn't realize that the situation with the boyfriend triggered old feelings of being abused, abandoned and unloved. Over the next two years, you attempted twice again once with aspirin and the other time by cutting your wrist. Nothing as serious as the first but the pain and lack of love simply never improved for you. You were a heavy drinker which resulted in exotic dancing and selling your body for a living. No wonder your life continued to spiral out of control until age 22. What a miracle!! This was the happiest day of my life. January 27, 1997, you went to church and gave your life to Christ. For the next 20 years, you studied and learned how to be a voice for the voiceless. You learned your purpose in life and became a true gem to those around you. You went on to write your first book *Don't Spill the Tea, One Woman's Journey from Abuse to Abundance* and began a non-profit for battered women called Rose of

Sharon Transitional Living for Women. You have preached the gospel of Jesus Christ, and will soon be known as an international speaker with your first overseas speaking engagement in France in April 2018.

When people see you now they have no clue of the past you lived, endured and conquered. I am so glad to be you. You have made me proud in so many ways. By walking with Christ you were able to fight suicidal thoughts and grit your teeth through the pain of life and still subdue it.

I now know my value and my voice will never be silent again. Had I left this world too soon, I would have never touched so many lives. With God's help, I will continue being a voice for the voiceless. Now I can say, it was so not worth it. To take the life that God gave you would have taken away a divine blessing from the world.

Thank You for living,

Rhonda A. Thompson

Dear Stacey,

You made it! You graduated from Georgia State University with a biology degree. You faced your fears and applied to grad school to get your Masters in prosthetics and orthotics. Did I mention that you have an interview for the University of Texas Southwestern and for California State University? Your dreams are slowly but surely coming true. I know it's hard to believe. Little Stacey Brown has a chance at grad school.

I know there was a point in time when you felt like you weren't going to make it. You felt as if life was too hard to deal with and healing was something that seemed so unrealistic. Did you spend a lot of time asking why me? Why did I have to be born with a physical disability? Why did I have so many scars? Why did I have to be different? You were born with congenital flexion contractures which means you were born unable to extend your arms. In the second grade, you had an operation on your right arm.

It consisted of a skin graph, metal rods being drilled into your bone, a cast, and a lot of physical therapy. Every day you wore a jacket to school to cover up your scars. Who would have imagined that you would soon have to have surgery again?

Remember what happened the summer before fifth grade started? You were in a car accident. You were on your way from Philadelphia to Maryland to spend the summer helping your grandmother at her ice cream shop. It was a two for one special, spending time with your favorite person and being around your favorite dessert. You were sharing a seatbelt when a black SUV hit your grandmother's car. If you didn't have that seatbelt on you would have flown through the front window of the car. It was a lot going on. Your stomach was in pain, you threw up your food all over the back seat. There was a lot of yelling and before you knew it you were in a helicopter headed to John Hopkins Hospital.

There you were again having another operation in another hospital bed. You soon found out that the seatbelt cut a part of your small intestines and that you weren't supposed to live through it. Your summer quickly went from ice cream and swimming pools to prune juice and needles. You were in constant pain... it hurt to sit up and you could barely walk. You had a scar going down your stomach and the surgeon decided to use staples instead of stitches. A month later, you were released from the hospital but that was only half the battle. School started in August, and you were a fifth grader! You should have been excited since it was the last year of elementary school. You were still healing from your operation. As a fifth grader, everyone was required to carry all their textbooks as they transitioned from class to class. They wanted to prepare us for middle school. The accident caused you to have back pain, so you could only carry your books in a rolling book bag. The other students didn't like that. They thought it was unfair. You were already getting teased for not being able to do a push up in gym class and now this. It's like people blamed you for your disability or felt that it was your fault for being in a car accident. You felt alone, and you felt like no one would understand.

In addition to all that was going on at school. Home didn't really feel like a home. It didn't feel like a safe space. There was a lot of arguing and once again you felt alone. You wanted to run away but there was nowhere to hide. You felt trapped.

You thought about taking your life. You knew that taking one of the kitchen knives and slitting your wrist would get the job done. No one would miss you, no one would look for you. You went to dinner with your mom, little sister, and stepdad and told your parents that you wanted to commit suicide. Of course, they thought you were just doing it for attention. The next day you were checked into the Rainbow

Center, a place for kids who are suicidal.
Your mom picked you up from school early that
day. You arrived at the center with nothing but
a plastic bag full of clothes. You slept in a room
with no TV. Every morning you had a nurse
give you medicine and take your blood
pressure. The other kids were there for a
variety of reasons. During group therapy, they
would say how their parents' divorce caused
them to be suicidal. You decided to go along
even though it was a lie. You figured if you just
told the counselors things like "I blame myself
for their divorce" the faster you would be able
to go home. In a week you were released from
the center. Still in pain, still feeling alone, and
still depressed.

From that moment on you struggled with
suicidal thoughts. When life would get too hard
you would think about jumping in front of the
train or slitting your wrist. Well, you made it to
the other side of suicide. You started to go to
counseling and this time you were honest. You

dealt with your pain and for the first time in a long-time healing became realistic. You not only learned how to forgive others, you also learned how to forgive yourself. You journaled and wrote poetry. Instead of looking at yourself as a victim, you began to look at yourself as a survivor. A survivor of depression, a survivor of multiple major operations over the course of your life, and a survivor of a near-death car accident. You began to thank God more for saving you. The most important part was that you began to read God's word. You realized that you're never alone because God is always with you.

 This past May you lost your cousin, Kevyn to suicide. It still hurts… You've never been in so much pain and your heart literally hurt. Suicide never hit that close to home before. Every now and then you'll think about Kevyn and you'll remind yourself to check in with yourself. You'll also remind yourself that suicide isn't an option and that it doesn't get rid of your pain it just transfers it to other people. You learned that depression doesn't control you. You are not broken and you do not need to be fixed. Last but not least, your pain has a purpose but your purpose is bigger than your pain.

Thank you for choosing me,
Stacey

Dear, Rob

When people look at you they may see a person in good health, great family, and friends, always a smile for everyone who passed me with a desire to promote health and fitness. Did I get that right? Well here's an example of, you never know what's behind a person's smile. I can tell you that 100% of what you SEE is superficial. What you don't SEE is a man who was very depressed and suicidal, yup, you read it right. Depressed. Suicidal. Being active in sports and going to the gym had always been the norm for me.

Until THAT day, that day in November, when that norm for me changed, it changed my life. My father had taken his own life. In some ways, I felt he had taken mine too. I no longer had the desire to do most of the things that I once found enjoyable. Words could not express the pain and the void it left in my life. The smile that everyone knew me to have was gone. The depression had won, I no longer wanted to hunt or fish and lost all motivation to function. It messed me up beyond words.... I didn't work for an entire year!

My memory often brought me to late 2011, I recall saying "I can't deal with this life without my pop". I figured I would drive to where my father killed himself and end it all there with him. Why not right? So I did. I took the drive there... I sat in the car for about 45 minutes and I just couldn't do it ... a part of me was still strong. It was like my dad was saying to me, "Slick, you have Liyah and you got stuff to do with your life, take your ass back home" after spending some time in the car dealing with my emotions, crying and then crying some more. I did just that. Went back home.

My name is Rob Brown. I'm 33 years old, a single father, entrepreneur, suicide prevention and mental health advocate... and I am also suicide survivor. On November 10, 2009, my father who was an army veteran and supervisor at the Veterans Affairs Hospital committed suicide as a result of his depression at the age of 52. I have always been active, playing sports and going to the gym, however, when my father took his own life. That messed me up beyond words. I didn't eat for days, I lost all motivation for sports and going to the gym. I didn't work for an entire year! For those that know me, know that I have never displayed any behaviors that would give someone the impression that I was suffering from this illness. That's because I wasn't, a life-changing situation caused me to fall into that dark place. I remember one day late 2011 at the age of 27, I said: "I can't deal with this life without my pop" and being that I had B.S in Health Science. I knew the body and I knew which way I could kill myself without it being painful to me... I figured I would drive to where my father killed himself and end it all with him. Why not right? I took the drive there... I sat in the car for about 45 minutes and I just couldn't do it... it was like my dad was saying to me: "Slick, you have Liyah and you got stuff to do with your life, take your ass back home". I went back to the gym, released stress and tension and never looked back. Fitness saved my life. I created my own fitness brand called ABSouluteFitness.

My goal for starting ABSoulute Fitness is to help save someone else's life in all aspects, whether it be mentally or physically. Suicide doesn't just affect one particular group, race or gender, it affects society in general! I sat down with my longtime friend and fellow suicide survivor, Army Veteran, suicide prevention and mental health advocate Miguel Sierra, to brainstorm the best way to continue serving as an advocate for suicide prevention. Being that I was already an established entrepreneur, founding my own fitness and wellness brand, ABSoulute Fitness, in 2014 to honor my father, a victim of suicide. It was only right to continue. After a few weeks of brainstorming and following the "mission readiness" format of the Army, we decided to create ABSoulute Life, a brand dedicated to improving productivity (mission) through interactive workshops that enhance skills in prevention of suicide, sexual harassment prevention, workplace resilience, and the correlation between physical and mental fitness. Our goal is to work with companies, schools, community organizations, colleges, churches, and any other organizations to instill in their members a sense of community, cohesiveness, and accountability for self and others. I had to find a way to build on that strength that allowed me to walk away from taking my life. So, to the gym I went and discovered a man who was strong enough, strong enough to fight back and walk out of that dark place that once held my life hostage. It was through my faith in God and my love for my own life that allowed me to be ok with Dad being in a different place. THAT was the true strength. I've never looked back on those dark moments, I hold memories only to reflect on what could've been, where I am now and my life has to offer through fitness and Health. Where I once wanted to use my knowledge in Health to take my life, I now dedicate it to saving many..... Fitness saved my life! My goal for starting ABSoulute Fitness is to help save someone else's life in ALL aspects of life, whether it be mentally or physically. Anytime I asked my pop for anything he would say "Absolutely, son" so that's the story and name behind my brand "ABSoulute Fitness" It's because of my father and how he and fitness saved my life! All that has happened has led me right where I am! There isn't ANYTHING that you cannot do! Whatever you are going through use that to motivate you. Everyone has a story. My pain, trials, and tribulations are not greater than yours. My story is no different, if I can do it, I'm telling you – you can do it as well!

Love,

Rob

Therapist Corner: Vaughn Gray, *LPC*

How Do We Address Suicide?

Suicidal ideation is a process of constantly thinking and worrying about how to bring finality to long-enduring emotional pain, with death being the ultimate solution. Many individuals that have ideas of taking their own life often don't communicate these thoughts or feelings with those around them. It is an intimate choice that one does not come too quickly nor easily, so much so that loved ones are often left asking the questions **"How did we not know?"** or **"What could we have done to help?"** There is no true face or look of an individual that is contemplating completion of suicidal ideation. People from all demographics experience stressors in life to the extent to where they feel an elevated level of despair and a loss of hope. *However*, there are many resources, training tools, and systems of support available to assist those in need and those who want to support.

As mental health practitioners, we consider three essential questions when assessing suicidal thoughts with our clients:

- **Does he/she have a reason and means for choosing suicide?**
- **Does he/she have a plan for completion?**
- **Does he/she have the ability to do so?**

Types of Suicidal Thoughts

Everyone's experience of suicidal feelings is unique to them. You might feel unable to cope with the enduring difficult feelings you are experiencing. You may feel less like you want to die and more like you cannot go on living the life you have. The Mayo Clinic notes that suicidal thoughts have many causes. Most often, suicidal thoughts are the result of feeling like one can't cope when faced with what seems to be an overwhelming life situation. If you don't have hope for the future, you may mistakenly think suicide is a solution. You may experience a sort of tunnel vision, wherein the middle of a crisis you believe suicide is the only way out. Some of these thoughts can include:

- Believing there are no other options
- Sensing your family or friends would be better off without you
- Thinking you've done something so horrible that suicide is the only option
- Experiencing unbearable pain that feels like it will go on forever
- Wanting to escape your suffering
- Wanting to let your loved ones know how much you hurt
- Wanting to hurt or get revenge on others.

Warning Signs: There are several warning signs that individuals can observe to determine if someone is contemplating suicide. They include:

- Feel hopeless, worthless, agitated, socially isolated or lonely

- Experience a stressful life event, such as the loss of a loved one, military service, a breakup, or financial or legal problems

- Have a substance abuse problem — alcohol and drug abuse can worsen thoughts of suicide and make you feel reckless or impulsive enough to act on your thoughts

- Have suicidal thoughts and have access to firearms in your home

- Have an underlying psychiatric disorder, such as major depression, post-traumatic stress disorder or bipolar disorder

- Have a family history of mental disorders, substance abuse, suicide, or violence, including physical or sexual abuse

- Attempted suicide before

Approaches to Coping

Hurting or killing yourself are not your only options. Professionals can help you learn new skills for dealing with your pain. These might include:

✓ developing new skills to cope

✓ seeing your problems in a new light

✓ improving your ability to handle intense and painful emotions

✓ improving your relationships

✓ increasing your social supports

✓ medications

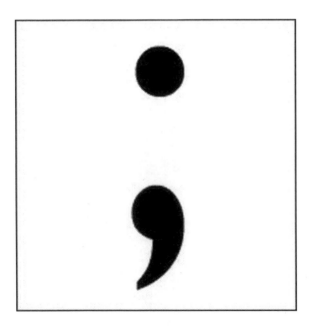

Ideation Coping Checklist

Take each day at a time. There might be good days and bad days. Try to focus on each day at a time and set yourself small, achievable goals.

Develop coping strategies that work for you. Self-help resources can help you to work through difficult feelings and learn coping skills.

Allow yourself to feel your feelings. Suppressing your feelings when they happen can cause them to build up over time and make them even harder to cope with. Think about what caused you to feel suicidal and share this with those supporting you.

Make a happy box. Fill a box with memories and items that can provide comfort and help lift your mood when you feel down. The box can contain anything that is meaningful and helpful to you, for example, a favorite book, positive quotes, photos, letters, poems, notes to yourself, a cuddly toy, a perfume or smell important to you.

Learn your triggers. Keeping a diary can help you to find patterns in your mood over time and help you to think about what might be causing you to feel suicidal. You can track your feelings by using an online mood diary.

Don't blame yourself. Many people who have tried or thought about taking their life feel guilty afterward, especially if they have worried loved ones. Try to accept that was just how you were feeling at the time, and focus your energy now on looking after yourself.

Write a letter to yourself. Include happy memories and mention the people who love and care about you. This can be helpful to read when you are experiencing suicidal feelings to remind yourself that things can get better.

Make plans to look forward to. Booking tickets to a music or art event or joining a club can help you to feel more positive about the future.

Build your self-esteem. Search for worksheets online that are free to download and use as healthy emotion exercises.

- Celebrate yourself. Write down your achievements and the things you like about yourself, however small. If someone compliments you, make a note of it.
- Do things just for yourself. Whether it's spending half an hour reading a book, doing a hobby or taking up a new one, try to regularly make time to do the things you enjoy.
- Seek support. If you're not already receiving support or don't feel the support you have is helpful, take a few moments to research available professionals in your area.

Let others know how you're feeling. Tell people what you find helpful and let them know when you are finding things difficult. It's okay to ask others to be with you if you need them.

Evaluating Suicidal Thoughts

1. **Dark or Depressing thoughts:** What are the troubling thoughts that I am having?

2. **Alternative Thoughts:**
    a. What I will tell myself (as reasonable alternatives to the distressing thoughts)?
    b. What would I say to a close friend who was feeling this way?
    c. What can I tell myself that will make me feel better, or remind myself of good things about me, my life, and the future?

3. **Alternative Actions:**
    a. What I have done in the past that helped.
    b. My coping resources.
    c. What will I do to help calm and soothe myself?

d. What can I do for the next 20 Minutes (and give it my full attention).

4. Call For Help

a. If I'm still feeling overwhelmed or out of control I will call the Suicide Hotline.

Release and Reflect:

Use these pages to journal your thoughts, share your affirmations and track your progress.

_____

_____

_____

_____

_____

_____

_____

_____

_____

_____

_____

_____

_____

_____

_____

_____

_____

_____

_____

_____

_____

_____

_____

_____

_____

_____

_____

_____

_____

_____

_____

_____

_____

_____

_____

_____

FINAL THOUGHTS:

Wow we actually did this! I have to first thank God for making me a visionary, a fighter, a survivor. I want to thank my amazing God sent blessing my parents, Reverend Harold and Brenda Guidry, My two sisters Latoya Bean and Breanna Guidry and my brother Harold Guidry III. I have to thank you for loving me through all of this, I know it has not been an easy transition but in this journey I never lost sight of the goal and that was to make you proud. I hope you are thus far and I will continue to press on for us all! Thank you to my brother in love David Bean Jr. for supporting my journey and creating a new family! To my niece, Abrielle Nicole, you are too young to understand but I thank you for filling the gaps I never knew I had until you came along! Everything I do is for you from here on out. To my family and friends, you all

are amazing people, all my old friends to my
new lifelines I ask God to bless you all more
abundantly and thank you for embracing my
journey. To Vaughn Gray our Licensed
Professional counselor who contributed to this
project, thank you so much for being a pillar in
society, for helping break the stigma of mental
health. To Jillian "JJ" Simmons, our contributor
to the forward, bless you for all the work you do
in your initiatives with Respect My Crown and
starting the conversation about healthy
relationships and women empowerment. To
my amazing contributors, survivors and now
family I thank you for being brave! I know it
takes a lot to tackle this road but you are
walking in it and if no one else tells you I am
proud of you! We are all connected as one.
To those who have purchased this book, I am
forever grateful. I wanted to take a different
route to self-help! This was a deep challenge
but we did it! I cannot begin to take credit! All of
us did this for you. There will be days where

you want to give up, DON'T! Pick up this book and apply these survivors' stories to overcome

I have placed journal pages in so you can track your progress, write out affirmations and have a guide to healing! It is my goal to make you the CEO of your NEW life! Always know you are important, your life has meaning, you are valued and someone out there needs you. We need you to survive. If you ever feel hopeless and don't have anywhere else to turn please get help. You are not crazy, remember you are a human battling your brain. Get the help you need! Find a support group, go seek therapy and speak out. My dear kings and queens you are so valuable and we want to see you win! We are so gracious you believe in your healing!

XOXO,

Bianca Danielle, Founder, Crying Voice Project

CONTRIBUTORS

Ajanae Udo

Dana Martin

Jameka Baker

Jason Pure

Kelly Patton

Latasha White

Rae-Lonni Hawkins

Richard Taylor

Sholante Carter

Rhonda Thompson

Stacey Brown

Robert Brown

If you need additional help:

Call the National Suicide Prevention Lifeline
1-800-273-8255

26098034R00085

Made in the USA
Columbia, SC
06 September 2018